Galvanizing Performance

Dearest Michael,

Thanks so much for your interest in my book! You are a dear, sweet human and friend.

Best,
Jill

Galvanizing Performance

The Alexander Technique as a Catalyst for Excellence

Edited by Cathy Madden and Kathleen Juhl

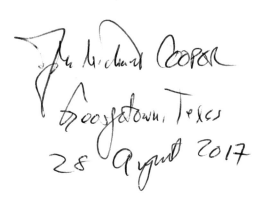

SINGING
DRAGON

LONDON AND PHILADELPHIA

First published in 2017
by Singing Dragon
an imprint of Jessica Kingsley Publishers
73 Collier Street
London N1 9BE, UK
and
400 Market Street, Suite 400
Philadelphia, PA 19106, USA

www.singingdragon.com

Library of Congress Cataloging in Publication Data
Title: Galvanizing performance : the Alexander technique as a catalyst for
  excellence / edited by Cathy Madden and Kathleen Juhl.
Description: London ; Philadelphia : Jessica Kingsley Publishers, 2017.
Identifiers: LCCN 2017027376 (print) | LCCN 2017009338 (ebook) | ISBN
  9780857012722 (ebook) | ISBN 9781785927201
Subjects: LCSH: Performing arts. | Alexander technique.
Classification: LCC PN1584 (print) | LCC PN1584 .G35 2017 (ebook) | DDC
  791--dc23

British Library Cataloguing in Publication Data
A CIP catalogue record for this book is available from the British Library

ISBN 978 1 78592 720 1
eISBN 978 0 85701 272 2

Printed and bound in Great Britain

To Alyssa-Lois and Edan-Hoelan
To Alice

Acknowledgments

The editors wish to thank all of the authors of this collection for their important, inspiring work. Thank you also to our peer reviewers. We would like to acknowledge the University of Washington School of Drama (particularly the students of Drama 455) and the Department of Theatre at Southwestern University. Special thanks also to Hannah Snetsinger at Jessica Kingsley Publishers as well as Matt Goodrich for his expertise and flair in preparing this collection for publication.

Contents

Introduction

Galvanizing Performance fills a need that until now has had expression only in specialty journals such as *Direction*, members-only publications of various Alexander Technique societies, and proceedings from the International Congresses of the Alexander Technique. The writings in this book are from teachers of the Alexander Technique (abbreviated throughout the book as AT) about the teaching process itself. Virtually all of the published literature explains the technique in some way, either on its own or in relationship to specific endeavors, such as performing arts or sports. However, the extant literature does not directly address the details of teaching AT. We get merely indirect, anecdotal glimpses of the teaching process.

What is missing in the literature are the voices of teachers who came after F. Mathias Alexander himself. It is our position that new approaches to teaching AT should be brought to light. The state of the art of teaching AT is evolving, and a great many teachers have done day-to-day, experiential, and heuristic research on what works well. Their research exists in disparate articles and anecdotes in books on particular topics. (Madden's book *Integrative Alexander Technique Practice for Performing Artists: Onstage Synergy* (2014) is an example.) *Galvanizing Performance* brings together the insights of an eminent group of teachers on the subject of teaching performers, revealing the specific details of how AT is taught.

Why teachers of performers? Because of the nature of performance training, some AT teachers represented in this book have taught the same individuals not for weeks or months, but for many years in venues such as university graduate programs and private practice. It is not unusual for these teachers to have had multiple generations of students. Over those years, they have had the opportunity to test new, innovative teaching approaches.

We want to more effectively preserve and disseminate the work of these pioneering teachers. This enables the next generations of teachers to build from the foundation their predecessors have so innovatively developed. Many of the chapters allude to the fact that new generations of students in all fields (not just the performing arts) are asking new questions and coming up with new puzzles and difficulties as they approach issues connected to what Alexander called psychophysical unity—what some call the mind/body problem. The teachers in this book have novel ways of addressing these conundrums—it turns out that AT, as John Dewey said, "bears the same relation to education that education itself bears to all other activities" (Alexander 1984 [1932], p.xix).

While the focus of this book is on teaching performers, the teaching ideas are widely applicable to other activities.

An Introduction to AT

For those of you reading this collection who are new to AT, this introduction offers a general background for the work and teaching process.

AT is a psychophysical change process using conscious thought to restore coordination and/or prevent miscoordination in human functioning. What F.M. Alexander (1869–1955) observed empirically is that the relationship between head and spine in movement is a key factor in vertebrate coordination—a fact that has subsequently been verified scientifically. Whenever a vertebrate goes out of optimal coordination, the system compensates with excessive work in the relationship between head and spine. Frank Pierce Jones, a Tufts researcher who studied AT, says in his book *Freedom to Change*:

> F. Mathias Alexander discovered a method (a "means-whereby") for expanding consciousness to take in inhibition as well as excitation ("not-doing" as well as "doing") and thus obtain a better integration

of the reflex and voluntary elements in a response pattern. (Jones 1997 [1976], p.2)

The goal of AT is to teach people to restore an optimal relationship between head and spine, and, when necessary, replace faulty concepts that cause the miscoordination—what Alexander called "mistaken beliefs"—with more accurate, constructive concepts. The results of this process include greater flexibility and grace in movement and speech, clarity of thought, and, for many, absence of physical pain and stress patterns. Again from Jones:

> The Alexander Technique opens a window onto the little-known area between stimulus and response and gives you the self-knowledge you need in order to change the pattern of your response—or, if you choose, not to make it at all. (Jones 1997 [1976], p.4)

It is in this miniscule moment of time, the "area between stimulus and response," that true honesty and creativity can emerge. As long as our responses are mitigated by habitual, unconsciously driven miscoordination, both what we think and what we express fall short of what is possible.

The causes of miscoordination include but are not limited to:

- imitation of family patterns

- imitation of teacher/mentor patterns

- mistaken ideas about anatomy and physiology

- learned patterns (e.g. from sports, music, or other training) that are misapplied to another activity

- attempts to use muscular contraction for tasks that do not require muscular contraction

- mistaken concepts about thinking

- compensation for injury (possibly compensation that is no longer necessary)

- trauma

- emotional armoring

- learned misuses, which F.M. Alexander calls "cultivated habits"

- "electronically raised" concepts of thinking and moving.

The sequence of teaching and learning AT involves an analysis of movement and thought in relationship to the desired goal, followed by synthesis of a constructive conscious plan for change and accomplishment of that end.

How It Is Taught: The AT Teaching Process

What we recognize as good coordination in human movement and behavior is recognizable as fluidity in movement, appropriate muscle tone for the activity, and clarity of thought and intention. This combination of qualities generates behavior illustrative of words attributed to A.R. Alexander (F.M.'s brother): "The hallmarks of the Alexander Technique are creativity, spontaneity, and adaptability to change." Ichiro Suzuki provides a model of what this kind of coordination looks like in baseball. Baryshnikov, in ballet, and Michelle Kwan, in figure skating, are other examples.

The teacher of AT needs to create the conditions in which these qualities can emerge from each student. The first tool is the teacher's own coordination. One of the unique factors in teaching this work is that the teacher herself must be using AT in order to effectively teach it. The teacher's own coordination functions in several ways:

- It provides a clear model of coordination for the student to imitate (possibly related to recent discoveries of mirror neurons).

- A clear coordination enables teachers to use their hands skillfully in teaching to guide the student's change process.

- Good coordination heightens the teacher's ability to observe, listen, and analyze.

- A psychophysically clear coordination enhances the teacher's "creativity, spontaneity, and adaptability to change" in the teaching process.

The tactile communication within AT is a primary way the teacher can help the student directly understand that thought and movement are inseparable. Teachers are trained to use a unique and refined system of teaching tactilely, communicating through a combination of light, informed touch and brief verbal cues. With the skillful use of their hands as an extension of verbal communication, AT teachers show their students how to make this association themselves. Most importantly, each teacher's full self-coordination models most profoundly the absolute unity of mind, body, and intention.

Variations of the Teacher's Art

Each of the authors of this book teaches uniquely. Their life stories, psychophysical histories, and fields of expertise inform how they define their teaching as well as the process itself. The editors of this book share with our authors the ability to teach via direct application. Yet we would not fully agree with all the viewpoints represented by the contributors to this book, nor would they necessarily agree with ours. Madden, for instance, strongly believes that certain commonly used AT terms contribute to misunderstanding AT. We do all share a core of information, and our experiences inform how we use the information. For this reason, we have asked authors to precede their chapters with a statement about their *AT perspective*, highlighting their values and approach to the work. As a result, our readers have in their hands a field guide to the diversity of AT approaches as well as a lens through which to contextualize each writer/teacher's contribution.

Direct Application

The editors acknowledge their bias: Both learned AT by using it as they did things directly related to either their daily or professional lives. Madden's early lessons were almost all theatre related—monologues, songs, dances, character walks, and so forth. Juhl's training focused on AT teaching processes specially suited for young actors and included applied work on the everyday life activities foundational to performance activities in theatre. Direct application is a practical, simple, related-to-life approach. Some people learn AT via a set of procedures that are limited in scope. While those who have learned AT this way sometimes can't imagine that you could apply the work without having mastered the procedures first, the editors (and others) embody confidence that direct application is an effective way to learn and teach—from the first AT class or lesson. A case could be made that the procedures might become an end in themselves, perhaps impeding the integration of AT into daily and professional life.

While the primary focus of this collection is not marketing AT to new students, one of the advantages of direct application is that the teacher can respond directly to students' life desires. In the case of performing arts students, these desires are usually related to skill development. F.M. Alexander said, "It is the wish, the conscious desire to do a thing or think a thing that brings about adequate performance" (1996 [1910], p.63). Without the desire to do something, the process of AT has no expression. Because it is only a "how," AT requires a "what"—something to do. For new students, direct application draws on the preexisting motivation and thus directly illustrates AT's value. When AT leads to better singing, acting, and dancing, desire is fueled by success.

In *The Power of Habit*, Duhigg describes the learning pattern most effective in bringing change to our daily and professional routines:

> The process within our brains is a three-step loop. First, there is a cue, a trigger that tells your brain to go into the automatic mode and which habit to use. Then there is the routine, which can be physical, mental or emotional. Finally, there is the reward, which helps your brain figure out if this particular loop is worth remembering for the future... (Duhigg 2012, p.19)

Madden rewrites this passage around the conscious use of AT rather than what the author calls "automatic mode" and "habit":

In learning to use the Alexander Technique for performance, and to cooperate with how we are designed to learn, it is useful to have an external cue (a cue from something in your activity or environment rather than just something you directly notice about yourself) to signal to yourself that you want to use the Technique. The Alexander Technique plan is the process. The reward appears either immediately or over time in the continued improvement in your coordination and your ability to use same in service of your desires. (Madden 2014, p.272)

With direct application, teachers are able to take advantage of the intrinsic motivation, the "trigger," to create an external cue that facilitates integrative practice. Anders Ericsson and Robert Pool describe the effectiveness of this "learning on the job" approach in *Peak: Secrets from the New Science of Expertise*:

One benefit of "learning while real work gets done" is that it gets people into the habit of practicing and thinking about practicing. Once they understand the importance of regular practice—and realize just how much they can improve by using it—they look for opportunities throughout the day in which normal…activities can be transformed into practice activities. (Ericsson and Pool 2016, pp.123–124)

By expediting the student's ability to use AT by taking advantage of their intrinsic motivation via direct application, the rewards are revealed through the evolving expertise of the activities themselves.

Direct Application Works!

In the following chapters, this group of experienced practitioners reveal the effectiveness of direct application. It is our hope that by seeing the range of possible teaching strategies, AT teachers can create their own approaches to direct application; teachers of all kinds recognize how direct or indirect collaboration with an AT teacher galvanizes their students' ability to learn; and performers (and others) are inspired to use AT directly to "shine up" their skills—their arts.

DEBI ADAMS

Debi Adams encourages deep respect and compassion for those who perform. An AT and piano teacher at the Boston Conservatory at Berklee and a performer herself, she generously shares her own experiences of learning to embrace her full and authentic self as teacher and pianist. In "Hands Last," Adams encourages a deeply holistic approach to experiencing the self in performance. Instead of thinking narrowly about accomplishing our activities with our hands, she reminds us that "many times throughout the day we reach for things before coordinating around receiving them." Each of these moments is rich with choice. "*Hands last* allows us a tiny window of time between stimulus and response to go ahead as we started, not do what we thought we would do, or do something completely different." Adams never suggests accomplishment as the end of learning. Rather, she advocates curiosity and discovery in the process, the journey toward excellence. She encourages her students to live broadly in the world, listening, aware of their surroundings and their human design. The glimpse Adams shares of her approach to teaching is practical, insightful, and wise.

SARAH BARKER

The strength and efficacy of Sarah Barker's chapter, "Full Embodiment," is her nuanced way of describing how she collaborates with actors to apply AT in the moment of performance. Barker chronicles her work with professional actors, students in Japan, and students at the University of South Carolina, where she is associate professor of acting. She rigorously applies AT as she asks students to work with acting principles developed by Constantin Stanislavski and those who based their teaching on his work. She focuses on helping actors use AT to free themselves of unnecessary muscular tension when they encounter conflict in the dramatic texts they are performing. Barker teaches actors how to benefit from psychophysical unity to free their imagination and create compelling performances. A step-by-step account of her approach to scenework is useful for both teachers and students. Barker says that "acting is a physical art." Her chapter clearly illustrates how students may inhabit their whole beings, moving through them in deeply creative and spontaneous ways.

CORINNE CASSINI

Corinne Cassini is a professional cellist and teacher of AT at Appalachian State University in Boone, North Carolina. In her chapter, "Confident Creativity," she details teaching exercises she has developed to encourage students' awareness of the ways their coordination is affected by their attitudes toward themselves as performers, toward the music they are playing, and toward their audiences. Cassini's exercises illustrate the effectiveness of compassionate communication in AT teaching. The first, "withholding definition," inspired by Cassini's teacher Tommy Thompson, helps students understand the relationship between thinking and experiencing. Replacing negative thoughts about themselves and their activities with a constructive approach improves their performance and heightens the pleasure they and their audiences experience. The "Storytelling as Freedom from Repeating Patterns" activity encourages students to let go of old stories about their relationship to music and create new stories that allow them to enjoy that relationship and perform comfortably and generously for audiences. Finally, students learn to value their talent and expertise through an exercise designed to help them accept compliments. Cassini demonstrates ways of encouraging students to improve their performance through kind and gentle attitudes toward themselves.

KATE CONKLIN

Kate Conklin is a highly skilled performer and AT teacher who sang with Cirque de Soleil and was on the voice faculty at CalArts. Rigorous research underpins her work. In her chapter, "Engaging the Expert Performer," Conklin generously shares and contextualizes a broad array of resources. Conklin also details her collaborations with expert performers from her position as an expert performer herself. "Affinity as a pathway" characterizes her work: She develops relationships with students based on mutual understandings of artistic processes and empathy. Embedded in her approach is a celebration of her students' considerable skills, talents, and insights. Her work with Cirque de Soleil performer Benedikt Negro began by celebrating his considerable skills, acknowledging that his approach to performance was already working. This celebration of and respect for her students' talents, skills, and expertise is inherent in the teaching process she details.

JULIANNE EVELEIGH AND PAUL HAMPTON

In "A Mirror, a Mask, and an Actor," Julianne Eveleigh, lecturer in voice, and Paul Hampton, lecturer in acting, at Federation University, Australia, describe a class in neutral mask through which students gain a solid grounding in physical and psychological presence, acting, and AT. Both trained at the School for F.M. Alexander Studies in Melbourne. Eveleigh is interested in the dynamic relationship between voice and physical expression, and Hampton studied mask work with Philippe Gaulier and Monika Pagneux in Paris. Their chapter describes interactions among mirror, neutral mask, and self combined with AT guidance in the first phase of actor training. The pedagogy Eveleigh and Hampton describe represents strikingly effective student discovery and training that "galvanizes many of the key skills we think are vital to the development of each new acting ensemble: mind/body coordination, playfulness, and freedom of choice." Eveleigh and Hampton explain in detail the stages of their work with students wearing neutral masks and responding to their images in a mirror. Their account is woven with insightful student responses that reflect the usefulness of AT for young actors at the beginning of their training.

JULIA GUICHARD AND HARVEY THURMER

Julia Guichard and Harvey Thurmer designed an AT class they call an "un-class." They have taught it for seven years at Miami University of Ohio where they are faculty members, Guichard in Theatre and Thurmer in Music. The class is offered for no credit and involves no requirements beyond mandatory attendance. As they describe it, their un-class challenges educational models that focus on end results to the detriment of process. In Guichard and Thurmer's un-class there is no expectation for results. Instead, students are encouraged to engage choice and process, which often has proved difficult for them. Many grew up with rigorous testing imposed by "no child left behind" approaches to education. Guichard and Thurmer were worried that students would be frustrated by the un-class because, in their educational experiences, they had been taught to focus on results. But when Guichard and Thurmer interviewed former students, they were enthusiastic and said they found AT useful for enhancing their music and theatre training precisely because it emphasizes process rather than results. Along with presenting the pedagogy they developed to make the un-class successful, in their chapter, "To Learn or to Un-Learn—That Is the Question," Guichard and Thurmer discuss the different ways music and theatre students respond to AT. This discussion is useful for thinking about ways to develop distinct AT pedagogies appropriate for these different learning cultures, also making a strong case for interdisciplinary teaching. Guichard and Thurmer present their pedagogy as an "alternative model of learning within the traditional structure of the academy."

MICHAEL FREDERICK AND ELAINE WILLIAMS (INTERVIEW FACILITATED BY KATHLEEN JUHL)

This chapter, "Alexander Technique Interventions for Stage Fright," documents an interview with internationally recognized Los Angeles-based AT teacher Michael Frederick and his colleague Elaine Williams, a senior teacher at the Baron Brown Acting Studio in Los Angeles, which focuses on ways AT can help actors overcome stage fright. Their lively conversation is anecdotal and rich. Frederick trained as an actor at the Bristol Old Vic Theatre School and as an AT teacher with Walter and Dilys Carrington in London. Williams studied AT with Frederick and deeply appreciates its usefulness for actors: "All work, especially for performers, is about 'smart relaxation,' is about mindful presence, and is about being able to see the opening to freedom. In acting, it is seeing and experiencing what is actually happening and being open and available to react and seize the moment." Frederick and Williams tell stories of an eclectic array of unusual students who benefitted from both AT and actor training: a homeless man who wants to become an actor, an almost penniless actor down on his luck, a man with a serious stutter who succeeded at actor training, a wealthy insurance executive who moonlights performing and directing in LA community theatre. Frederick and Williams describe improvising with each of them in ways that effectively addressed their stage fright and led all of them to pursue actor training.

KATHLEEN JUHL

In "Mindful Bananas and the Alexander Technique," Kathleen Juhl urges theatre students to "play to make a play" and embrace the risk of slipping on proverbial banana peels that propel them into the present moment where, surprised and off balance, they must right themselves. To help them avoid falling, she and her students organize their classroom environments in ways that encourage coordination and set the stage for engaging AT processes and understandings. Juhl is professor of theatre at Southwestern University in Georgetown, Texas. Inspired by her AT teachers who studied with Marjorie Barstow, she encourages students to apply insights they gain from AT to improve performance in the moment of activity. She invokes Jon Kabat-Zinn's work with mindfulness practices, the play theories of Johan Huizinga and Richard Schechner, Stephen Nachmanovitch's approaches to improvisational music making, and Mihaly Csikszentmihalyi's definition of "flow." Virginia Woolf's description, in her memoir *Moments of Being*, of the "shock" of insight and recognition that inspired her writing serves as an inspiration for Juhl's teaching. Using AT to mediate a relationship between play processes that rely on "banana time" and mindfulness practices, she describes in detail two teaching approaches—"Core Practice" and "Round Robin Improvisation"—that are based in part on the work of these innovators. Her pedagogy encourages spontaneous creativity through "paying attention on purpose."

CATHY MADDEN

Cathy Madden studied extensively with Marjorie Barstow and is well known internationally for her innovative AT pedagogy. She is principal lecturer in the Professional Actor Training Program at the University of Washington and also directs and performs. Her book *Integrative Alexander Technique Practice for Performing Artists: Onstage Synergy* is a detailed guide to direct application in the performing arts. In *Galvanizing Performance*, she opens the door of her classroom, revealing her process for a class she taught in the summer of 2016, vividly depicting the detail and nuance of her approach to group teaching. Her chapter, "Report on a Five-Day Introductory Class for the University of Washington School of Drama," describes a pedagogy of discovery, using direct application from the beginning, encouraging her students to be AT explorers. The chapter details her plans for each of five three-hour classes, chronicles the activities of the classes, and shares student responses. In this chapter, you will discover purple people while peering into a classroom where AT becomes a simple technique for living a coordinated life with great fun.

In a second chapter, "Glimpsing the Collaboratives," Madden surveys another approach to direct application—AT teachers working with teachers of other disciplines. She describes her many experiences with colleagues at UW, then offers stories from three other AT teachers (Belinda Mello, Jennifer Schulz, and Kate Conklin) on their work with a second teacher. Survey comments from students who have experienced this type of teaching affirm the effectiveness of this teaching strategy.

PATRICIA O'NEILL

In this lively account of an approach to AT teaching steeped in metaphor, singer Patricia O'Neill, professor emeritus at Louisiana State University, describes teaching that encourages students to embody AT concepts while appreciating the power and beauty of singing processes. "I find that metaphor transcends my students' beliefs and preconceived ideas, inserting itself with a purity and simplicity that disarms, enlightens, transforms, and sparks the imagination." O'Neill's teaching weaves a rigorous application of AT principles with fierce attention to individual students for whom she chooses or discovers metaphors appropriate for their journeys toward discovery and artistic excellence. The chapter, "Metaphorically Speaking," is infused with testimony from former students that honor the efficacy of metaphor for learning singing and AT. O'Neill begins with a delightful story about her attempt to understand what a teacher meant when he said, during a voice lesson, "Yes, that's it!"—a common but elusive metaphor for accidental artistic accomplishments or, as O'Neill speculates, discovering optimal coordination. She says that metaphor sparks rich imaginative insights that AT clarifies in more concrete terms. One of O'Neill's most powerful metaphors describes using AT as being in the center of a hurricane: "Profound in its stillness, it contains all possibilities and therefore facilitates the emergence of a direction while remaining open to all other directions." O'Neill uncovers a poetic of AT teaching processes.

ROBERT SCHUBERT

Robert Schubert begins his chapter, "Of Testing Times and Hoped-For Miracles," with an anecdote from his own career as a professional clarinetist. He was playing a clarinet solo in Beethoven's Fifth Symphony for a temperamental conductor who criticized him harshly the first time he played the solo in rehearsal. Schubert prepared for the second go-round—fiercely. On the second attempt, when he was overworking to *show* the conductor he was capable of playing the solo beautifully, the solo went badly. Before the third time, Schubert remembered his AT training. He told himself, "It doesn't matter what this sounds like. I'm just going to direct myself [use AT] while I play." Process rather than product became his focus, and he played well. Schubert, a lecturer in woodwinds and the Alexander Technique at the Victorian College of the Arts and Melbourne Conservatorium of Music in Australia, depicts clearly and in detail the musical challenges of his students, quickly diagnoses problems, and succinctly describes the insightful solutions he offers. His work is deft and unintrusive, matter-of-fact, uncomplicated. He asks himself, "Can I remember to think about my use of myself and let the 'ends' take care of themselves?" Schubert's question characterizes the pedagogy he describes: Focus on process means inevitable change for the better.

CRISPIN SPAETH

Choreographer/producer/AT teacher trainee Spaeth led the Crispin Spaeth Dance Group from 1992 to 2007 and continues to make dances when the stars align. Her chapter, "Is This Dance Made of Cake?" is a journey through an AT-infused creative process in making dances using what she describes as "the broader applications of AT, including application to thinking itself. Having a tool to improve my thinking means an improved creative process. Simple as that." She leads us through the rehearsal process, describes using AT to solve a partnering dilemma, lauds the role of AT in deciphering the mixed messages of dancer training, and shares its utility for communication and leadership. Her chapter concludes with detailed descriptions of some open-ended dancing experiments. For each of the three structured improvisations, she and her fellow dancer ask, "How can I use AT while I am dancing?"

Galvanizing

Galvanizing is a word that describes the moment when performers (and others) use AT to do what they are doing and, suddenly, it is as if they start to shine! When we are with them, we experience the contrast between what they were doing and what they are doing now. This moment inspires exploration. Even if the former moment was going "pretty well," what is happening now has a new spark. Using AT has stimulated a whole-self-fullness that facilitates success and what Marjorie Barstow sometimes called "putting a little pep into it." The moment is pleasurable, effective, affective, and just a bit contagious.

AT galvanizes our ability to follow our dreams. Using AT directly to do what we care about moment to moment spurs us to continue using it because the pleasure, effectiveness, and growth that is revealed in our actions assures us that we are on our desire's path. Whether in the everyday enjoyment of life, or in the building of expertise, the direct application of AT honors our personal journeys to mastery.

References

Alexander, F.M. (1984) *The Use of the Self.* Downey, CA: Centerline Press. (Original work published 1932.)

Alexander, F.M. (1996) *Man's Supreme Inheritance.* London: Mouritz. (Original work published 1910.)

Duhigg, C. (2012) *The Power of Habit: Why We Do What We Do in Life and Business.* New York: Random House Publishing Group.

Ericsson, K.A. and Pool, R. (2016) *Peak: Secrets from the New Science of Expertise.* New York: Houghton Mifflin Harcourt.

Jones, F.P. (1997) *Freedom to Change: The Development and Science of the Alexander Technique.* London: Mouritz. (Original work published 1976.)

Madden, C. (2014) *Integrative Alexander Technique Practice for Performing Artists: Onstage Synergy.* Chicago, IL: Intellect, University of Chicago Press.

Hands Last

Debi Adams

AT Perspective

The Alexander Technique, developed by F.M. Alexander, is a method for making choices in how we do what we do. It is dependent on our kinesthetic sense, the sense that is responsible for telling us where we are, including our position and movements. As we cultivate our kinesthetic sense, we gain a greater awareness of our habitual choices. With this awareness, we are faced with new choices. Alexander looked specifically at how our head is balanced on our spine as a reflection of our freedom to make choices. He was interested in the sequence of movements that resulted from freeing our neck, rebalancing our head, and thus decompressing our spine and limbs. This sequence of free movement enables us to redirect habitual choices into more desirable ones. This is the basic premise of AT: We have choices in how we do what we do.

In my work lately, I have been interested in our sense of safety and how that contributes to the ease in our head–neck relationship. If I feel safe, I feel balanced. Movement comes easily. If I perceive danger, I don't feel balanced or able to make choices in how I move. In the students I work with, the danger is most often perceived rather than true. This recognition enables them to find safety in the moment and, hence, their freedom to choose.

One of the most important truisms of AT is that it is based on *non-doing*. This is at once a simple and challenging concept. The work to *not do* something can seem more difficult than the act of *doing*. Why is it so hard not to reinforce a familiar response? That's why so many of us study this for so long.

Working with musicians is an honor. We are part of the same tribe. My experiences as a performing musician as well as a musician who recovered from injury enable me to speak to other musicians with an honesty and understanding that we both appreciate. Many Alexander Technique teachers come to this work because of a personal experience of struggle and recovery. I am no exception. For me it was a severe case of tendonitis that interfered with my graduate studies in piano performance. The experiences I had with AT during my years of recovery have greatly influenced my manner of teaching the technique. Here are two major lessons I learned:

1. The integration of our being is real. Searching for solutions in the physical realm alone does not suffice.

2. The organization of our system is deeply dependent upon our head–neck relationship.

I believe my story of recovery may clarify why these two principles are so important to the way I teach.

Like many others, my first approach to recovery was via a traditional medical route—visiting a neurologist, having an electromyography, seeing a physical therapist, and gradually increasing my time at the piano. I was advised to play no more than ten minutes per day while I still had pain. Attempting to prepare a graduate piano recital—with pieces lasting as long as 45 minutes—on ten minutes of practice was the ultimate challenge. I learned how to practice efficiently during those ten-minute intervals, and this has served me well to this day.

I was fortunate to find an AT teacher after graduation, while teaching in a college music setting. It became apparent that I needed to train to teach this technique. For years I had heard piano teachers speak of "free arms" and "arm weight." I wanted the ability to give my piano students a direct experience of what these words meant. The hands-on work from my AT teacher helped me to understand these phrases, and I wanted to do the same for others.

I studied AT for several years before I found myself able to play and perform again without pain. I had abandoned performing for teaching; I got married; I had children. I wasn't attempting to play all that much. I did play on faculty recitals at the institutions where I taught but was cautious about the repertoire I chose. Because I could barely play, I felt a bit like an imposter instead of a pianist.

A few years into my teacher-training course with Tommy Thompson, I complained that even after all the AT I had done, I could still feel a whiff of my old injury returning after only 30 seconds at the piano. He responded that it was all in the attitude I brought to the instrument. Who knows why, in certain moments, things become clear? I went home, sat at the piano, and as I raised my arms to play, I suddenly saw myself. I was becoming *someone else* in order to play. It felt fake and dishonest.

Now I often tell my students, "You can be only who you are, where you are." Just being *me* at the piano was all I needed. Once I saw who I had become (Tommy referred to this as the *created self* rather than the *true self*), I knew it was not what I wanted. It wasn't me. From that moment on, the pain disappeared. Whenever I tell this story, it feels almost made up because it sounds so quick and simple. Indeed it was! Once I reached this understanding, I easily shed my created self. I always needed to call upon my conscious awareness, however, for my habitual persona was never far away—at least for a while.

One principle of AT is the importance of freedom in your neck so that your head is moveable and decompresses your spine. The list of what causes our neck to tighten is much too long for this chapter. I often look at young children and see their ultimate ease in just being, their momentary upsets disappearing in a flash. Perhaps their lack of responsibilities allows them this freedom. They have no mortgages to pay, no deadlines to meet.

Our patterns of use are reflective of our whole selves. In contemplating Alexander's primary control (his discovery that the relationship between head and spine is of primary importance in determining the quality of overall human functioning), I had gotten lost in the physicality of it all. I encourage you not to waste your time trying to address your body as though it is out there on its own; it is not. It is integrated with every bit of you. I was mistaken when I did not embrace this truth. I didn't think I was separating myself into parts, as I had learned to address the *whole person* through AT. Even so, I was more often attending to *physical* freedom in my work at the piano. I thought that if the pain was physical, the solution must be hiding in the physicality of my playing. Most people hold similar beliefs: We have experiences and teachings that cause us to believe that our physical self operates alone. But all our parts are one—we are simply *us*.

While Alexander was one of the first to apprehend the unification of our selves, he did place importance on the head–neck relationship. I had experienced the magnitude of this relationship long before studying AT. When I was in college and doing some physical exercises one night, I suddenly felt something snap across my right ear. I fell to the floor and was unable to get up. It made no sense to me—I didn't feel badly hurt and could move my limbs, but could not rise from the floor. Eventually my roommate came home and, after calling the emergency room of the local hospital, put warm compresses on my neck. Gradually I regained the ability to move. If you injure an arm or a leg, you may not be happy, but you are not completely incapacitated. If you injure your neck, however, there are potentially serious consequences. It took years for me to make the connection between the experience of this small neck injury and Alexander's primary control. I have since learned the simplicity of this relationship and the important consequences it has for our coordination.

Before I studied AT, I had a piano teacher who taught me to release unnecessary tension at the piano. It changed my playing completely, and I was so grateful for this. However, I learned later that without a central coordinating mechanism, I was endlessly releasing parts. By integrating the movements via the primary mechanism (head–neck relationship), I had long-lasting releases that resulted in a simple integration of my movements. Having musicians attend to this mechanism while not separating themselves into parts is my mission in teaching them AT.

How I Teach AT to Musicians

Several years ago, I teamed up with a friend and colleague to create "The Well-Tempered Pianist" workshops and performances. During the course of workshop preparation, I realized that certain principles of piano playing showed up repeatedly. Thus was born my 12 Commandments of Piano Playing (Adams 2014). I teach an AT for Musicians course at the Boston Conservatory at Berklee, where I have found these commandments transferable to other instruments and voice.

I will now highlight a few of my commandments and other suggestions, pairing them with some AT maxims. You will see that each idea addresses what I feel are the most important aspects of this work, such as the integration of our whole selves and organization of our system around a central coordinating principle (our head-neck relationship). As much as I describe new ways of thinking and challenging our perceptions in order to effect change, the essence of the AT is in *non-doing*. This philosophy undergirds all the suggestions here.

> ▶ *AT is a tool that helps us experience a synchronicity of our sensory systems.*

> ♫ *If you can't hear it that fast, you can't play it that fast.*

A key intention is to synchronize the senses. For example, almost every time we struggle with a fast passage, the issue is not that our fingers can't move fast enough or that we haven't practiced enough. Rather, it is that we can't hear the passage as fast as we are trying to play it. I have used this commandment successfully with many instrumentalists and singers. All I have them do is hear the music in their head, making sure each and every note is clear and pitch perfect. This is always a slower tempo than they had previously attempted to play. When they play the music at the exact tempo they just imagined, it's always cleaner. Then I ask them to speed up the tempo in their head, but not beyond what they can clearly hear. They usually realize that they can't hear it as fast as they thought they could. So they practice by imagining the passage without actually playing it until they can hear it with clarity at the desired tempo. Voila! Works every time.

> ▶ *AT teaches freedom through our relationship to the world around us.*

> ♫ *Use your environment to inform your practice.*

We are motivated by sensory experience. Often you hear an AT teacher say that the head moves first and the body follows. I think something happens before that. We are brought to attention by a sensory experience, that is, we hear, see, or smell something. Our head moves in response. As previously stated, I look at the AT work as synchronizing the senses. When all of our sensory mechanisms are working in an easy relationship to each other, everything *makes sense*. How limiting to think that something making sense appeals only to our intellect. In fact, situations that make sense often do not seem logical.

When practicing an instrument, it can be helpful to awaken the senses to what is usually unnoticed or intentionally blocked. Can I include the sound of traffic outside and the smell of coffee brewing? If I can include these aspects of my environment while practicing, then I can include the sight and sound of my audience when I perform. In my early piano studies, I had a teacher who advised me to block out my audience. Unfortunately, such advice, a belief that if we focused our attention inward we would avoid distraction, was popular. My desire now is that I want to *be there* in performance. That's why I'm doing it. If we try to block out our audience to create a protective bubble for ourselves, then anything unexpected that happens outside that bubble may distract us. There are no surprises if you choose to include what's around you. There is just flow from you to your audience and back. Frank Pierce Jones spoke of the *unified field of attention*:

> The organism has at various times been divided and subdivided into a great many parts and categories—the mind and the body, the five senses, the vascular system and the like. Though for purposes of study these categories are convenient and perhaps necessary, there is always a danger of thinking that the divisions are real, and it is customary nowadays to start any treatise on human behavior by affirming the unity of the organism. There is one division, however, that is seldom questioned—the division between the self and the environment. It is regularly assumed that attention must be directed either outward into the environment or inward into the self...
>
> I should like to take a strictly Unitarian approach to the problem and deny the necessity for making any such division, even for convenience. Information about the state of the body and the state of the environment is being recorded in the brain at one and the same time. Attention is ordinarily directed either one way or the other but there is no reason why this need always be the case, since the organism is capable of selecting the stimuli to which it will respond. (Jones 1997 [1976], pp.176–177)

I live in Boston, where winters can get pretty cold. One of my favorite days of the year is the first one that feels like spring. I like it not only because it feels great, but also because I enjoy observing everyone else feeling great. On that day, we are happy to be where we are. We may have closed down a bit in the winter, perhaps trying to shut out the cold. By separating ourselves from the world around us, we unintentionally retreated inward—in our thoughts and in our bodies. The natural lengthening response of that first day of springlike weather resembles what happens in an AT lesson. We are moved to expand our attention into the world around us *because we want to be there*. We feel expansive, lighter, and happier. We have a fresh, new perspective on life. Everything we do seems easier. Musicians spend so many hours in solitary practice that it can become "winter" all year long. Allowing ourselves to expand our attention to include the space around us can invite the same sense of expansiveness and fresh perspective we get from the first spring day.

Another time to explore the unified field of attention is when we attend to details in practice and performance. Pianists are notorious for sitting at their instruments for hours on end. We don't have the choice to vary our position from sitting to standing as so many other instrumentalists do. Often a sore neck or back is the only stimulus to get up from the bench. But what if pianists, in addition to noticing what's happening between their fingers and the keyboard, were simultaneously aware of sensations throughout their neck and back? They may recognize a relationship between the sound they make, or the difficulty in making the sound they want, and the sensations they notice throughout their body. Integrating the self and environment enables one to gain insight into our stimulus and response patterns. I might not realize that every time I approach a particular passage I tighten in a way that actually makes it harder to play. If I'm not listening to myself as well as to the music, I might miss this.

> ▶ *AT helps us acquire skills that give us the freedom to choose our responses.*

> ♫ *Practice makes permanent.*

Too many musicians overlook the reality of this statement. Sometimes we are so busy attending to one part of a piece, or one aspect of playing it, that we discount the effect this repetition is having elsewhere. Many musicians work repeatedly to get a passage "note perfect." In the process, they may be missing something in the rhythm or phrasing they will need to address later. By the time later comes, their practicing has unintentionally reinforced the incorrect rhythm and phrasing. Practicing via repetition will solidify *everything* you're doing at the time. If you suddenly stiffen in reaction to a difficult note pattern, you are practicing this stiffening as well. With a soft awareness of everything, you can prevent yourself from learning something you actually don't want. I can attend to learning the notes and other musical details *and* be aware of myself in the space around me. This might seem counterintuitive, but it is a natural, efficient, and pleasurable way to learn music.

I mentioned earlier my ability to utilize ten minutes of practice to prepare a piece that was 45 minutes long. My *practice makes permanent* philosophy directly relates to this. Before the injury, I had spent most of my practice time playing through pieces without the awareness of what was being reinforced. When limited to ten minutes, I would choose one or two spots that I knew needed attention. When it was the only section I was practicing, I could tackle it more completely. Now, with my knowledge of AT, I integrate this type of practice with a new understanding of myself. I can look at a small section from every angle and recognize the bits that are unconsciously reinforced. The beauty of this type of practice is that it sticks. While I don't advocate practicing in ten-minute intervals to learn long pieces, I believe we can use our time more efficiently when we understand that practice makes permanent.

> ▶ *AT is learning to move in accordance with our design.*

> ♫ *The shortest distance between two points is a curve.*

The piano keyboard is four feet wide. In order to navigate this territory, you need to take advantage of the spiral nature of movement. Too often we try to get from the low end of the keyboard to the upper end by moving in a straight line. Contemplate your anatomy. There are no straight lines. Bones aren't straight, and neither is connective tissue. Our forearms rotate. Turning a doorknob is a simple way to observe this. The same movement you use to turn the doorknob gets you from point A to point B on a piano keyboard: a curve. If you try to move laterally, you end up pushing against yourself and will have trouble arriving on time. But if you acknowledge the spiral nature of movement, you will follow a curved trajectory. The movement is free and speed is increased. The shortest *and fastest* distance between two points is a curve. I'm sure you will notice, if you are checking, that your neck tightens when you try to move in a straight line.

This idea is not piano specific. I have seen it work on oboe, clarinet, violin, viola, bass, marimba, guitar, and even trombone. The slide may appear to move in a straight line, but the arm that is moving it needs to acknowledge the curve. Notice that I wrote *acknowledge*: You don't need to *do* anything. You just acknowledge the truth of your design.

▶ *AT introduces us to our continuous movements.*

♫ *There is no right posture.*

Another aspect of our design is its *tensegritive* nature. *Tensegrity* is a term coined by American sculptor and photographer Kenneth Snelson (1927–2016) and American architect and designer Buckminster Fuller (1895–1983). It combines the words *tension* and *integrity.* I and a host of others believe it is a more accurate description of how we are designed to move than the compression model of building blocks stacked in proper alignment. A tensegrity structure is an interdependent structure—movement in one area is reflected throughout the whole. It is also held together by a tensional balance—just like us. We don't relax when we learn AT. We coordinate appropriately around the activity at hand. Acknowledging our tensegrity prevents us from interfering with the easy tasks of movement.

My musician students are usually stuck somewhere between compression and tensegrity models as they play their instruments. They ask, "What is the best position for sitting?" or "How shall I achieve the best alignment for singing?" There are no positions in AT. Improved alignment is a result of good *use* rather than some end to gain directly. The violinist will rest the violin on their shoulder, like a shelf, and compress the left side of their body beneath that. Then they expect to move freely around that shelf in order to play. That's very difficult! When I convince them that the whole of them moves, as well as the fact that their bones are not their only support, they release the compression and are able to move freely everywhere. This makes their playing so much easier, enabling their bow arm to move more freely and have better contact with the strings. The clarinetist will compress and squeeze the middle of their torso, creating a compression structure. Once they relinquish the need to do that, they move as a free and integrated whole, with deeper support from the floor. Their sound becomes richer, breath is fuller, passages gain clarity, and rhythm is more precise.

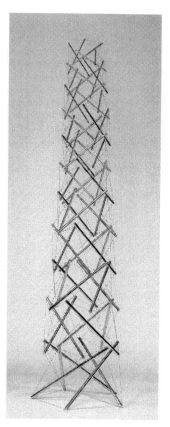

Penta Tower
Source: photo © Kenneth Snelson

Resonance is another way to experience tensegrity. In my next life I hope to play the cello. There is something about that instrument

GALVANIZING PERFORMANCE

that is close to our emotions. It's big—you get to hold it with your body and can feel its resonance everywhere. Feeling vibration from your instrument is magical. As a pianist, I don't get much of that, but many instruments allow you to feel their vibrational essence. Noticing vibrations can help you listen to a musical moment in a full and rich way. As you allow yourself to notice the resonance, it both brings you out of and deepens your awareness of yourself. Your bones resonate. Violinists and violists, instead of feeling like you create some sort of stable base for the instrument from which to move your arms and hands, you can follow the resonating buzz in your bones and feel all the movement within you while your instrument sings. And cellists, you will easily feel the resonance in the floor and in your feet. What a wonderful way to connect with your tensegritive nature and your support.

Tensegrity can be applied to how we make use of *all of us*, meaning that an intention to stand there is no less important than the connective tissue providing movement. A tensegritive structure is always movable, always responsive; it responds as a connected whole.

▶ *AT is a tool that helps us experience groundedness.*

♫ *Acknowledge your support.*

Support is key to all that we do as performing artists. What do we mean by support? Is it the floor beneath our feet? Is it our family and friends? This is a personal definition. We each have our own sense of what is and isn't supportive. You may find support in the way you prepare a program. I like to think most often of the support I receive from gravity because I know I can count on it. I wake up each morning knowing that if I roll out of bed I'll land on the floor—and that's a good thing. The day I don't will be a scary one indeed. Sometimes we act as though we need to push ourselves onto the floor, but we don't: There is nothing that will take us up from the floor unless we jump. Other times we act as though we need to hoist ourselves up from the floor, as though we are avoiding the very thing that helps us feel secure. There are many reasons for this. Perhaps we've had an injury that caused us pain whenever we put any pressure on a foot. We still walked on the floor but avoided that part of our foot. Once we've healed, we might still avoid that part of the foot because it's what we've practiced (remember *practice makes permanent*). I had a student who as she released into the support of the floor realized she had been tiptoeing around in order not to disturb anyone. As a young girl, she had been told that she made too much noise and would awaken her father who worked a late shift. While she wasn't actually on tiptoe, she was not allowing the floor to support her through her whole foot.

Several things can help reinforce our perception of gravitational support. Try dropping something. I did this when walking with a friend after some sort of emotional shock. Reminding myself that even though I felt unsupported, gravity was still working, I repeatedly dropped my small tote bag. Each time I did, I found myself releasing into the support of the ground. I like to tip over a half-full bottle of water, seeing that the water stays close to the floor. Seeing and feeling the water and its relationship to gravity helps me experience it in myself. I can let my arms and shoulders behave like the water by letting them flow to the "bottom of the bottle."

Another tool involves a series of awareness experiments that begin with a pen. Try this experiment: Take a pen (tip closed) and rub it on some different surfaces—your chair, your arm, your hair. Notice that you can actually sense the differences between these surfaces *even though you are not touching them directly*. The pen almost acts as an extension of your hand. A clear example of this is when people who are blind use a stick to stay safe in their surroundings. While their hand is on one end of the stick, the sense they get of where things are from the other end of the stick is important (Doidge 2007). To continue the experiments, stand behind a four-legged chair. Balance the chair on its one leg that is closest to you. Balance it lightly, without a tight grip. Notice that you can sense the floor through the chair's leg. You are supported by that same floor. Now balance the chair on the two legs closest to you, taking the time to notice the support from the floor, then go to all four legs as it was when you started. Isn't it interesting that you can now tap into that gravitational support? You are using the chair to notice the floor. If you can sense the support of the floor through the chair, then when you touch your music stand or a part of the piano (singers, this is for you), you can notice the ground it is on that also supports you. It is not about *doing* anything, but rather *acknowledging* what's going on.

One more thought on gravity: Many of us grew up being told that gravity pulls us down. This is not the whole truth. There are complementary forces at work: us and the gravitational field. If gravity only pulled us down, we would not be able to respond to it with the easy lengthening and expansion we can access. There is a force responding to our pull toward the earth that moves toward us. When you are exploring your relationship to the planet, remember that it comes up to support you.

Years after my discovery about a created persona, I was pondering the role of support in teaching. I am referring now to emotional support and the realization that a loss of that support may have contributed to my injury. Two years earlier, I had finally found a piano teacher who was guiding me on a path toward playing the piano as I had always wanted. He helped me find an ease and freedom of movement in playing that I had not thought possible. I returned to the school I had attended for undergraduate studies in order to study with the same piano teacher for my master's degree. During my second year of graduate school, however, unexpected circumstances forced him to leave the school. Learning anything is like learning to ride a bicycle: You may begin with training wheels, but the real learning isn't solidified until the training wheels are removed. He was an extraordinary teacher, but I had not studied with him long enough to own what I learned from him. I still needed my training wheels; I didn't feel ready to continue my piano studies without him. I felt unsupported and reached for support in the only way I knew: I created a false persona. The teacher never actually stopped supporting me, but my perception was that I was left on my own. How interesting that my perception of losing support may have resulted in an injury and ultimately a new direction in life—one where support is vital.

My most recent investigation into support involves its relationship to our sense of safety. When I don't feel safe, I compromise that easy relationship between my head and neck that is so important to effective functioning. Here's a simple experiment. Stand up but lean back a bit off your center of balance. At some point you will lean far enough back that you fear falling. What happens to your neck? Sometimes when we play our instruments we feel unsafe, either because we are off balance or have interpreted a situation as perilous for other reasons. Why, when we play, do we do so as if someone is threatening our life? We can laugh at this, but it happens. I would repeatedly remind one of my piano students of her safety during her lesson. For some reason she typically played for me as though her life was on the line. It was just a lesson! Each time she reminded herself that she was safe, her body eased greatly and of course her playing improved. It was more enjoyable to play that way too!

▶ *AT is a technique grounded in the reality of our design.*

♫ *Know that you are suggestible and use the information wisely.*

Suggestibility is a topic that fascinates me since teachers have relied on it for generations. Music teachers are notorious for using imagery and metaphors to elicit a new sound from a student. Some of these suggestions are quite useful; others may be less so. If they contradict our actual design, they can be problematic. I had a student tenor who was told by his voice teacher to imagine his diaphragm was an exercise ball and to push down on it. You can probably imagine the effort he put into his singing. I'm sure his voice teacher thought the suggestion was useful, but it clearly caused the student difficulty. As AT teachers and students, we are often faced with having to translate our music teachers' instructions into real and useful suggestions. Sensory suggestions can be helpful, but they carry responsibility. I prefer sticking to the truth of our design over images. Reality has not been distorted by my suggesting that the support of gravity is recognizable when I put my hand on the piano. I have not said that my diaphragm is an exercise ball. I have only enabled someone to realize what actually *is*. That is all that is necessary. When the tenor discovered that his diaphragm was not shaped like a ball and that he could not push it down, he began to allow his natural design to take over. The result was a free and rich voice.

How we use suggestibility becomes extremely important when it comes to *Body Mapping*. This term was coined by two AT teachers, Bill and Barbara Conable, to help students clarify their anatomical makeup (Conable and Conable 1995). The premise is that if students have misperceptions of how they are designed, they will use themselves according to those misperceptions. For instance, if I think my jaw hinges close to my chin, I may be apt to sing with a partially closed mouth. Probably the most startling example of a mismapping I encountered was with a student who came for lessons because of a limp. She had been to several doctors, and no one could find a reason for the limp. At her first lesson, she told me that she had a prosthetic eye. I gave her a pencil and asked her to hold it vertically at the center of her face. She held it in front of her good eye. When we went to the mirror so that she could see what she was doing, she gradually moved the pencil to her nose. And then when she walked, her limp had disappeared. She had been organizing her movement around her good eye.

A flutist came in to her lesson one day exclaiming, "I have pain in my right wrist!" The interesting thing was that she was pointing to her arm—about three inches toward her elbow from her wrist. I asked her to point to her left wrist—no problem there. I asked her to point to her right wrist, and again she pointed to the spot three inches away. When I asked her to look at what she was doing, she was amazed, then traced the space with her finger from her "false wrist" to the right location. So much tension dropped away in that moment, because she could finally move her wrist.

Body Mapping is significantly different from studying anatomy. While anatomy is the study of the human body—learning its form and function—it is not necessarily the same as understanding the form and function of *your own body*. And that is Body Mapping. You may have no clear conflict with a picture of the human body, but your internal understanding might not quite match up with reality. In other words, your personal experience may be quite different from what you're seeing. Getting in touch with that personal experience can be extremely important. Body Mapping aims to connect your perceptions with the reality of your makeup. Because so many of us have mismapped ourselves, I think it is important to stick with reality when it comes to suggestions. We already have enough misconceptions about our design. Adding other falsities to the mix can be confusing. Suggestibility works best when it comes from the truth. When that happens, the change in patterns of *use* can be extraordinary.

▶ *AT cultivates an openness that allows more information to become available.*

♫ *Open yourself to musical memorization.*

One day while attending an AT workshop, I was using the break time to memorize a piece of music. Although not a difficult piece to memorize, it still required work. I had just experienced three hours of AT and was feeling open, free, light, grounded, and all the other descriptive words we use to describe the indescribable to others. I played through the piece, using the written score before deciding what parts to memorize. As I read the piece, I realized that my openness was allowing me to absorb more than the usual amount of information. I felt as though I was absorbing the entire score. When I was done, I closed the book and played the entire piece from memory. I remembered it the next day and even the day after. I am not able to do this so easily with every piece I memorize, but I learned that day that the openness we bring to the task enables us to see, hear, and remember so much more.

When working with students in my musicians' classes, I always ask them to have a score handy even if the music is memorized. The muscular patterns we have associated with a piece are deeply connected to its memorization. *We have memorized these patterns and coupled them with all the other parts* (notes, dynamics, phrasing, and so forth). We are an interconnected whole: If we change one aspect of our movement, it affects the rest of us. Often as we make the changes that free our physical movements, we challenge the security of our memorization. We rely so much on kinesthetic memory that other musical landmarks may disappear. Understanding this link between muscular patterns and musical memory can be extremely helpful. Attending to patterns of use in the learning process can solidify memory. I can make an intentional gesture for a particular sound and know that my consciously choosing that gesture secures its memory—muscular pattern and notes.

Because memory and kinesthesia are closely related, exploring the security of a memorized passage in ways that challenge the relationship to the kinesthetic experience can be revealing. I don't do this because I need to but because doing it brings a deeper trust in what I have prepared. For example, play the notes of the right hand with the left hand and vice versa—not at the same time. If you can do this, you are learning to trust that you know the notes independent of the muscular patterns. Knowing the notes that way is not connected to how it feels. Once you return to using the appropriate hands, the knowing *is* connected to the feeling, and it is a deeper knowing. I can now trust that if I have a slip of the finger, recovery is easy because I don't rely solely on my muscle memory to get me through. I know my pieces well enough to change muscular effort without losing the memory. If I play a note with a different finger than usual, it does not throw me off as it once did. There is a newfound confidence in the memory that frees me to play as I wish.

▶ *AT teaches us not to interfere with reflexes that allow calmness to permeate our system.*

♫ *Consider excitement versus anxiety as a path toward improved performances.*

What happens to you when you are anxious? Does it affect your breathing? Your sense of support? Your body temperature? Your heart rate? Your field of attention (narrow versus expanded)? What happens to you when you are excited? Does it affect your breathing? Your sense of support? Your body temperature? Your heart rate? Your field of attention?

Try this experiment: Breathe shallowly and rapidly—maybe even pant a bit. These short quick breaths will cause you to feel anxious.

Conversely, if you intentionally slow your breathing to a fuller exhale and inhale, you will feel this anxiety diminish. Your breathing mechanism is both reflexive and voluntary. You don't need to think about it when you are sleeping (reflexive), but you can alter it to sing a long legato phrase (voluntary). Because the breath is responsive to your intentions, you can alter it to calm yourself down. You will believe you are less anxious when your breathing is not behaving the way it does when you are anxious. If you start with exhalation, the letting go of the breath, this practice corresponds with the lengthening of your spine, allowing for a greater and easier inhalation.

When you have spent months preparing for a performance, you are eager to play well. You have worked hard, and in some cases, you get only one chance to get it "right." Even if you have multiple performances of the same program, you only have one chance on a given night. You might be a little excited, causing you to breathe differently than you did in practice.

A tensegrity structure is an interconnected structure. Remember that change in one part affects the rest of it. Understanding this allows you to reroute your physiological responses (in this case, breathing) by recognizing that they are your *excitement* and not necessarily your *anxiety*. You have prepared, and preparation is the surest path to believing in excitement over anxiety. Performers who assume their symptoms are those of anxiety become more anxious. They will interpret the change in breathing as anxiety. It is your interpretation of the symptoms that can lead to trouble. Excitement and anxiety have similar physiological attributes, especially at the beginning. If you can inhibit your interpretation of the symptoms, you may recognize your excitement. When you are excited, the symptoms don't escalate.

One definition of Alexander's inhibition is what Tommy Thompson calls *withholding definition*. We often define our experiences before we actually have them, basing this definition on a past experience rather than the one we are having in the moment. If we expect to be nervous during a performance, we may indeed become nervous. This is what happens when we make assumptions about changes in breathing patterns. A past interpretation of the symptoms as those of anxiety probably led to an uncomfortable outcome. But when the symptoms show up again, we can withhold definition. We can accept the experience we are having in the moment. By accepting what is, we can prevent it from becoming what we might otherwise fear it will become.

▶ *AT allows us to redefine our priorities.*

♫ *Reconsider the priorities of your performances.*

Musicians often expect their performances to be perfect. I regularly challenge my definition of what *perfection* is. Is it getting the right notes? I don't think so. Is it playing a piece exactly as you played it last time? I don't think it's that either. For me, perfection is a direction: I am moving toward performances that increasingly satisfy me. I measure my ability to stay present and am pleased with a performance when I am truly *there*, responding to the music in the moment, listening almost as if it is my first time hearing it. There is a freshness and responsiveness to the music when we are present. I used to experience what I called momentary blackouts—tiny moments when I disappeared. Now I am much more successful at being present with the experience I'm having. Sure, I want to get the notes right! But if I miss one, it's not a failed performance. There are so many details to practice that we all hope will work well during a performance. It seems that the recording industry and its technology (hence, corrections) has made us believe we ought to be able to play with that type of perfection all the time. Our humanness includes imperfection. It is this attribute that allows for spontaneity and excitement in performance. Without taking risks, a performer can sound robotic. By prioritizing those elements that lead toward more satisfying performances, we can redefine what a perfect performance is.

▶ *AT allows us to perceive the usual in an unusual way.*

♫ *Musings on how to read a score:*

One day in my AT for Musicians class, a student was playing a piece with high and fast-moving sixteenth notes. She was not a singer, but the higher the range, the more anxiety showed up. Then she commented on how fast the notes were moving. I looked at her score and suddenly saw it in a new way: The noteheads were on top, and the stems hung down into the two groups of four sixteenth notes beamed together.

I saw the noteheads as heads—*my* head. I saw the stems as the rest of me connected to the deep black of the double beams. These beams were the ground. Although it may seem a bit absurd, as I looked at the notes that way, I felt more support from below. I saw all the black dots as free and movable heads totally *supported* by the ground. My student was able to see this as well. When she did, she stayed calm and supported while playing these fast notes. How does this work when the stems protrude up from the noteheads? I'm not sure yet, but I know that my perception is changeable and my experiences change with my perception.

▶ *AT is a tool that helps us stay present.*

♫ *Thoughts on listening:*

I had a piano teacher who, after giving me a suggestion, asked:

"Did you do it?"

"I tried."

"I *know* you tried. But did you *do* it?"

What a fantastic question. I didn't know. I only knew what I was attempting to do, but I was not available to hear whether or not I had actually done it. This seemed ridiculous to me. Why was it so hard to *know* if I did it? I needed to rely on taping my practice sessions in order to hear what I was doing, and sometimes I was surprised by what I heard. Then, after practicing AT for some time, something interesting started to happen. When I played back a recording, it was exactly as I had heard it while playing. What a wonderful experience.

What a relief. It didn't require hard work to achieve this. I needed only to get out of my own way and be present throughout my playing.

> ▶ *AT is a simplicity of being where we are fully supported, integrated, and coordinated around any activity we choose to do.*

♫ *Hands last.*

Hands last is related to Alexander's *end-gaining* principle. It is amazing how many times throughout the day we reach for things before coordinating around receiving them. As soon as we have an intention to do something, our system says, "Oh, I know how to do that!" *Hands last* allows us a tiny window of time between stimulus and response to go ahead as we started, not do what we thought we would do, or do something completely different.

Instrumentalists tend to focus on their hands. Sometimes the focus is so great that they exclude the rest of themselves. I used to ask my classes to draw self-portraits at the beginning of the semester and again at the end. Then we compared their self-perceptions. One semester a young violinist drew her hand—just *one hand*. That was how she perceived herself. At the end of the semester, she drew the front of her body along with things in her surroundings on one side of the paper, and the back of her with the things behind her on the other side of the paper. She clearly learned the concept of hands last. Her sound became so rich and full when she attended to her whole self in the world.

Hands last is also a guide in improvisation. As soon as I give myself permission not to behave in the way I start to behave, endless possibilities for other behaviors appear. In a split second I can alter my musical direction. In improvisation, this means there are new possibilities for notes to be played or rhythms to explore. In classical music, where we tend to reproduce the notes and rhythms of the masters, we are invited to explore the interpretations of these seemingly restrictive patterns. If I apply my *hands last* principle, I can find myself playing a piece for the hundredth time as though I am experiencing it for the first time.

Whenever we use our hands to do anything we can have a similar experience to playing a musical instrument. I find that because we are eager to use our hands for so much of what we do throughout our day, our complete coordination is often unavailable to us. It is part of our desire to reach our end goal before we are appropriately coordinated to do so. Often, because we are less committed to the results of a non-musical task, we can explore *hands last* in relation to simpler activities in life. My commitment to how I tie my shoes is nothing compared to how I play a musical phrase meaningfully. I learn a lot about my responses in daily activities that can be applied to my music making. By applying *hands last* to other activities, I become more keenly aware of how I use my hands in relation to my instrument. In music, I need my full coordination in order for my hands to have meaning. There is a movability, stillness, and flow of energy that comes through our hands, rendering them expressive. Hands are a convenient way to touch, though the action begins from a place deep within us. Our hands come last.

How Can Musicians Access These Principles on Their Own?

One of the most common questions I am asked is "How can I do this on my own?" This is where the simplicity of the technique shines. It may not always be easy, but it is simple.

Acknowledge What Is Important

This might be the simplest route to wholeness that there is. It is easy to think that our awareness of ourselves is less important than the activity we are involved in, such as playing an instrument. We find our wholeness when we can acknowledge that our sense of ourselves is *at least as important* as what we are trying to do. Attention to all the details is still very much possible.

Take the Time to Listen to Yourself and Not Just Your Music

This is similar to the suggestion above, but I repeat it here because the listening can go deep and is an ongoing event. What we listen to, how we listen, what affects our listening is ever-changing. Renew the listening again and again.

Know Where You Are and What's Around You

Orienting yourself to the space around you can be a powerful experience. Taking a few seconds to sense where you are and what is around you can thwart distractions as well as help you expand. We can easily lose focus if there is an unexpected sound in the hall. You can prepare yourself for the unexpected by knowing where you are.

Find an Open Window to the Primary Control

I use the image of the open window as a reminder that everything is connected. When I notice tightness somewhere in my body, I may become frustrated trying to release it. But there may be movability somewhere else. Rest assured that everything is connected. I allow myself to sense movement *where I can*, whether in my thinking or in my body. That's the open window. While many windows feel shut or inaccessible, there is usually one that is open—even just a little bit. As I begin to sense movement and release in that one area, it can spread to parts of me that I was unable to access directly. I gain access to more of me via the open window.

It is important that these releases take me to an easier relationship between my head and spine. I spent years freeing myself of unnecessary tension at the piano before I studied AT. This was useful to a point, but there was no central coordination around it. I would free one arm, then another, then a leg. I was putting out fires every few seconds in order to continuously find freedom to move. Once I discovered the organization from the head throughout the rest of me, it became so much simpler. Find an open window. Allow the release to spread and find its way to the primary mechanism.

Embrace the 2 Percent Solution

This is an idea I received from one of my first trainers, Bruce Fertman. When I first began my AT studies, I felt different after a lesson, and I wanted to feel that way all the time—100 percent. Bruce encouraged me to feel satisfied with 2 percent. This was very helpful. It was always clear to me that tension accumulates over time. What I had never considered was that the freedom from tension also increases.

Acknowledge Your True Design—Spirals and Tensegrity

We often lose sense of the spiral nature of movements. Tapping into that spiral—just acknowledging it—can bring tremendous relief and insight into what we are trying to do. Pause for a moment and consider where the spirals are and see what happens. Remember that you are a tensegritive being.

Use the Balance Disc and Any Other Tools That Work for You

I'm always looking for different ways to help students find their sense of support. One that I have a lot of fun with is the balance disc. It's a fitness aid that people use to develop their core strength. We have what many call "I don't want to die" reflexes. When we stand on a balance disc, our deep postural muscles receive a great challenge, and they will do whatever it takes not to die. I have instrumentalists play while standing on the balance disc—on flute, violin, French horn, trombone, you name it. When our system is trying not to die, the interference that is usually there for music making disappears. Your system prioritizes these activities for you: *Not dying becomes more important than playing.* The sound that everyone produces on the disc is amazing. This may seem counterintuitive. When the most important thing becomes not to fall off that disc, our customary habits of micromanaging our playing disappear. We may not feel in control, but we produce a beautifully free sound. One of my favorite aspects of this experience is what happens to students once they step off the disc. Suddenly they sense their gravitational support as never before. The stimulation they receive through their feet while on the disc heightens their awareness of the support that is always there. There is nothing to *do*. They play again with the ease that comes from feeling truly supported. Standing on the disc is like surfing. Your shoulders drop as you just sense the balancing challenge below. It requires that all the water flow to the bottom of the bottle.

Ask the Right Questions

When we are pleased with our playing, we usually ask ourselves what we did to make it happen. I think it's more useful to ask what we *didn't do* that allowed the new experience to take place. By asking what you didn't do, you won't try to recreate a feeling, probably the most common response to a lesson. You are better served by exploring the *conditions present* that allowed you to play freely. If we can recreate the *thinking* that was behind the new experience, then we may have an even better experience next time. Why limit yourself to reproducing a great feeling when a better one may be just around the corner?

Accept

This is one of the most powerful ways to achieve what you desire. David Gorman wrote one of my favorite articles on AT: "The Rounder We Go, the Stucker We Get" (Gorman 2012). In it, Gorman describes a typical pattern of noticing something because a symptom appears. The first thing we do is try to get rid of the symptom. We think it is wrong and so make changes to feel better, but soon enough the symptom returns. As we continue the loop of trying to fix ourselves and finding the symptoms reappearing, we never question what we do in the moment when the symptoms show up. We judge. We don't accept that moment. *Accepting doesn't mean liking.* It means deeply acknowledging what's happening and not judging it in any way. Accepting includes objective observation, and it removes so much of the conflict that we bring to ourselves. Acceptance is a practice. It has levels of awareness. It can be transformative.

Let Go of Judgment (Isn't That Interesting?!)

Whenever my students notice something about themselves, I always tell them there is only one suitable response to the moment: *Isn't that interesting?!* It is all very interesting. Without judgment we are free to observe ourselves with a true freedom to make new choices. As we stop judging ourselves, we become less judgmental of others, and that is a beautiful way to live.

The Bottom Line

F.M. Alexander was a man in search of solutions to his own vocal problems. He did not *invent* anything. Rather, he *discovered* some basic principles inherent in our design. I find this reassuring. He did this without an AT teacher. As much as I encourage you to seek a teacher for support and guidance on this most interesting path, I hope you can recognize that it is all within you to discover this work on your own. It requires curiosity and deep interest without judgment. As I help my students on their journeys, it is *their discoveries* that are most important. Everyone finds their own way in life—and in AT.

References

Adams, D. (2014) *The Twelve Commandments of Piano Playing*. The Well-Tempered Pianist. Accessed on March 21, 2017 at https://thewelltemperedpianist.files.wordpress.com/2015/07/12-commandments-of-piano-playing.pdf

Conable, B. and Conable, W. (1995) *How to Learn the Alexander Technique: A Manual for Students*. Portland, OR: Andover Press.

Doidge, N. (2007) *The Brain That Changes Itself: Stories of Personal Triumph from the Frontiers of Brain Science*. London: Penguin Books.

Gorman, D. (2012) "The Rounder We Go, the Stucker We Get." In *Looking at Ourselves: Exploring and Evolving in the Alexander Technique*. Toronto: Learning Methods Publications.

Jones, F.P. (1997) *Freedom to Change*. London: Mouritz. (Original work published 1976.)

Full Embodiment

The Actor's Way

Sarah Barker

AT Perspective

My work with F.M. Alexander's discoveries and acting has
provided me with a clear and practical understanding: The
actor's imagination is magnified when fed by a simple act of
release into balanced coordination. A delicate adjustment
of one's head in relationship to the top of the whole spine
causes a cascade of reorganization throughout the torso
followed immediately by a lengthening in the limbs. I call this
balanced coordination. Whether beginning acting students or
seasoned professionals, all actors experience a deeper, more
connected experience when they support their performance
with a conscious triggering of balanced coordination.

In order to serve every level of actor, I introduce the
conscious AT tasks they can use in a sequence. In the first step,
they free the neck in order to release the head lightly away
from the top of the spine. Beginners can find a powerful change
in their performance with just this step. In these situations I
draw on the power of kinesthetic imagery. Imaging how the
body moves through space and time (kinesthetic imagery) is
a fundamental aspect of movement imagery, a well-defined
construct in the sports sciences. Movement imagery refers

to the kinesthetic as well as visual properties of movements that are rehearsed mentally in the absence of overt physical movement (Hall 2001). I give participants precise images of the connection between the top vertebra and base of the skull and how it can subtly move to improve balance. To that I add images of the full surface area of neck muscles, giving ways to think of those muscles softening or releasing. Participants learn to pause or suspend action for a split second before launching into a performance in order to keep these images in mind while acting (this is the equivalent to Alexander's *inhibition*). I have used this approach to great effect in introductions to AT and acting at conferences, including the Southeastern Theatre Conference and the Association for Theatre in Higher Education, where few participants have any knowledge of the technique.

The second step includes allowing the whole spine to lengthen and the torso to expand through outward release in response to the movement of the head. Again, I direct the actors' attention and imagination to construct a self-image in which they sense their back, sides, and front in full dimensions. They are aware of the unity of their whole body from the bottom of the feet to the top of the head. Actors need to have studied AT enough for this to be an action they can take without detracting from the performance they're executing. As an actor pursues an action and reacts to the acting partner, they see (internal image) the whole body in motion moment to moment. When successful, their presence and ease of action are visibly increased.

In the third step, the actors expand their field of attention. They learn to focus on their physical experience while at the same time attending to the environment around them.

I have been strongly influenced by my training with Marjorie Barstow, whose pedagogical technique was to teach AT while a student was performing an activity. It is not necessary to achieve a state of "good self-use" *before* applying it to activities. Instead, directing one's self to allow a new relationship of ease becomes the initial step for action (physical or psychological).

In this context the activity is acting. I teach an art of acting combining the actor's authentic, personal responses to the character's inner life with full embodiment through physical imagery in the actor's body. As I come to understand what the actor believes the character is experiencing psychologically, I ask, "Where do you feel that in your body?" and "Describe it with imagery." This is always linked to the actor/character's need to do something to another character. In order to accomplish this need, AT direction initiates the action and combines with the inner character imagery.

Reference

Hall, C.R. (2001) "Imagery in Sport and Exercise." In R.N. Singer, H.A. Housenblas, and C.M. Janelle (eds) *Handbook of Psychology* (2nd edition). New York: John Wiley & Sons, Inc.

This chapter illustrates my coaching of actors with attention to their self-use and acting process. My method is to respond to each actor's personal process for embodying the story, character, and language. The Alexander Technique powerfully helps actors physically manifest what is in their imagination. I guide actors in using principles of AT to free themselves of unnecessary muscular tension as they explore the psychological conflicts inherent in dramatic texts. AT also helps actors consciously increase their sensitivity to other actors and the audience, thus moving the audience powerfully.

I will begin with a basic classroom project of physically interpreting poetic texts that, with AT explorations in movement and word, become easier and more deeply felt. Second, I describe private coaching with an actor to develop a daily practice that eliminates habits of unnecessary tension. He then applies new patterns of self-use to perform a speech by Shakespeare's character Oberon with ease and specificity. Working in Japan with conservatory actors on naturalistic scenes from classic

20th-century American texts, I show how including AT supports psychological character work and expands actors' field of attention to increase sensitivity to each other and the audience. Finally, I describe my work with a professional actress preparing a challenging emotional and physical performance and how I helped her free her voice and refine her final performance.

In all these cases, my intention was to work with each actor's personal creative process. Based on our initial conversations, I came to understand how each actor interpreted the character and text. My coaching aims to create moments of freedom that encourage creativity and novel choices during an actor's rehearsals and performances. As noted in the AT Perspective, my training with Marjorie Barstow helped me understand that exploring the new relationship of balance throughout the body becomes the means-whereby the actor carries out the performance. It is not necessary to achieve a state of "good self-use" *before* applying AT to rehearsal and performance. Instead, exploring the new relationship of balance throughout the body becomes the means-whereby the actor carries out the performance. Directing one's self to allow a new relationship of ease becomes the initial step for action (physical or psychological). Through practice over time, actors' self-use improves, particularly in relation to their performance.

In coaching, I rely on particular aspects of AT. Two of these are unity of the whole human organism and greater freedom of movement. When these goals are achieved, they inevitably create compelling performances. When there is fragmentation and excess effort, performances seem mechanical and overplanned.

Beginning with freedom in the neck enables the positive change in the head's balance on top of the whole spine. Exploring and experimenting with the relationship of the head to the whole spine, a person can unlock a mechanism of total integration throughout the spine/torso and limbs (primary control) (Fischer 2000 [1942]). In the moment of that release (upward flow in the spine and reflex lengthening out the limbs), the actor (or anyone) unifies mind and body and moves with ease. Exploring the principle of AT inhibition encourages actors to allow a split-second pause before launching into a performance, helping them replace habitual patterns of effort with greater self-awareness and new creative impulses.

Expanding the field of attention affects the interaction between actors as well as how the audience is affected. Frank Pierce Jones's description defines it eloquently:

> I had to expand my attention so that it took in something of myself and something of the environment as well. It was just as easy, I found, instead of setting up two fields—one for self (introspection) and another for the environment (extraspection)—to establish a single integrated field in which both the environment and the self could be viewed simultaneously. (Jones 1976, p.9)

The Particular Acting Aesthetic with Which I Work

My approach to acting processes is based on Constantin Stanislavski's work combined with contemporary physical acting approaches such as those of Michael Chekhov. I teach students to produce acting that combines heightened naturalism with full embodiment of the character's inner life. The process mines the actor's authentic, personal responses in an imaginary situation. It privileges spontaneity and experiences of discovery.

Once an actor develops a neurological connection between physical movement, thought, and feeling, the work is fully embodied and impulses emerge from the body's center and extend throughout the limbs. Beginning actors usually notice that their movement does not fully express their thoughts and feelings (or inner impulses or inner life). However, I teach them to develop thinking in the body and use it in rehearsal and performance. Trained professional actors appreciate the links between the inner life and the physical expression that develop gradually through movement investigation in rehearsal. Expert actors and beginners find the improvisational movement explorations I give develop the connection between thinking and moving. This work was inspired by Kristin Linklater's sound and movement exercises and Jerzy Grotowski, Joseph Chaikin, and Richard Schechner's movement improvisations.

My goals for the art of acting are: 1) full-body involvement in expression rather than isolated segments of the body; 2) believable, authentic expressions of inner psychology; 3) more compelling expression with less effort; 4) greater precision and fluidity in movement; 5) spontaneous and surprising reactions in character relationships along with unexpected nuance in communication; 6) greater sympathy and responsiveness between actors.

Young Actors Work with Poetry

This exercise illustrates how young actors' physical responsiveness to textual images can be developed. The final phase of the exercise applies conscious AT direction to the exploration. In this phase, the actors transform the quality of their performance both in their personal experiences and the experience of the audience.

With my guidance, the actors prepare a short poem for presentation. I ask the actors to move in response to images or feelings that each word evokes. They are not to act out literal interpretations like miming digging with a shovel for *dig* or flapping their arms for *fly*. A less literal interpretation often occurs if they start with the separate sounds in each word, physicalizing the sensation of the sound, first in the mouth, then extended into the whole body. Linking these movements together produces movement that expresses the whole word. Continued improvisation gradually alters the movement until a satisfying repeatable gesture is established. All of the words in a phrase are developed in this way, then are linked into a physical phrase. Throughout the improvisations, full-body movements evoke emotional or psychological responses, affecting the face and voice. The audience sees it in the face and the quality of motion, and hears it in the voice. At this point in the explorations, the gestures need to be large enough that an audience can see them clearly. In fact, I explicitly ask the actors to stay aware of the audience.

Before AT is introduced, this developmental process and the resulting performances ordinarily use muscular effort that interferes with unity of mind and body. The gestures seem difficult, and the phrasing is disjointed. Challenges such as maintaining the large scale of the gestures, effort of expression, and self-consciousness with being watched compete with the actors' attempts to allow emotions to naturally arise from the images and movements. So after the first presentation, I work with the actors to integrate AT directions to remove these obstacles and facilitate the connection to feelings in the performance. The other students watch and give feedback to support their colleagues' learning.

Here is one example: Grace Fennell presents the poem "Blue Sky" by Pasckie Pascua, in which the poet talks to his absent mother. Grace sinks to the floor with weight and struggle. She is alone, abandoned. Then she grasps an invisible rope and begins to draw herself upward, off the floor, saying, "I want to touch the sky and feel your face/where streaks of rain used to flow freely." She describes her mother as "on ebb tides and full moons: you come and go/to and fro like wind and rain and sun and snow" (Pascua 2014, p.29). Her body becomes these elements as she floats in the remembered comfort that is no longer there. It is an evocative performance that seems difficult to perform. I use AT to help Grace ease the execution of her movements, enhancing audience reception of her performance.

As she repeats the presentation, we explore how AT helps her improve her physical awareness and expression throughout her body. I ask her to focus for a moment on letting her neck be free. I place my hands on her neck just long enough to assist her in releasing the tension in her performance. As she begins to fall to the ground, she takes an extra split second to release her head forward and upward until she senses her spine freeing and lengthening upward. Again, I manually support rebalancing her head. In addition, a moment of hands on her torso reinforces her back and spine becoming more fluid. She lets this new condition continue as she falls to the floor. Then, to grasp the imaginary rope, she renews freeing her neck and balancing her head. As her spine follows her head, her arms become free and reach up. She creates the impression that she is struggling to pull herself up on the rope, and her joints and muscles remain fluid while she moves.

Of her experience, Grace said:

It made it feel more graceful and effortless. When Professor Barker sent me off into the "ocean," I felt like I was really riding the ocean for a second and as if my movements were just natural and I wasn't really trying to do them. I also just really like what I did. I felt like it was so much more beautiful and soft. It didn't feel like I was trying to remember my moves for a performance and act them out; it felt like I was really just being pushed around by the ocean. One instance when I applied AT was in my movement with the rope. At first when I tried, it was very difficult and required a lot of effort. I was tense in my neck and shoulders. I thought this was because I had to act like I was climbing a rope, and that itself requires effort. Professor Barker told me that you in fact are not supposed to use effort but just appear like you're using effort. I held my neck free and lifted my shoulders to give the appearance of struggling to climb the rope when in fact I wasn't struggling that much.

This process encourages the performer to attend to the manner of execution. The actor now adds self-observation and self-direction to whatever else they do. This leads the performer to pay attention to each moment of the performance. Attending to freedom and flow of movement reduces excess effort. At the same time, the actor is increasingly able to create mental images and react to them emotionally. I describe excess physical effort as creating mental static. When static is reduced, communication between the actor's thoughts and movement, and between the actor and the audience, improves. Less muscular effort leads to more capacity for imagination and characterizes the goal of this work. The effect is that actors share their experience with the audience with clarity and emotional impact.

When working this way, actors feel they are taking more time than usual to execute an action. Sometimes they are concerned that during the performance they take too much time to keep the audience's attention. However, in the poem presentation just described, observers did not report a sense of lagging or slow movement. Instead, the audience saw more detail, and the story affected them more emotionally than the first time they saw the poem, although the performance took nearly the same amount of time.

A Young Man Works on Oberon's Speech

A second case involves a student actor, Leroy Kelly, who took private lessons with me after participating in the coursework just described. Our work began by applying AT skills to his self-use. A disciplined body builder, he employed the same quality of pressure and strain in all of his acting work. He would need to practice AT every day to eliminate the extreme habitual muscular contraction and compression he used in his body-building work. He needed to repeat the new physical organization to replace his well-practiced habits of strain. Once he made some changes in his physical use, we could work on a monologue.

I had him lie on his back on the floor to help him eliminate the body's struggle with gravity and experience release. I asked him to calm himself, letting the weight of his body release to the floor. This work is based on AT table work, in which the teacher's hands guide the body to release and lengthen. But our activity quickly focused on simple movements the student can do on his own to encourage lengthening and widening. My prompts were: 1) gently lift and lower one arm at a time, finding ease and length in the arms and neck; 2) let the ribs move flexibly with the breath, imagining them softening toward the spine; 3) move the arms over the head, allowing the ribs (especially the lower ribs) to stay close to the center of the torso, preventing them from lifting up and out; 4) maintain the torso as a unified whole from the bottom of the pelvis to the top of the spine, all parts in balance with the integrity of the spinal curves; 5) let the neck remain easy, shoulder blades rooted in the back while still remaining wide apart.

Next he stood and I encouraged the upward support of the spine to follow the slight release forward and upward of the head. We also explored how he could lift his arm without fixing/contracting the muscles (especially of the upper arms and shoulder) to prepare for arm gestures in expressing text. This set the stage for performance work.

He presented a part of Oberon's speech from *A Midsummer Night's Dream*, Act II, Scene 1. He had connected large physical gestures to the images, and I manually helped him to support each gesture with AT head/neck/spine coordination. In particular, he found that he drew his shoulders together for many of the full-body gestures. For example, he worked with "sleeping eye-lids laid" with a gesture of delicately smoothing, then quickly shifted to antic movement on "madly dote":

> *Fetch me that flower; the herb I shew'd thee once:*
> *The juice of it on sleeping eye-lids laid*
> *Will make or man or woman madly dote*
> *Upon the next live creature that it sees.*

(Shakespeare 1968 [1623], p.167)

But the excess tension in his shoulders restricted his ability to create an impression of gentle, tender application of the flower's juice. In addition, the tension restricted his breath and voice. The transition was stilted and unclear. To change this, he released his head away from the top of the spine so that his torso lengthened upward as he began the phrase. He brought his shoulders up and forward as his arms and hands lengthened forward on "eye-lids laid." The student reported, "My movement was more open with more space to move in. My gesture was easier and clearer and more emotionally engaged."

The actor experienced significant changes beyond the specific work on Oberon's speech. His report of the global changes in his attitude and acting skills gives an idea of how AT can affect an actor's future work and performance success. Of the work, he said:

When I use AT I feel different, a different self. My gestures are lighter. When I am doing a speech, I don't have to decide to make a gesture, they happen. As I work, I go through the images with greater time and space to move into. I don't have to work to create the images that go with what I am saying— they just come into my mind. I am not planning as much as letting them happen. Each image moves/flows into the next. Within the structure of the text I am able to improvise. I now see other actors planning too much the way I used to. They looked stilted and as if watching themselves. This is how I used to experience self-doubt. Doubt comes through all the time, but with AT it's that release in my head that's starting to happen. I'm discovering more of myself and letting go of the inner demons. This also allows me to mix imagery of the text and personal memory. I'm learning to personalize the images. They become very clear and emotional connections happen.

When Leroy directs his attention to a unified self he is less likely to critique his creative expression during performance. It may seem logical for one to expect the actor to "look stilted as if watching themselves" if he uses conscious control. But the effect is the opposite. He is no longer simultaneously judging his theatrical expression while performing. Instead he enjoys the freedom he creates by integrating AT directions with his portrayal of textual imagery. I train actors to find personal connections to the ideas they communicate. Leroy refers to this as personalization. I teach actors to imagine seeing, hearing, tasting, smelling, touching whatever they refer to. They link spontaneous emotional reaction to these sensations. As this develops, actors also link AT directions (neck free, head releasing forward and upward, torso lengthening and widening) to each imagined experience. The actors become more and more proficient at creating active thoughts and imagined experiences that stimulate a variety of new physical behaviors.

Coaching Actors at the New National
Theatre Drama Studio of Tokyo

These young actors had had one or two years of actor training. They had studied Sanford Meisner's repetition exercises and scene work, voice work, singing, and movement work including Lorna Marshall's physically based acting techniques and AT. Their acting teacher, Minako Ikeuchi, says that Japanese actors are forceful and strong in their playing. The theatre culture rewards effort in expression, resulting in an underlying sense of pushing or rushing to meet the director's demands and the play's emotional heights (Ikeuchi 2015, personal interview). In response to these circumstances, I helped the actors explore AT concepts in order to honor their authentic experiences and further explore them with less force and manipulation.

The first concept is nurturing self-awareness in place of self-consciousness. Simply put, self-consciousness tends to create negative judgment and assessment of self. Self-awareness is impartial, curious observation of self. I began with an exercise I call "Listening to the Body" to develop actors' active self-awareness.

Listening to the Body is subtle work the individual actor undertakes to respond to physical movements latent in the body. To begin, they notice places of pressure or tension in their muscles. They often think they have to keep that tension in order to stand or maintain good posture. I ask them to notice what they are resisting, such as an urge to twist or bend or collapse. The actor makes small adjustments to slowly, bit by bit, allow the urge their sensed body desires. After each adjustment, they pause, observe sensation, and discover the next movement the body seems to need. Many report that they inhale spontaneously and fully as they release into the body's requests. I encourage them to allow twists and bends and off-center movement or tiny, repeated movement like a finger flicking or eyes blinking. The experience of moving without commanding and controlling one's body leads to feeling the body as a unified whole, a slowing of the nervous system, and, most likely, stimulation of the parasympathetic nervous system. An actor will usually feel more in tune with emotions and physical sensation, as well as more interested and often surprised by how they move. Generating movement this way emphasizes the importance of listening to their natural impulses rather than controlling movement dictated by their own intellectual analysis or a director's instruction. In later coaching sessions, I refer to the quality of self-awareness and mind/body unity they discover in this exercise. This lays the groundwork for actors to explore rather than force behavior as it relates to exploring a character's behavior in the world of the play.

The second concept is becoming conscious of and releasing an individual's habitual patterns of effort.

The observation exercise "Exploring Preparation: Ready, Set, Go" helps the actor discover their habits of preparation and the effects of inserting a split-second pause (inhibition) the moment before performing an action or speaking. The actors begin with the intention to perform a prepared audition monologue or speech with high intensity and volume. I ask them to imagine a high-stakes situation such as an important audition or a performance in front of a large audience. Then I lead them through four different experiments/observations for getting ready to perform the monologue. Steps 1 and 2 are the same each time:

1. Get yourself ready in the moment before you begin.

2. Focus on doing the best performance possible.

Step 3 is different each time:

3a. Perform the first line of the monologue. Then stop and observe what you have done physically and mentally to prepare. Discover what has been the effect of your preparation.

3b. When it is time to speak, don't, but suspend or do something completely different. Notice what changes in your physical set pattern. Observe for changes in attitude.

3c. When it is time to speak, don't, but use AT directions to release upward. Notice what happens as the release upward stimulates lengthening and widening throughout your body.

3d. In order to speak, pause for a moment, initiate AT directions, and maintain them as you speak. After speaking, compare your experiences in experiment 3a and experiment 3d.

In the final experiment, 3d, I define the AT concept of inhibition as a pause or moment of suspension. In the setting of the Japanese studio, we discovered it is similar to "Ma," a central concept in the traditional Japanese aesthetic meaning the void between (space, pause). Allowing Ma introduces an element of time to create and experience a moment deeply and with little effort. Within the pause, the actor observes, staying open to new possibilities of reacting. Attending to Ma leads to greater imaginative and authentically felt character experience.

To conclude these preparations for scene work, the actors walked around the studio applying the basic AT directions with hands-on guidance from AT teachers who assisted me. Thus the stage was set for me to coach scenes.

A Streetcar Named Desire

The first scene from *A Streetcar Named Desire* (Williams 2004 [1947]) demonstrates how I work with each actor's rehearsal goals. All of the actors in this studio intensely prepare their emotional state before beginning a scene. They are highly focused and keep in mind the given circumstance of the play and characters' needs. They easily discuss the power dynamics between characters and their complex conflicting needs. After they performed part of the scene, I asked what I could help them with or "How did it go?" This gave me a focus for coaching.

Two actresses played sisters Blanche and Stella in the opening scene of *A Streetcar Named Desire*. They reported that they had trouble connecting to their partner. The actress playing Blanche was personally nervous and tried to use the feeling for the character, but it got in the way of her reacting to the other character. The actress playing Stella kept losing her focus—her attention jumped all over the place. I observed a subtle forcing of emotions in both actresses as they looked intensely at each other without being truly affected by one another. They did not draw the audience into their world, instead creating a solid fourth wall.

Blanche is in fact very nervous, so that behavior or feeling is appropriate to the character. The trouble comes because the nervousness the actress felt was general, unattached to the given reality of the play. Stella is also likely to be distracted and overwhelmed by many feelings: seeing her sister in this deteriorated state, embarrassed by her messy house and Blanche's reaction, puzzled by the aloofness she sees in Blanche. The actress playing Stella, like her acting partner, needed more specificity in communicating her experience.

The actors needed to root the experiences in the body. I asked Blanche to start the scene by taking two stiff drinks of alcohol before her sister arrived. This would give her a strong reason to be nervous when Stella entered the room. I pointed out that she, as Blanche, was attacking the glass to pour the drink, diving forward with her shoulders and chest—pulling down. Her quick reaction was to think she shouldn't move that way. But I encouraged her to continue this action. I explained that applying AT does not mean she must be in good posture in order to perform. AT lets her shape her body as Blanche, to attack the glass while keeping fluidity and ease. I touched her neck and asked her to think of her head moving away from the top of her spine so her spine could lengthen, and her whole body lengthen and widen. As the lengthening began, she again attacked the glass and closed the shoulders—but now with greater ease.

To help the actress playing Stella be affected by Blanche, we examined the way she used her eyes. She was carefully watching Blanche but then would look around the room to consider Stella's discomfort with the state of her home. She would lose her awareness of her sister—she could not pay attention to both. By using the heightened physical awareness that comes from working with AT, we were able to change her focus. This aspect expands the field of attention from focus only on self to focus on the self within the entire room. At the same time, the actor can include the other actor's body and movement into their personal awareness. The expansion begins with noticing freedom in the neck, allowing new balance of the head, and new fluidity and expansion in the whole torso. I asked the actress to imagine sending out energy beyond her body, into the room, and finally, surrounding the other actress with the energy. The simple change in perspective had a powerful effect on the actress's internal life. She was now simultaneously able to respond sensitively to Blanche's every move and make decisions moment by moment about what she, Stella, should do.

The Odd Couple (Female Version)

The second scene I worked with was *The Odd Couple* (Female Version) by Neil Simon (1986). Act 2 Scene 3 begins with the roommates silently antagonizing each other with deliberate actions. Florence Unger is trying to eat a meal. Everything must be precise. Olive Madison deliberately antagonizes Florence, spraying air freshener all around the meal. The actress playing Florence faces a performance dilemma. She wants to be free of excess tension, keep her voice free, and expand her awareness of and presence in the performance space. However, Florence's most natural reaction to Olive's antagonism is to cringe. She tightens and contracts her arms and neck. Her gestures convey a building anger and need to control. Her voice tightens, her attention narrows. Neither the audience nor Olive can receive the full impact of Florence's struggle to control her anger. What I wanted to offer to her was using AT (freeing her voice and expanding her field of attention) to support her spontaneous reactions. As she is imaginatively engaged, her character reactions originate from the subconscious, spontaneously, and with believable complexity. Asking the actress to consciously release her neck and direct her head to move forward and upward would likely distract from that valuable link to her own inner life. I felt it important to approach the solution obliquely, indirectly. Assuming she is imaginatively engaged, her character reactions originate from the subconscious, spontaneously, and with believable complexity. Rather than risk breaking that valuable link to her own inner life, I approached the solution obliquely, indirectly.

I asked the actress to evoke Florence's best in-control moment. She performed Florence as satisfied, easy, and enjoying an ordered and peaceful meal. Her body naturally began to release and balance. Together we reinforced this physical state with AT directions. My hands were on her head, neck, and shoulders. She carefully organized the placement of her plate, napkin, and silverware. Her back released back and her whole torso became balanced on her sit bones on the chair. She reported that Florence/she was pleased with her state. She was attached to and pleased with the dinner setting. I reminded her of one simple objective—to keep order. She imaginatively committed to this goal. Then I surprised her: I reached down and scrambled the silverware in front of her. Spontaneously and immediately she recoiled and compressed, a natural reaction for the actress and character. We repeated the sequence: She organized the silverware, I scrambled the place setting. I asked her to observe what she did physically and where she directed her attention. I wanted her to tell me exactly where the compression was and what happened to her neck and spine. She reported this accurately. Then I asked her to create the same movements in the body, the same body shape of compression by using AT directions to get there. She started from an easy, open state. Then, as I helped her with my hands to use AT, she slowly curled her shoulders, narrowed her chest, and thrust her head forward. She did this fluidly, with as much lengthening as possible. When she completed the transformation, she reported that her breathing was free and that she still felt easy and balanced. However, the audience still saw her character, disturbed by what was happening, recoil and compress. This is key to understanding how actors can use themselves well while still portraying a character whose story affects the audience. Actors can create the essence of the human experience rather than having to fully experience the strain and effort that would occur in the real situation. The actor playing Florence contorted her body in reaction—but with the greatest amount of ease and length possible.

Working with the actor's field of attention strengthens the actor's presence on stage and captivates the audience further. I asked the actress to draw from her experience in another exercise we did to prepare for scene work. In this exercise, the actors explore awareness of volume and space. The purpose is to expand the field of attention in all directions and strengthen the actor's presence on stage.

The actors walk a random path through the space, crossing through the middle frequently. I guide them in four different ways to imagine and become aware of the whole space:

- As you walk, notice that you can see the floor and ceiling at the same time. As this stimulates activity in your peripheral vision, become more aware of how much you can see to the sides as well. If you are moving through the space with a group, heighten your awareness of people as they pass by you without focusing on any individual.

- Imagine that you can feel the density of the air. As you walk toward a wall, imagine feeling the air pressure increase. At the same time, imagine the pressure behind you becomes lighter and lighter as you walk away from the wall behind you. If you prefer, imagine a color in the air that intensifies or deepens in front of you and gets lighter and lighter behind you as you walk.

- Feel the light breeze that you create as you walk at a brisk pace through the space. Become aware of the eddies and turbulence you create as you walk. If you walk closely past someone else, you will feel a greater disturbance in the airflow. Imagine the swirling of the air increasing as the currents rise to the ceiling and corners of the room. Imagine the turbulence returning around you as the air bounces off of the walls.

- Imagine that your whole body emanates light as if you were a human light bulb. Imagine the light strong enough to illuminate the walls and ceiling. Fill the room with your light. If there are other people in the room, imagine that you are surrounding them and including them in your light.

Using this exercise, the actress becomes aware of her back, her sides, top of her head, her feet. She pays attention to the room all around her and the other actor moving about her. Expanding her field of attention magnifies what the audience sees when she reacts to the other actress during the scene.

The actress can use AT during the performance to emphasize her reactions in one more way. She can insert AT directions into the moments her character, Florence, recomposes herself after each attack of Olive's spraying of deodorizer. After she recoils, she can allow her neck to free and lengthen her torso in coordination with rebalancing her head forward and up. Technically, this is a brief rest for the actress. But it also helps the audience see the character's intention to return to control. I asked the actress who plays Olive to expand her field of attention to include Florence's minute changes and to mirror them and respond accordingly with Olive's desires to disturb Florence. This improved the actors' focus and the amount of detail that the audience saw.

Coaching a Professional Actress for Performance

A colleague, actress, and vocal specialist, Erica Tobolski, asked me to coach her for an upcoming performance of *The Other Place* by Sharr White. She described a problem in her rehearsals: She felt like she was choking herself and restricting her voice in moments of high conflict. We discussed what Erica might be doing physically to interfere with her vocal performance. When she came to the most deeply felt, difficult moments in the play, she psychologically connected with the character but her body was stopping her speaking clearly and expressively. This is a normal human reaction many actors must find ways to overcome. In ordinary life, when people feel deep emotional pain or anger, the natural reaction is to suppress the feelings in order to stay in control. An authentic reaction happens, and unconscious responses kick in to repress the feelings. When we discussed this during our working session, Erica also worried that the huge emotional event in the script was demanding more than she could give.

We began with the most intense moment. As Erica entered into the character's action, her chin rose and her shoulders lifted slightly inward, toward her ears. As she touched into emotion, she felt it rising in her, a truthfulness that carried pain and loss, and her breathing was restricted. Despite her strong intention to do otherwise, she shut down the feelings as soon as they came up.

I said what she was doing posturally was right for the character's psychology. What lay before us was to find a new pathway to that physical shape. I asked her to initiate the lifted chin and narrowed shoulders by freeing her neck and allowing her head to move delicately up. As her spine softly lengthened, she completed the physical shape of pain and loss. Then as she spoke the lines, I asked her to find moments where she could slightly release her shoulders and tip her chin down. When a breath came in, she lengthened and widened her torso.

As we worked, she saw that constriction and freedom are not fixed states, that there can be a fluidity going to constriction, then back to free flow and ease. "If I felt myself go back to a constrictive pose or constrictive place, I could notice that and then I could make an adjustment. It wasn't that I had to place myself in a particular position." The key was in the realization that she did not have to maintain an open posture to perform the character with ease. "You can't act from a place of good posture, alignment. Because there's no truth in that. That would be an actor directive layered on top of your creative impulses." She described the challenge:

What I know about acting is to follow an impulse. So if I have the impulse, I go with it. If my own pattern is stopping me, then I've got to find a way to adjust in the moment so that the impulse can flow through me and the breath and the voice can be expressed. If a physical pattern of resistance or control stops/blocks me in the moment, I make an adjustment so breath and body can fully express that impulse.

As we worked together, I encouraged her to repeat the pattern of resistance and emotional experience deeply and fully. Several times, she let herself find the impulse to contract and arch, letting it fully manifest. Our session proceeded with the basic AT directions, to begin speaking with less muscular contraction. Technically, she went into the physical form, the movement, of the emotional expression. She lifted her chin, and her shoulders still contracted but with more mobility and length. Then she could breathe fully—and with freer breath she could experience the emotional life of the character. This way of working let her release this emotional life through her body. She saw the possibility for change and variation every step of the way. She said:

It's almost that the very flexibility of the spine, allowing that flexibility to be a living thing. Just like thoughts shift and morph, emotions swell and recede—the very thing of life. The body itself does that and the spine does that. There are surges and retards, just like the breath rises and falls, the spine moves with the breath. Allowing for that to happen rather than saying that I have to be a certain way.

She also explained that this helped her practice what Arthur Lessac called atom to atom movement (Hurt 2014). "If you feel yourself veering off the road you don't jerk yourself back on the road. You might tip over. You don't stop and start again. You just gently guide yourself back onto the road."

She said my hands-on guidance gave her feedback, a gentle suggestion to try something different, as if to say, "Try this instead." The AT coaching encouraged her to release muscular tension. "If I unconsciously go into restriction, I can just as easily consciously come out. Then I could imprint the new physical sensation to what I wanted to feel." As she crafted her performance, she responded with thoughts and emotions that in the past had stimulated restriction. She could instead associate a release in her neck, throat, and shoulders with the emotional reaction, so that she associated it with the new sensation. She said, "My job is to rehearse the path so that I can get there again." The hands-on work gave her a new experience, enabling her to achieve what she aimed for. She rehearsed telling herself, "'I need to, I can, release those muscles so I can breathe and move into the dramatic moment.' I found the way to get there was through the breath." By her opening performance her breath was happening unconsciously and well.

During rehearsal, Erica was concerned whether she could go to the emotional states demanded by the script without forcing. Taking time was another part of the lesson—to allow ourselves to breathe. She said:

The actor's sense that "I need to hit this mark NOW!" put an undue amount of pressure on the performer. If we don't give ourselves the time to breathe, we're going to have to artificially manufacture the emotional state, it's not going to be authentic. We need to trust that the audience will hang in there with us.

We both agreed that the audience also needs time to go on the emotional journey. In a way, the actor gives the audience time to breathe.

When I saw the performance, Erica took time to lead the audience into these experiences. Here is an excerpt of one particularly powerful moment that we worked on in which the character, Juliana, responds to being called "Mom":

Juliana: What horrible things must have happened to you. (*A silence. Something in this affects the Woman deeply.*)

The Woman: Hey. Look at me. Look at me. Nothing…bad. Happened to me.

Juliana: Well, then, why didn't you come back?

The Woman: Because. Because everything that happened to me was…so wonderful.

Juliana: And can you tell me that…wherever you are. You're happy? (*What follows is a deep untruth that is, at the same time, a profoundly earnest fantasy.*)

The Woman: Oh, I'm so happy. I have…such a wonderful life. Richard. And I. We're. We're so happy together. And we're…so in love with the girls. And they can't wait to meet you. I've told them all about you. I've told them how wonderful you are. And I've told them what a…what a wonderful. Wonderful. Mother you've been, Mom. (*Juliana sobs. This is the forgiveness she has been waiting so many years to find. The Woman gently puts her arms around Juliana and rocks her. Gently.*) It's OK, shh shhhhhh. (White 2011, pp.39–40)

The Woman, a stranger, calls Juliana "Mom" because, even though Juliana is not her mother, she realizes that Juliana, struggling with dementia, needs to hear it. Once the Woman says "Mom," the actress playing Juliana changes profoundly. This was a transformation the actress made by sinking onto the floor from a couch. We worked on this moment using AT (freeing her neck, letting the head move into a new balance) to release and surrender to the moment. In performance it was immensely moving. The look on Juliana's face released, softened, letting tension melt away. We could see it in her whole body. Later, Erica reflected:

It's essentially accepting it, almost giving over, surrendering to the psychological release rather than fighting it. I think it is probably a scary place to go, because one doesn't trust that it will be what it needs to be, the audience won't be patient with me—it won't be enough. I don't want to be rejected by the audience.

As the performer, Erica was confident that she could handle the large feelings, but it took specific skills to bypass the normal psychological pattern of suppression.

Conclusion

The coaching I have described springs from my philosophy that acting is a physical art. It is consistent with Stanislavski's teaching that access to the subconscious or superconscious of the actor comes through physical action (Stanislavski 1961). Physical actions emerge through cultivation of the actor's imagination in relation to the text or script that is being interpreted. If the physical objectives and actions the actor plays are not rooted in the real experience of the actor, they lack believability or truthfulness. AT, when used in the ways that I have described in my coaching, provides the conditions for the actor to deeply experience the imagination in the body. As you have read, AT adds a dimension to the actor's practice that creates a richer portrayal of the drama.

References

Fischer, J.M.O. (2000) "Notes." In F.M. Alexander *The Universal Constant in Living*. London: Mouritz. (Original work published 1942.)

Hurt, M. (2014) *Arthur Lessac's Embodied Actor Training*. New York: Routledge.

Jones, F.P. (1976) *Body Awareness in Action*. New York: Schocken Books.

Pascua, P. (2014) "Blue Sky." In *Red is the Color of My Night*. Asheville, NC: Loved by the Buffalo Publications.

Shakespeare, W. (1968) "A Midsummer Night's Dream." In *The Norton Facsimile of the First Folio of Shakespeare*. New York: W.W. Norton and Company. (Original work published 1623.)

Simon, N. (1986) *The Odd Couple (Female Version)*. New York: Samuel French.

Stanislavski, C. (1961) *Creating a Role*. New York: Routledge.

White, S. (2011) *The Other Place*. New York: Dramatists Play Service.

Williams, T. (2004) *A Streetcar Named Desire*. New York: New Directions Publishing. (Original work published 1947.)

Confident Creativity

Corinne Cassini

AT Perspective

The Alexander Technique as developed by F.M. Alexander is a means to support our recognition and awaken our appreciation of the value of changing patterns of behavior. What I am calling patterns of behavior are the habitual ways in which we go about our daily activities. Our desire for a more rewarding and fulfilling life is largely impeded by these patterns. AT brings about the conditions for new and different choices to become available. We are more often than not unaware of how these patterns of behavior affect our functioning. Our thoughts and emotions determine the ways in which our bodies coordinate themselves and move through life in response to our desires. AT is a means to efficiently engage the "how," or the process of fulfilling our desires, that best matches our inherent design. AT gives us an embodied experience—physical, mental, emotional, and potentially spiritual—of the differences between an unexamined habitual reaction and a response or action chosen out of awareness. The awareness gained in reaching a new experience gives us a choice relative to the new experience. We are therefore able to create a new experience for ourselves and retain the freedom to choose or not choose this new experience.

There were several key moments in F.M. Alexander's own learning process—which started with the desire to heal his recurring hoarseness while he acted on stage—and in his teaching. These turning points later became what we AT teachers often call "principles" or other words we create to describe our individual interpretation and application. Alexander realized that it wasn't sufficient simply to make a decision to change his habits; he first needed to know these habits more intimately—how they affected him and especially what triggered them. The principle of inhibition, which my teacher Tommy Thompson and I also call *withholding definition*, enabled Alexander to pause and reconsider his commitment to his initial intention or desire. This pause created a space between stimulus and response, enabling him to notice whether the intention relative to his desire to speak was indeed serving the desired outcome. This led him to a moment of choice between his familiar outcome and what he might experience with an unknown and potentially improved outcome. He also discovered that thoughts connect with physical coordination and that the relationship between the head and back via the neck determines the quality, efficiency, and freedom or fixity of movement. When thoughts are open, relaxed, and present to the moment, the relationship of the head and the spine tends to be fluid and free. In other cases it manifests various degrees of tightness, impeding overall coordination and movement relative to our activities.

Practically, in my own teaching, I offer visual observation, verbal feedback, and guided touch to expand students' awareness of choice and possibility relative to their intentions, beliefs, and desires. This teaching process invites students into a deeper sense of freedom, confidence, and presence of being while they consciously choose how to engage effectively in the activities of life. Most recently, I have been particularly interested in how students' thoughts and their relationship to activity influence the ease and presence with which they perform their activities.

> Music students who gain insight into their true intentions behind music making are confident and present in the midst of their creative process. This level of awareness opens them up to their potential for free expressivity.

In teaching the Alexander Technique, I am interested in guiding music students through various ways of becoming aware of their states of being while engaged in their professional activity. As students become aware of their attitudes toward themselves, the music, and the audience during music making, they experience how their states of being determine their coordination or "use." Once they gain this awareness, they are freer to shift and choose their thoughts about themselves and their relationship to their activities, the environment, and their audiences. What follows is more creativity through improved coordination, ease, and self-confidence.

This chapter describes four of the practices I offer in my AT classes for musicians at the Hayes School of Music at Appalachian State University in Boone, NC. My aim is to help release each performer's creative potential through attending to their thoughts and self-confidence.

Withholding Definition as an Inhibitive Moment

Withholding definition[1] teaches students how to observe themselves or the situation, being present to whatever is happening in and around them without amplifying, dismissing, or judging. This distances them from their habitual reactions to specific situations and any previously defined outcomes based on past experiences. When we withhold definition of any experience, there is room for a new experience to emerge. This inhibitive space of withholding definition affords an opportunity for artists to transform challenging situations into experiences where confidence and creative freedom are a reality.

I introduce "withholding definition" to a class with a "can and can't" game. The sequence goes as follows:

1. To begin, decide if you would like to do this activity standing, lying down, or sitting. Then notice your shape and where you are contacting the floor or chair to establish a sense of position and place in the room. Sense your body's contact with whatever is not you: Notice the floor under your feet, or the ground under your head and back, or the chair under your sit bones. Sense the air and space around you. These are reference points for your relationship with yourself and the room that you can tune into at any moment. This will give you information relative to yourself and the experiences you are about to have.

2. Now think of an activity that is a challenge for you, something you feel you "can't" do, something you've defined as "too difficult" to achieve.

3. As you are thinking about this activity, notice outside sensory stimuli (sense of balance, relationship with sensed support, and what you hear or see). Notice any emotions and what happens to your relationship with yourself and the room.

4. Notice what changes the most when you think, "I can't do X." Once that's registered, let the thought go.

5. Next, engage in thinking about an activity you've been able to complete successfully, something you've done well or something you are looking forward to and confident you can achieve easily.

6. Similarly, notice outside sensory stimuli (sense of balance, relationship with sensed support, and what you hear or see). Notice any emotions and what happens to your relationship with yourself and the environment.

7. Again, notice what shifts the most when you think, "I can do Y." Once that's registered, let the thought go.

8. You now have two contrasting experiences: one relative to something you presently feel incapable of, another relative to an activity that you define as possible to achieve. Notice that

these contrasting experiences are different only because of your perspective on and the definitions you have assigned to each activity.

9. Now, consider the thought "I can't do X" while you withhold definition, or "inhibit" this thought from being defined as it was earlier. As you withhold definition, connect with any sensory and emotional experiences and allow them to come over you. Then do the same withholding definition of the "I can do Y" thought, noticing your experience and the differences.

10. Finally, to integrate this experience, allow the understanding and insights gained from the experiences of withholding definition to permeate, influence, and transform your initial definition of what you saw as challenging. Notice if your experience of what is possible has shifted as well.

The goal of this exercise is to bring to students an awareness of how their thoughts about an experience define and create this experience. They realize that by using inhibition or withholding definition, they have a choice between their definition, with its resulting habits, or the creative potential that lies in the absence of such a definition. In the absence of definition, they gain insight into new ways of relating to themselves, their environment, and especially their activity.

One student, for instance, felt overwhelmed by the number of activities he had to get done in addition to practicing in order to succeed as a music major. Because he approached these activities with an "I can't" attitude, he procrastinated. When he withheld definition of the "I can't" attitude and considered how he enjoys practicing as a process (an "I can" thought), he experienced positive responses in his body (clearer vision, improved sense of balance) and in his emotional response (eagerness) to getting his homework done. He reported that his school activities became simpler, more straightforward, and easier to accomplish while withholding definition. He became able to choose a new habit of completing his work well before the deadline, enjoying it and learning.

Learning to observe the connection between thinking and experiencing empowers students in performance situations to let go of their habitual definition of how things have been. When students withhold from defining their experience, they open themselves to embody and express "who they might become in the absence of the definition and apart from what they typically experience" (from a workshop with Tommy Thompson). In this open state of observation, using "withholding definition" as an inhibitive moment, lies great creative potential for the artist.

The Inquiry Process

The inquiry process is a systematic and analytical procedure inviting performers to use their own intelligence to see and understand their thought patterns and beliefs. These beliefs may be constructive and useful or bothersome in ways that interfere with performance activities. The presence and thus relationship of musicians with their audience, context, or environment, for instance, is often experienced as an interference when it is a reason why artists perform and potentially a source of great support.

This activity is inspired by my reading of Krishnamurti along with Plato's Socratic method. I developed the activity as a way of teaching AT through my own inquiry work on myself. For this I used similar questions to those asked by Byron Katie in *Loving What Is* (Katie 2003) and by David Gorman[2] in his "Learning Methods" classes. Thanks to all these influences, I experienced the transformative powers of my own thinking about my coordination, as well as my relation to myself, with my playing, and with the audience while on stage. The experience had a positive impact on my confidence and stage presence, so I decided to combine, adapt, and include this way of working for my classroom teaching at Appalachian State University.

Similar to my own experience, my students often assume they have a clear and constructive guiding intention for their performance or practice sessions. The inquiry process reveals underlying expectations or beliefs of which they are unaware and that can override or interfere with the intentions they assumed or hoped were guiding them. Whether conscious or not, the most prevalent state of being for students engaged in any activity is what is organizing their use or overall coordination during activity.

There are up to eight students in each of my four classes, so everyone gets to perform at least twice in a semester. For the inquiry process, I work individually in the context of a performance on whatever aspect of music making is relevant to the student while the group observes. The following dialogue is a compilation of several actual experiences with students as I engaged them in the inquiry process.

Corinne: What was your experience of playing just now?

Student: Not great. I was nervous because there are people here listening to me. I messed up here and there.

Corinne: This is true, but why does playing for people make such a difference?

Student: It's nothing like practicing! There are people listening, watching!

Corinne: Yes…but why do you play?

Student: Because I love music.

Corinne: Are you saying that it's enough to love music for yourself, playing in your practice room your whole life?

Student: Not really…

Corinne: Why not? What's missing?

Student: Sharing, somehow. The better I get at a piece in the practice room, the more I wish to share it, to have others hear it!

Corinne: Playing for others seems like a natural outcome of learning and getting good at what you love doing. When does this change?

Student: I want others to hear what I have to play, that I play it well, but I get nervous when I'm about to perform for an audience.

Corinne: Let's be very specific here—this is a crucial moment. When you come in front of others to play, where has your attention gone?

Student: I'm thinking more about them and about not messing up. I'm not just playing the piece or loving what I'm doing.

Corinne: Exactly, and how are you thinking of the audience?

Student: The moment I think of them I feel I have to impress them or that they are evaluating, maybe even judging me in some way.

Corinne: Evaluating is useful under certain circumstances. When you are in the practice room, who does the evaluating?

Student: I do, and it's usually constructive. It helps me know what I need to work on.

Corinne: Yes! When you are performing are you still doing the evaluating?

Student: No. Suddenly I feel as if the audience is doing the evaluating and I become more demanding of myself. I have no idea what they are thinking but I assume it's bad.

Corinne: Do you see how there has been a shift from the music and a natural desire to improve and share what you love and are good at to thinking, "How well am I doing here? What are they going to think of me?"

Student: Yes.

Corinne: Good. What is that experience like kinesthetically? How are you experiencing the worry that they are judging you? What does this thought or emotion feel like?

Student: I am almost paralyzed really and breathing is shallow. I feel stiff and tight in my legs and arms and just below the sternum… I feel vulnerable. I feel very small up here as if I shouldn't be here in front of you.

Corinne: Great! Bringing the interference to your awareness is essential here. Can you imagine playing your best under these circumstances?

Student: Not at all!

Corinne: Exactly! Now think of the piece you love and your desire to share it. Think of the practice room and go into the actual experience, sensing in your body, naming the thoughts and the emotions of playing what you love. Just like you did for the experience of being judged.

While the student is connecting with their thinking, I might use touch to provide support for this exploration. It's not always necessary because the main focus here is the effect thinking has on coordination. But it enhances awareness on a psychophysical level and allows the student to let go of the tightness experienced earlier while playing and talking about feeling judged. My intention with touch here is to provide more safety and grounding while the student is exploring this new way of thinking and being relative to performing.

Student: I'm calmer and more grounded. My body feels more open and I can feel my feet. I feel like something big shifted for me in my thinking about playing. I almost feel excited!

Corinne: Indeed, you've just let go of a habitual thought or definition about performing. Why don't you play the part you just played with this in mind: "I want to share all this that I love and I would like you to listen." That simple!

[Student plays. When she finishes there is a big smile on her face.]

Student: Wow! That was different.

Corinne: It was indeed! How was it different from what usually happens?

Student: Well I was just in the music. I was just playing. I wasn't trying to get it right. I wasn't worried about the harder bits. And those actually worked out too! I changed the way I was thinking about the whole thing. It seems I don't feel that tightness below the sternum and in my arms and legs when I'm not worried about the audience. So I stayed with the music and felt connected with the audience in a good way.

Corinne: Yes, you changed your intention relative to the activity of performing and you changed how you were thinking about the audience. The inquiry process helped you understand your thoughts and touch helped you sense the direct effect those two ways of thinking have on your use. Once you felt it, you could let go of the habit of defining a performance as an experience of being judged by the audience. Let's now ask our audience so they can share their experience. You may then see how you were probably creating this perception of reality quite on your own. [To the class:] As the audience, what was your experience?

Classmate #1: I wanted you to play well the whole time, but I was nervous for you the first time.

Classmate #2: I was more interested in hearing your playing this time.

Classmate #3: The second time was so much more interesting. I felt drawn in and connected with you and the music.

Classmate #4: I could tell you were really enjoying yourself.

Corinne: Your whole self and experience changed by changing your thinking. Can you sense how the way you think of yourself and the audience or the intention with which you perform is either in the way or supportive of you sharing your art? Practicing wasn't a factor between the first and second time you played. Yet I think you played at least as well, if not better than you are used to playing in the practice room. Is this the case?

Student: Indeed. I don't feel I've played with this much ease before, but I have imagined or wanted to feel this way while I play.

Corinne: Good. I suggest you experiment further with this activity to get clear on what happens in yourself when you think one way and what happens when you think the old way. You can use a friend as your practice audience. Thank you!

In the classroom setting I could continue the questioning, helping students become aware of what they specifically enjoyed and loved about what they just played. I ask what they would like to express through playing the piece—the character or mood for instance. I might go into the reasons they play music in the first place, guiding them to reach the deeper reason they are presently in a performing career.

The inquiry process helps students identify an interfering thought pattern or belief and transform it into a constructive intention. This constructive intention allows the students to bring their attention during practice and performance time to musical expression rather than technical perfection or negative self-assessment. I have found valuable learning in this process. Performers shift from reacting to their thoughts and suffering the consequences expressed physically through difficult coordination to being present to the experience of playing. They become aware of the influence and ease a constructive intention brings to their physical coordination and creative flow.

Artists may guide themselves through this inquiry process on their own, first identifying the habitual but less conscious interfering thought patterns. Usually there is a misinterpretation or unreliable appreciation of reality, as I just illustrated. The audience comes to be entertained, appreciate the music, and enjoy the performance. Players who believe otherwise set themselves up to experience stress because their attention is not on their art but on what the audience thinks of them or on the expectations they have set up for themselves.

As an AT teacher, besides guiding the conversation during this process, I am determining through observation where the students' quality of attention is being embodied or showing up in their use. In these moments, my hands are guided to tense shoulders, contracted facial muscles, tight legs, or a head pulled back, but only with the intention of bringing the student into deeper awareness of themselves through their coordination. I ask students to "listen" to my hands as they register the quality of their attention. Then based on our previous conversation, I ask them to think of a word that best expresses what they wish to share about the music or what they love about the piece they are playing. Their intention can be general or specific depending on what they are ready for and able to connect with. This part is done without playing.

Figuring out what performers love about music or want to express is an intention-setting process. Through setting this constructive intention, they are choosing to shift their attention away from interfering thought patterns and back to themselves and the present-moment experience in which they are involved. I encourage students to become aware and sensitive to the improved quality of all aspects of their musical experience. Once I see and sense a shift in students' attention, I ask them if they are sensing the shift as well and remain a bit longer with touch to support them in the newfound awareness of their own experience.

Just before taking my hands away, I tell my students that they have just been given an experience while being supported. Although the experience is unique and cannot be duplicated, the awareness of the experience is their own to come back to without my needing to be present. The awareness belongs to the students and empowers them going forward in their ability to access a similar experience of ease while playing. They follow the steps of identifying the interfering thought or attitude ("I have to play perfectly"), then they set a constructive intention ("I love to share this piece") that leads to a shift in the quality of their attention ("I am now open and available to the moment"). Out of this process and the ensuing experience, an awareness is born. This awareness is accompanied by a quality of attention that students can learn to reproduce on their own.

Storytelling as Freedom from Repeating Patterns

In my own experience as a musician, certain performances have stood out either because they went exceptionally well and showed me new horizons or because they brought forth my shortcomings and limitations. These outstanding events turned into stories that shaped and have continued to define me in ways I haven't always consciously chosen or desired.

It was while assisting Tommy Thompson in the context of his work with actors that I was first introduced to "story work." Shortly thereafter, I experienced firsthand letting go of stories I kept telling myself as a reaction to past performance experiences. Instead of learning from the stories and allowing them to serve my growth and music making, I let these stories hold me back. Moving from the story as a reaction to the experience to the story as insight into the experience changed my relationship with performing. This shift brought me the necessary space and freedom to experience a variety of new ways to perform based on learning, rather than on old fixed ideas about performing.

I use the Storytelling as Freedom from Repeating Patterns activity with my students as a way to invite them to let go of patterns they have been repeating and that are holding them back from their potential as performing musicians. This storytelling activity has several points in common with *narrative therapy*, a branch of psychotherapy developed in the 1970s and 1980s by Michael White and David Epston (White and Epston 1990). Both share the idea that the stories we tell ourselves shape who we are positively or negatively—and that they can be changed. This process is therapeutic because it leads patients to create new and different stories about themselves that are helpful to them. In addition, both narrative therapy and my storytelling activity involve a supportive audience of peers that have been through the process and are now witnessing as a mirror while the patient or music student shares similar experiences. Tommy Thompson's important *withholding definition* teaching principle and F.M. Alexander's principle of inhibition accompanied by the use of touch gives this activity a depth that is not shared with narrative therapy. What follows is an example of what takes place during my classes when I lead the storytelling activity. It will illustrate how I use the medium of storytelling and touch as an AT teacher to free students of repeating patterns.

I start out by asking the class to consider the different experiences—turned to stories—that continue to shape who they are today. I invite them to look for the stories that still shape their experiences onstage or around playing and practicing. Then I ask for volunteers willing to share their stories while the class is present and listens.

A singer whose teacher regularly tells her to sing out more shares the story of why she doesn't dare to let her voice be fully heard in performance:

As a kid I was very enthusiastic and energetic. I loved to sing loud and speak a lot. My dad would often tell me to be quiet and that I was too loud. I thought I had a nice voice but gradually I became very shy and quiet when around people and especially around my dad. Eventually I didn't dare to say much of what I felt in general. I'm still shy to speak up or sing out in public because I'm afraid of being too loud.

When my student has finished speaking, I first ask her to notice and tune into her "felt sense," a term coined by Eugene Gendlin. The felt sense encompasses more than a kinesthetic experience of a given situation in a given environment. As AT teachers, we talk about the present-moment psychophysical experiences, and to me the felt sense combined with the psychophysical experience comes closest to what I am inviting students to notice during this activity. Eugene Gendlin defines the "felt sense" as:

> not a mental experience but a *physical* one. A bodily awareness of a situation or person or event. An internal aura that encompasses everything you feel and know about the given subject at a given time—encompasses it and communicates it to you all at once rather than detail by detail. (Levine 1997, p.67)

Peter Levine in his work with somatic experiencing (SE) asks his patients to tune into this same felt sense as part of the SE facilitation process in releasing traumatic experiences.

When I use touch as an AT teacher, I am tuning into my students' felt sense and psychophysical organism through my own felt sense along with all the information it is giving me about myself, the students, and the situation we just shared. Students tune into their own experience before I use touch to bring them into a deeper awareness of their felt sense. I touch students where I feel intuitively drawn. It matters less where I touch than how and with what intention I am touching. My intention is to give students the necessary support while they become aware of their felt sense and the psychophysical experience of their stories. During their initial experience of the events that would become their story, they most likely were not prepared to respond to the experience with openness and freedom, especially if the experience was a challenging one. Their response was narrowing, diminishing, or a protection of some sort. This is the experience I ask them to tune into after they have related their story. I also invite the rest of the class to check in with their respective felt sense to see if the story has struck a chord within their experience.

In this example, I am interested in touching the part of her she felt she needed to protect. I am being present to the part of her that shied away from freely expressing herself in this case. But I am also looking to communicate with the part of her that loved to sing and speak, the part that she thought her dad experienced as "too loud." My intention is that her perspective about the story will shift. I ask her to connect with what she feels she has learned from her story, especially relative to who she has become. I invite her to consider how this story has affected the direction and the choices she's made in her life while she withholds definition about how this story may or may not need to continue to affect her singing. Once I sense the shift in perspective from a definition of herself to an opportunity for growth and learning, I ask her to tell the same story again from the new perspective she has just become aware of. I invite her to allow the insight she has gained during hands-on work to permeate her story and guide her retelling of the story. Usually the new story is shorter, simpler, less emotional, and more compassionate toward the teller and all involved:

I sense it's okay to open up and let my voice be heard while singing now. The audience wants to hear my powerful voice! My dad must have been tired a lot and probably didn't understand what it was like to be me as a kid. I was just doing what kids do! I love my voice, and in the practice room I sing my heart out like I used to, alone in my room, as loudly as I wanted behind closed doors. Now I'm ready to let others hear my voice because it's not too loud!

In the course of this storytelling activity, students often shift from reacting habitually to their stories, to responding more freely and with insight. Students no longer identify in negative or interfering ways when a situation resembling the one in their story comes up. They allow new perspectives on the events to emerge. A new story is born out of the learning and insight that takes place during the listening process with the support of touch from the AT teacher. As in the example, the new story demonstrates a clear purpose and course of action in a new direction that is useful for the students' future choices.

I ask the other students to give their feedback on their experiences of both versions of the story. Many are touched by, feel connected to, and are engaged in the new story. They learn from relating it back to their own experiences. Here are a few responses:

- "Your whole way of sitting while you were telling the second story became more confident."

- "Your voice was fuller and more resonant the second time! It wasn't too loud at all. The first time your voice was shy and a bit too soft. Now it's more assured."

- "I believed you the second time and could tell you also believed what you just shared."

- "My parents liked my playing but not the practicing, so I can relate to the way you opened up. You said you wanted to share your voice with the audience and not keep it hidden in the practice room, and you did that!"

Students frequently relate more to the second story—it has a more universal scope. Even someone who hasn't had the same experience can feel empathy for the teller and their story.

Through Storytelling as Freedom from Repeating Patterns, students' experiences are reorganized relative to present realities rather than past habitual realities. The shift from reacting habitually to the past as if it's still present to responding from a present-moment perspective on the present situation involves the ability to withhold definition and the principle AT teachers call inhibition. Students register the *absence* of their habitual use associated with the past experience (old story). This brings them to relate to their stories not from the point of view of the person they were or how they used themselves in the situation they were in, but from that of the person they have grown to become thanks to or in spite of their experiences. When they acknowledge being present to themselves in the absence of their (old) story, they use themselves differently even in situations related to their story. The new use creates new experiences that open their awareness to new and different choices. In this freedom to choose their responses relative to and in the present moment, they find a space of confidence and creativity.

The Confidence-Giving Power of Accepting Compliments

In the highly competitive and critical world of performing, students are quick to criticize or judge themselves, easily spotting flaws in their own work or feeling inadequate, as shown in the inquiry process. They seem much less eager, even uncomfortable, to appreciate who they are, their dedication to playing music, and the high quality of their work. I am surprised how few positive qualities they notice, not to mention use, that would otherwise enhance their creativity and confidence on stage. Learning to sincerely give, receive, and accept compliments allows performers to acknowledge and own the positive qualities being reflected back to them. Their ability to evaluate and assess themselves becomes more constructive, leading them to realize more of their potential as musicians.

As a performing musician, I experienced during a workshop with Tommy Thompson how recognizing my strengths through receiving compliments gave me not only a better appreciation of these qualities, but also more confidence and assurance in my expressive abilities on stage. I decided to use this activity with my music students in the classroom. The confidence-giving power of accepting compliments uses the principles and builds on the learning from both the withholding definition and storytelling activities described above. All three activities use experiencing oneself through observation, felt senses, and a kinesthetic and embodied way of listening. The compliment giving and receiving activity is a way of showing students the strengths they already possess. They gain the ability to see, recognize, and embody their potential. They may use this awareness to further their confidence during performances or life in general.

The exercise works like this: Students form pairs, sit across from each other, and exchange compliments. I ask them to notice and experience habitual reactions to being complimented, such as laughing, deflecting, rejecting, justifying, explaining, or feeling embarrassed.

Once they've noticed some tendencies, I ask them to pause in order to connect with the support of the chair underneath them and with a general sense of poise above their sit bones. I invite them to withhold definition about who they think or believe they are, to connect with themselves beyond their habitual ways of being and seeing themselves. This opens them up to receiving what their partners will say to them during the activity. I also encourage them, if they are feeling comfortable, to make eye contact with their partners.

As they resume the exchange of giving and receiving compliments, the students receiving compliments withhold their habitual reactions, instead pausing to notice the areas in or on their bodies where they sense the compliment has reached them or "landed." Similar to the way one is sensitive to tone of voice and body language, a compliment, criticism, or any remark spoken to someone is not only received through the person's ears, but also is sensed kinesthetically in or on the body. What I am asking of the students is to sense and register the kinesthetic experience of the compliment. To help them connect with the kinesthetic experience rather than the habitual reaction, I ask them to place their hands on the area where they sense the compliment lands. I invite them to acknowledge and receive the compliment more deeply than they did the first time through their own connection with the area they are touching.

Once the compliment is acknowledged, while maintaining their hand position and the connection with the kinesthetic experience, I ask them to give their partner the next compliment from the kinesthetic experience of having authentically received the previous one. The exchange continues in this manner.

Sensing the compliment in the body, along with the self-directed kinesthetic listening, allows the students to leave habitual reactions from the first exchange behind. Noticing how and where a compliment is taken in by using their own hands to locate and connect with the kinesthetic experience helps them acknowledge, receive, and accept the compliment authentically. The self-recognition present in this moment, facilitated by their mutual relationship as each other's mirrors, allows them to own positive qualities or strengths they may previously have halfheartedly believed about themselves. The more students are at ease receiving a compliment, the more they are able to trust that aspect of themselves that is complimented. And further, the more aware they are of their strong points and the more open they are to compliments pertaining to those very aspects of themselves. The response to the compliment received and returned comes from a place of trust and connection created between the two partners in the present moment. The compliments evolve, becoming less automatic and more authentic. Each compliment, spoken from a place of self-acceptance and recognition, gradually becomes closer to the truth, reflecting the depth rather than the surface of who each student is. It is especially impressive and touching to see how students show their strengths to each other by opening up and being vulnerable. Students often come to powerful realizations as to whom they believed themselves to be versus who they really are.

When students understand how a belief they have held about themselves, such as "I have to be perfect," has been standing in the way of their progress, they become open to questioning and ultimately letting go of that belief. The compliment activity helps students realize how they might better appreciate themselves through what they appreciate in others and others appreciate in them. It builds trust and fosters a sense of shared experience with other human beings. It enables students to become more familiar with their own qualities rather than habitually focusing on what they are still unable to do. For example, if "perfectionists" are able to receive and accept compliments for something they don't see perfection in yet, they will understand how the way they see themselves doesn't match how others see them. They might also understand how the statement "I have to be perfect" is an expectation that interferes with their progress. The situations (onstage, at auditions, in a lesson) in which musicians and performers tend to fear criticism most are also the same situations in which they may receive compliments. Being open to compliments is a quality that connects musicians more to their audience, especially when they meet audience members backstage. Acknowledging the compliments shows respect toward the people giving them and is an opportunity to be reminded that the audience is there to appreciate their art. It's also an opportunity to see if musical intentions were well expressed through the performance. The more performers are aware of their strengths, the more they are able to rely on and use these strengths to further their confidence during performances or even in life. This sense of mutual respect between performer and listener strengthens musicians' genuine connection with the audience, giving them increased confidence in their creative potential.

It is my intention as an AT teacher to guide students through the process of becoming aware and conscious of their whole self as this self engages in any activity, especially performance activities. By whole self, I mean their entire being: its physical sensations, emotional feelings, thought processes, and ability to gain self-awareness.

The four activities I've described are central to my teaching and how I guide students through their individual processes of becoming confident and free in the moment they need it most. Withholding definition helps them let go of beliefs and opens them up to new and different ways of thinking and being. It gives them choice and is a foundation for what follows. Certain beliefs present more resistance to withholding definition alone. With these beliefs or set ideas students move through the inquiry process and inspect their perspectives for logical validity and usefulness. Other patterns have an emotional history. Students discern their repetitive emotional states through awareness of the event that created what has become their story. Seeing this connection allows them to be present to their circumstances rather than repeating past ones. Finally, through learning to authentically accept compliments, they learn to be open to relationship, seeing their audiences, and being seen and heard by them.

My use of touch comes in as a support to any of these activities. In my experience working with students, there is always an observable moment when a shift in perspective or an opening happens for them. AT teachers might identify this as a positive release or reorganization or rebalancing of the whole organism. Although meaningful, this beneficial shift in overall coordination is only a symptom of the more important change in students: that of the quality of their attention and presence to the moment. In choosing to shift their intention and attention, they become more freely coordinated, aware, and available to themselves physically, emotionally, mentally, intellectually, and possibly even spiritually. When students empower themselves to choose their perspective on their performance, they are present, free, and confident in their creativity.

Notes

1 Tommy Thompson of the Alexander Technique Center at Cambridge first introduced withholding definition as a way of teaching inhibition. See his website at www.easeofbeing.com.

2 For David Gorman's Learning Methods see www.learningmethods.com.

References

Katie, B. (2003) *Loving What Is: Four Questions That Can Change Your Life*. New York: Three Rivers Press.

Levine, P.A. (1997) *Waking the Tiger. Healing Trauma: The Innate Capacity to Transform Overwhelming Experiences*. Berkeley, CA: North Atlantic Books.

White, M. and Epston, D. (1990) *Narrative Means to Therapeutic Ends*. New York: W.W. Norton.

Engaging the
Expert Performer

Affinity as Pathway

Kate Conklin

AT Perspective

Short Description of the Alexander Technique

I describe the Alexander Technique as a tool that can be used to do something with quality. What follows is my current description of AT as well as definitions of relevant terms.

AT is conscious, constructive thinking, cooperating with design[1] as a creative response to desire.

Desire represents what we want: generally, as in to find out what else is possible; or specifically, such as a particular way of landing a jump or executing a musical phrase.

Creative response means an adaptable, flexible framework that provides easily varied and spontaneous ways to act.

Cooperating with design means to comply willingly with our own structure and functioning—anatomy, psychology, and so forth.

Conscious, constructive thinking means thinking that is purposeful and active. The initial step of the process is cognitive; it also is an action that is positive.

Key Design Information and Concepts

- *We are whole.* Humans are complex, living systems.

- *We are alive and moving.* We are always in movement, even when relatively still. Understanding this about the human system is essential if you wish to guide it in specific ways.

- *We are embodied thinkers.* Thinking and movement are not separate; they are an integrated, interdependent system.

- *We are relatively literal thinkers.* How we understand and interpret ideas and movement depends greatly on how we understand the words used to describe something. We have psychophysical definitions for many existing words, so it is of utmost importance that we articulate our observations and plans (directions) in ways that are appropriate, specific, and constructive.

- *We experience and observe with all our senses.* There are 21 generally accepted senses.[2] I am available to using all of them in observing the quality of coordination and performance.

Key Terms and Definitions

The following terms are defined as I use them.

COGNITION

The mental action or process of acquiring knowledge and understanding through thought, experience, and the senses.

CONSTRUCTIVE

Serving a useful purpose; tending to build up (Online Oxford English Dictionary [OED] 2017)

COORDINATE

1. Bring the different elements of (a complex activity or organization) into a relationship that will ensure efficiency or harmony

   1.1 Negotiate with others in order to work together effectively (OED 2017)

CREATIVE

Creativity is a key property of all life; it is inherent in all forms of life. How I use this word includes inventiveness, imagination, and innovation.

PERFORMANCE

I use this word to mean intentional communication with an audience.

PROFESSIONAL

I use this word somewhat idiosyncratically to mean engaging in an activity with something where demands are placed on one's skills. It's meant to refer to a level of skill and execution consummate with a primary occupation or profession, whether or not it is compensated.

QUALITY

I use this word in all of the following ways, as per the Oxford English Dictionary.

1. The standard of something as measured against other things of a similar kind; the degree of excellence of something

   1.1 General excellence of standard or level

2. A distinctive attribute or characteristic possessed by someone or something

2.1 (Phonetics) The distinguishing characteristic or characteristics of a speech sound

2.2 (Music) Another term for timbre (OED 2017)

RELEVANT DESIGN INFORMATION

I describe information about anatomy, functioning, cognition, and neurobiology this way. The qualifier *relevant* refers to the timing and amount of information, insofar as useful to the situation at hand.

SKILL

1. The ability to do something well; expertise

1.1 A particular ability (OED 2017)

Performing is one of the most exciting and fulfilling human experiences. In performance, we make creative choices using technical skills to communicate with an audience. We are entirely in charge of our actions while also wholly integrated with a predetermined structure, making continuous, subtle adjustments; responding to internal and external stimuli; recovering and rerouting moment to moment.

I approach the process of learning and refining performance skills as a continuation of the desire to perform itself. Engaging a performer's curiosity and what they already care about—along with their existing skills and expertise—establishes fundamental, necessary links between creative choice, resourcefulness, skill, techniques, and new information. I refer to this as using "affinity as a pathway." It's part of the process I use that seeks to engage existing expertise, build additional skills, celebrate the desire to perform and improve, and develop self-reliance.

Performers usually pursue coaching to improve their performing and, in many cases, to improve their overall well-being in support of their creative and life goals. In my experience both as a student in formal and private training and as a teacher in a wide variety of contexts—private, university, conservatory, and independent training capacities, having worked with over a thousand performing artists—I have observed many models that intend to help performers in practical ways, but in fact deprive them of practical performance skills by separating the elements of performing from the act of doing so. These models tend to focus (perhaps inadvertently) on studio practice, procedure, and exercises separate from the context of why we learn these skills. Thus, performances become rare, exam-like events, and dependence on the guidance or approval of teachers, rather than on the effectiveness of the performance and integrated skills of the performer, becomes emphasized. Performance itself is its own skill that needs development, reliable strategies, and practice. Helping someone with performance by working on performing itself synthesizes the skills and coordination necessary to serve their performance demands, creative intent, and relationship with their fellow performers and audience. Working in this way defines the learning process as a constructive choice, optimized for personal empowerment. Giving full value to a performer's skills helps them to do so as well, so that they feel the full force of their readiness and bring those skills to bear consciously on the task at hand. Self-awareness, freedom of choice, and resourcefulness are made explicit and central.

The American composer Morton Feldman said, "I am interested in how the wild beast lives in the jungle, not in the zoo" (Feldman 1969, p.76). I include this quote to crystalize my intent, and as a nod to the field of ethology, which emerged in the early part of the 20th century under the wild assertion that it might be useful to study animal behavior in a natural habitat rather than a laboratory environment.

The Alexander Technique is, at its heart, a creative act. AT is a tool performers can use to do what they wish to do with quality—particular qualities that serve their specific artistic work and overall life desires, by way of a coordinated whole self. It was designed as a tool to be used, in life and activity, by a performer who wished to do something extraordinary—recite Shakespeare—with particular quality in order to communicate with an audience. For performers, AT is an incomparable tool. Using the technique is a choice we make to engage our curiosity, senses, and intelligence to respond to our desires as well as the world around us.

Using AT to help performers is its own complex skill. There are significant and meaningful differences between using a technique as an end in itself and using it as a practical tool. For me, AT must be immediately useful in life and art.

This chapter is for performers, teachers, and coaches as well as anyone curious about the intersection of coordination and performance. In it I describe how I have developed my particular way of using AT in creative collaboration with performers from acrobats to opera singers, illuminate the needs of highly skilled performers and the special skills needed to work effectively with them, and provide a rough template of how I conduct lessons and coaching.

Flying Lessons

My catalyst to study AT was performance. I am a singer, and I went to my first AT teacher with a clear desire: I wanted to achieve electric, inclusive performing all the time. I had glimpsed the transcendent alchemy of my vocal and musical skills merging with those of other performers such that we and the audience seemed to be together in flow state. At those moments, I felt like I was flying—controlled, free, and blended with the infinite. I wanted to find a way to do that reliably and on purpose, any time. I had no idea if this was possible. My teacher said it was, and I believed her.

She was right. What I had sought in vocal study—a clear, reliable process through which to realize and further develop my artistic potential—I found in AT. I was singing for Cirque du Soleil's water show, *O*, when I began to regularly use AT. I was singing two shows every night, ten shows per week, in a myriad of musical styles, surrounded by some of the most spectacular performers in the world. The show provided me an ideal laboratory to implement what I was learning in a rich, multifaceted biofeedback environment. When I varied my strategies and attention in warm-ups and performances, I noticed how I responded, how the other performers responded, and how my fellow musicians responded. I also received varied feedback from the company's artistic and management teams, depending on their various aesthetic preferences. I also perceived a palpable response from the audience. I more regularly experienced my performance as a live entity that could morph and change at will.

Working this way got me wondering about the other performers. I wondered how they did what they did night after night, how it worked for them. Observing and talking to my colleagues at *O*, I discerned more detail about how they went about their work, what they did for training and warm-ups, between acts, and on their days off. There was a phenomenally high level of skill and experience, accompanied by a wildly variable array of understanding about technique, performance, and coordination. Some people had no idea how to articulate what they did—they could just do it—while others were incredibly detailed and studied. As in any field, some had any number of outdated, inaccurate, and even destructive ideas about movement and were dutifully doing what they'd learned. Others had taken it upon themselves to reapproach and reinvent their craft, seeking out information and additional skills, evolving with their art.

I also sensed and directly observed a tragic and false duality: the pitting of health and sustainability against artistry and commitment to performance. A director would quote the adage, "work smarter, not harder," then in the next sentence give the instruction that when holding a prop umbrella onstage, "your arms should be fully flexed—it should hurt!" These were the same athletes who were to throw and catch each other in the very next act. The idea that they should tire from such a simple movement seemed dangerous and absurd considering what they had to do immediately after. Coaching and feedback given to performers in their particular skill was often limited by their and their coach's lack of deep or accurate understanding about coordination. The coach might have seen awkwardness in their movement, but lacked the resources to help them alleviate it. Impediments also came from a top-down approach to artistic direction. Acrobats lamented that artistic directors regularly made changes without asking them what performers needed to do their jobs and perform optimally.

A brief, frank conversation with the artists and crew, using their experience and expertise, could have easily allowed the performers to receive the support they needed.

Observing these world-class performers, it seemed audacious to think that I could help them, but there was such a clear gap in available, meaningful help for performers of their caliber that I felt compelled to act. I saw the deep desire of artists to keep developing their work dynamically in order to be safe, healthy, and satisfied. I felt that desire myself, and I wanted to respond to it. The questions that emerged, with respect to myself and the other artists, were as follows:

- How do we get help?

- How do we develop criteria by which to understand, filter, and discern helpful feedback (sometimes from wildly varied and questionable sources)?

- How do we undertake the process of recalibrating our instruments (our sensory and all other systems of feedback) while maintaining a high level of performance, not significantly disrupting our ability to do what we do?

- How, if I can effectively work with my own performance and skill, do I make myself useful for my fellow performers? How do I become a trustworthy resource so they can ascertain if using AT in their work and lives is useful?

- How do we get so we can trust ourselves?

With these questions began my life's work.

The Hottest Fire

A technique must be tested to know its true usefulness. Its durability and scalability, as well as its limits, must be discovered. I call this "the hottest fire"—the process of exposing the technique to the most extreme cases possible. I needed to see if AT could help me achieve what I truly wanted: to be more coordinated and sustainable in my movement and singing while exponentially increasing my artistic ability. I used the technique to sing opera, avant-garde music with extended vocal techniques, and, most demanding of all, the highly ornamented and precise vocal music of Bulgaria. Within my specialty of Bulgarian singing lies a virtual wonderland of unusual vocal sounds—yips, yodels, slides, pulsation, exquisitely intricate ornamentation, rhythmic and metric precision, and inconceivably long phrases (sometimes entire songs) that seem to afford no opportunity to breathe. I tested AT in every context I could come up with, thinking, "If it doesn't work, I need to know that. If it does, I need to know how and why." I found nothing that the work could not be adapted to, so I explored how the technique would fare for highly skilled performers in other fields.

Thus began my collaboration with Benedikt Negro, a pantomime and the lead actor in O. He plays the role of an ancient theater owner whose physical appearance is hunched and gnarled, eventually transforming into a younger, more vital version of himself. He is highly skilled in stylized movement, extremely athletic, and a rascal. He needs to do physically and athletically demanding things on stage while portraying an apparently "inefficient" character along with subtle, nuanced acting. Observing Benedikt in action made it absolutely clear that any useful technique would need to facilitate both wildness in artistry and technical precision. No rigid models would suffice for the task. Collapsing and compressing to achieve the desired visual effect, enduring inefficient movement, was completely impractical for the athletic feats he had to perform. This was the hottest fire I could have imagined to test the value of AT for extraordinary performing.

So Benedikt and I got cracking. Benedikt explained the artistic values and techniques in various types of mime, and how he worked with them in the context of this particular character and the show. He shared his performance and aesthetic needs, as well as the demands of the show. We played with using the specific aspects of his character as an entryway to coordinated, precise movement. Our ten-year collaboration taught me myriad lessons that I use every day.

Lessons Learned

IDENTIFY WHAT'S WORKING

When I saw Benedikt employ a particular technique, I asked, "What does that do for you? What do you like about it?" I was curious about how he was already addressing his desire to perform with quality, and what his art form offered in terms of practical techniques as well as ideals. This was where I learned to depend on the expertise of the performer I was working with—I respected Benedikt's artistry and integrity, which served as the basis for our collaboration. My aim was always to begin the process with what was working, what we could keep that he was already doing, distilling a clearer, more direct, and more comprehensive plan as needed.

One night I noticed Benedikt preparing for the part of the show where he leaps all the way across the stage with impossibly high vertical jumps. When doing this, he seems to be suspended by cables. Backstage, right before this moment, he was moving his wrists in a loose, supple way. When I asked him about this, he said he did this to check that all his joints were springy, that he was ready to jump. It was a cue he used to get his whole body tuned for what he was about to do, and it was working beautifully. I suggested that he might include in his preparation process the thought that his head moves delicately on top of his spine as a pre-condition to his supple wrists. Including a coordinated primary movement pattern enlivened his entire body, making his jumps even more astounding.

On another occasion, I noticed a curious heaviness in his initial setup when he would assume a "neutral" starting position to go into a pantomime routine. When I asked about it, he told me he was "getting grounded." I asked him what he meant and what in particular he wanted in his preparation. He described that he desired mobility, flexibility, and energized readiness. With a quick review of a few relevant design features (the design of particular joints as well as the overall organization of movement), we devised a strategy that placed his goals at the forefront. Ultimately, he achieved these goals more precisely than he had with the old plan.

SUSTAINABILITY IS NOT THE ENEMY OF ARTISTRY

Extraordinary performers require a process to help them understand what might be possible, as well as various ways these possibilities might be achieved. To explore the possibilities of Benedikt's character, we experimented with using a more fluid movement quality to exaggerate the curvature and asymmetry of his form. To our mutual fascination and delight, he felt and moved better, yet the character looked even more extreme. Using principles of efficiency to cooperate with, rather than fight, apparent inefficiency, we were able to make the result even more potent.

IT'S NOT WHAT IT LOOKS LIKE; IT'S WHAT IT IS LIKE

Good sound and movement quality are not fixed variables; they vary based on what the performer is aiming for. A character choice might look like a contorted, hunched shape, but, done in a coordinated way, it can be mobile and sustainable. Conversely, the rigid erectness of a dancer might look like certain traditional models of "alignment" but, if poorly coordinated, does not support the flexibility and vitality needed to dance.

A supporting method must be useful for performers, increasing their overall enjoyment and the sustainability of their performance. It needs to work clearly better for them and their audience than what they were doing before. While an abundance of somewhat useful techniques exist (and I have benefitted at times from many of them), I was interested in pursuing only that which was profoundly practical and infinitely scalable. Using AT in my own performing before learning to teach it enabled me to experience its value firsthand, equipping me to help performers respond creatively to their goals. The extreme generosity of Benedikt and the hundreds of other artists who have shared their art with me has been the primary reason I can be useful to them in return.

Essential Skills for Working with Highly Skilled Performers

Observing and Analyzing the Quality of Coordination

As I continue to work with performers and help other teachers do the same, three things have emerged as necessary skills to work effectively with performers. These skills are interdependent, meaning that fluency in one impacts and enriches the others, increasing skill and adeptness in all of them. "The better your own skills, the more deeply you understand the skilled performances you witness" (Blakeslee and Blakeslee 2007, p.169).

Essential to helping performers is the ability to appreciate what they are doing, in the full sense of the word. This includes seeing, hearing, sensing, and analyzing subtle aspects of the process behind the result; imagining other possibilities; understanding how their coordination affects the artistic outcome; and foreseeing future implications of a way of doing something. This "omnisensory" process is observing the quality of coordination—sensing the relationship between head and spine, and how this relationship affects overall coordination and movement quality (including movement of the limbs and joints) and the overall execution of the task. It is possible to discern information about the quality of coordination through sound, quality of performance, precision, speed, liveliness, and spontaneity. All of these are clues about coordination.

Appreciate

1. Recognize the full worth of

2. Be grateful for (something)

3. Understand (a situation) fully; recognize the full implications of. (OED 2017)

The more deeply I can understand the nuances of the skilled performers I work with, the more insightful, practical, and appropriate my ideas can be. Along with my skills as an AT teacher, the most powerful tools I can bring to this collaboration are deep knowledge of a particular skill and the skill-building process; experience with satisfying, effective performance (my own and that of other artists); and fluency in coordinating appropriately to achieve these things.

Key to skill building, performing, and coordinating effectively are well-developed mirror neurons. Mirror neurons are neurons that fire both when one acts and when one observes the same action performed by another. The neuron "mirrors" the behavior of the other, as though the observer themselves were acting. It is argued that mirror neurons are the neural basis for empathy. Blakeslee explains it in this way:

> Your mirror neuron system becomes more active the more expert you are at an observed skill. When pianists listen to someone else's piano performance, the finger areas in their primary and premotor cortex increase about their baseline activity. The same thing does not happen in the brains of non-musicians. While they can certainly appreciate the music deeply, their experience is inevitably shallower than the pianists in at least one way, because they are not experiencing what it is like to actually produce it...

As Blakeslee details, expertise helps us to imagine into the activity of another by exciting neurons in us. This can happen even when it isn't our particular skill. The extent to which we have experience with the components of an activity is reflected in our mirror neurons, and understanding skill building in some expert way allows us to more effectively help performers. It is, therefore, a much more meaningful collaboration when both teacher and performer have lived, active experience in skilled expertise.

> When you learn a new motor skill, you see the world differently. You understand actions differently. (Blakeslee and Blakeslee 2007, pp.169–170)

Developing Skill and Process of Refinement

The more direct experience one has with performing, the more one can understand the predicaments of the performers one works with. Having a lived experience of developing and refining a skill for performance creates a holistic empathy with the performers, as well as a deeper understanding of the process itself.

This understanding includes empathizing with the difficulty of an artist's choice to apply AT as a way to reimagine and refine a specific, highly skilled process that has worked for them in the past and been praised by others, in service of their own satisfaction and sustainability. Engaging in a process that may unsettle a performer's beliefs about their art, technique, and self, that may temporarily disrupt well-established pathways, can be as harrowing initially as it can be ultimately rewarding. Doing this requires optimism, bravery, and grit. It is invaluable for a teacher to have been through the experience themselves and kept going with their art professionally. Teachers and coaches who perform professionally in a well-coordinated way (by "perform" I mean any kind of intentional communication with an audience that places demands on their skills) are much more likely to understand what performers are going through, and what they need to do their job. Because of their dedication and training, elite performers can recognize quality. They can identify and relate to someone who is skilled at something themselves and thus demonstrates credibility. Living what I teach is the best way to be qualified and useful in working with extraordinary performers.

Communicating a Clear, Reliable, and Adaptable Process

The ability to communicate an adaptable process depends upon the teacher's direct experience of using it, as well as learning about the experiences of others using that process. I often think of how designers and architects use drawing as a tool for understanding; they draw in order to see. When one has reproduced something independently, one understands more about how it truly is. Specific, clear articulation of a process can be a key tool to use, particularly when one cannot demonstrate the activity itself. For example, if I am helping someone do a series of backflips, even though I myself cannot execute that task exactly, I have applied AT to enough kinds of movement and observed others doing such movements that I can effectively demonstrate portions of the activity. I can articulate the components sequentially at a micro and macro level to help the performers through the process. The ability to perform a skill with quality and coordination is inestimably helpful in dissolving the clutter of rhetoric about whether an approach is effective. If I can demonstrate, partially or entirely, a well-coordinated, excellent execution of something I am working on with a performer, this act speaks volumes about the potency of the idea I wish to communicate.

Guiding Principles

> My commitment is to truth, not consistency.
>
> Mahatma Gandhi

Developing and refining techniques and strategies are part of a fluid and dynamic process. As my own skills and understanding change (as well as scientific information itself), I have become accustomed to the need for a cyclical disorganization and reorganization of ideas and techniques in order to integrate new information. To be the kind of trustworthy resource I want to be for myself and fellow performers, I have evolved an emergent process by which I validate, negate, develop, and organize ideas and information. Following are some of the ways I explore and verify information and techniques.

Cooperate with a Holistic Worldview

I encountered the work of physicist and educator Fritjof Capra when I was about 16, and it has profoundly informed my art and life ever since. Capra's theory of living systems is a holistic worldview. This ecological (relating to living systems and their relation to each other) way of thinking has been a catalyst and guiding paradigm for me as I have developed a framework and criteria for performing and working with performers. We are whole, we are interconnected, and any technique or approach must be in accord with these principles.

Ultimately—as quantum physics [has] showed so dramatically—there are no parts at all. What we call a part is merely a pattern in an inseparable web of relationships... The new paradigm may be called a holistic worldview...seeing the world as an integrated whole rather than a dissociated collection of parts. It may also be called an ecological view, if the term "ecological" is used in a much broader and deeper sense than usual. Deep ecological awareness recognizes the fundamental interdependence of all phenomena and the fact that, as individuals and societies, we are all embedded in (and ultimately dependent on) the cyclical processes of nature. (Capra 1996, p.6)

My choice to study AT is an example of this. I was interested in pursuing the work only when it was clear to me that it was consistent with a holistic, scientifically coherent, and practical paradigm.

Find Multiple Sources

Finding numerous sources of information helps to clarify what is consistent across disciplines or activities, versus what is specific to a style or activity. In developing criteria for understanding the principles of human movement and extraordinary performance, I find that once something fits within the framework of wholeness and interconnectedness, it shows up from credible sources in multiple fields. For instance, information about anatomy and functioning should be easy enough to verify across sources.

This way of researching from a performance standpoint evolved from my work in Bulgarian music. I always made sure I had at least three distinct, reputable sources for a song, since this would help me know its origin and evolution, as well as understand the essence of the song within multiple interpretations. I do this any time I find relevant information about neuroscience. For example, I look to several reputable scientists to determine how reliable the information is and what various interpretations exist. If I find interesting information from a nonscientific source, I seek out that writer's sources and research those.

Seek Contrary Views

Finding contrary views and understanding the thinking behind them helps me refresh and refine my perspective about my own work, identify contradictions, and think through alternative approaches or techniques. What are the benefits and limitations of an alternate approach? Even if I disagree with the premise or effectiveness of something, seeking to understand its perceived value helps me better understand people's behavior.

For instance, singing presents some ways of achieving a "powerful" sound that are clearly suboptimal by my standards: They involve muscular force and pose a risk to the voice, compromise overall coordination, and produce pale imitations of true resonance. However, to diminish or dismiss them and their users isn't particularly helpful. In learning about what these strategies offer singers—they do increase loudness in a limited spectral range and therefore do have an effect—I can better understand how to help my students retain the effectiveness of approach through a more fully coordinated whole self.

Expose My Work to Experts in Related Fields

It's essential to share, practically and theoretically, with other members of my community for the purposes of collaboration, exchange of ideas, and (if applicable) validation. Doing this enables me to vet ideas with scientists and other experts, as well as further my understanding about their work. This helps me gain insight about how others work with performance, singing, and movement.

For instance, I have a trusted colleague who is a voice pathologist and voice therapist, and is also an active singer. I frequently seek her feedback about specific issues, approaches, and clients. She has been generous and insightful about how to help singers recover from injury and fatigue, vocal hygiene and usage, and courses of action for rehabilitation and treatment.

Research Other Fields of Science

Neuroscience, stress physiology, flow/optimal performance, anatomy, and other related areas are invaluable in helping provide a fuller, more dimensional, and thorough understanding of people and the world. Researching across disciplines helps alleviate the myopia that can come from being inside a particular field, giving us access to ways of thinking that can enrich our own thinking, as well as reveal limitations in our thinking.

F.M. Alexander, neurophysiologist Sir Charles Sherrington, and ethologist Nikolaas Tinbergen all put forth groundbreaking work about human movement and behavior. Neuroscientist V.S. Ramachandran, neurobiologist Robert Sapolsky, and psychologists Daniel Kahneman and Mihaly Csikszentmihalyi have all made significant, meaningful, and continuing contributions to our understanding of how people think, move, play, learn, make decisions, and change. Their work has been particularly illuminating and enriching for me.

Recently, talking with a physicist at a party, I asked him how he would explain and demonstrate Bernoulli's principle (a principle cited often by voice teachers relating to pressure, flow, and potential and kinetic energy). Hearing his way of articulating it, outside of the voice field bias, gave me a fresh perspective on how the principle works and how it specifically applies, and in some ways does not apply, in singing.

Pursue Learning in Other Fields

Thinking across categories requires listening to experts in other disciplines, seeing how they think about what they do, and hearing what connections they see. This involves learning new things, playing, and lots of time observing and learning from others—all opportunities to renew coordination in new frontiers. Directly and obliquely, learning how to do new things helps us to see and experience what principles emerge that are harmonious or discordant, contributing to understanding our own field and its organizing principles. Learning new skills has given me the invaluable opportunity to constantly be a beginner, continually refreshing my perspective and excitement.

A couple of years ago, I took juggling lessons from a friend and colleague. It was a frustrating, hilarious, and transformative experience. I was a true beginner and fell victim to all the classic blunders. I found little contrivances to get the result I wanted faster, but was coached expertly by my friend who caught on to my tricks immediately and said, "You don't want to do that. It won't work for anything in the future." I was struggling with just three balls, so he deftly grabbed four, five, even six balls to show me exactly how my plan was limited in any context other than what I was working on. It was a pleasure to be taught by someone who could see ahead to all the next steps of the process and guide me through them with a keen eye and constructive feedback. It also proved helpful in my singing—I found ways to move and think that were new, and I experienced revelation and synergy.

All Together, One After the Other

A recent example using all of these guiding principles was in preparing to teach a Performance Readiness workshop. I specifically revisited several related texts: *Flow* by Mihaly Csikszentmihalyi, *Why Zebras Don't Get Ulcers* by neurobiologist Robert Sapolsky, *The Body Has a Mind of Its Own* by Sandra and Matthew Blakeslee, and a newer book, Kelly McGonigal's *The Upside of Stress: Why Stress Is Good for You, and How to Get Good at It.* I listened to interviews with Anders Ericsson, psychologist and researcher in expertise and human performance, and with neuroscientist V.S. Ramachandran. I researched and learned training and pre-performance routines from performers and athletes, including Olympic athletes hurdler Michelle Jenneke and swimmer Michael Phelps.

To get specific feedback on the content of the workshop and my understanding of the subject, I consulted with Dr. Paula Thomson, researcher, clinical psychologist, sports psychologist, kinesiologist, and choreographer, as well as Cathy Madden, actor, acting teacher, and AT teacher. All this in preparation for one three-hour workshop.

Teaching

Much of the process I use when working with performers is similar when I work with non-performers as well. All elements are synthesized and varied spontaneously to best accommodate the person with whom I am working.

Initial Conversation

When I first work with students, I ask them what brought them to see me. I ask them what they are interested in, curious about, and/or working on. I ask them how they are currently responding to their goals. Having this conversation initially and then throughout our collaboration helps me get to know them holistically. We are establishing their desire, curiosity, and the overall why of what they do. This also communicates clearly that this enterprise is their choice.

If they are there to improve their performance, I listen to their constructive critic (the part of them that wishes to transcend their current abilities), celebrate the desire to change and explore, and respond with a nourishing approach.

If they come because of pain, I ask them what they wish to do with better quality and more comfort once the pain is managed or gone. I do this because I have observed that while pain can be a powerful catalyst, it's not a sustaining motivator, because it represents something unwanted. If pain is the only trigger to use the technique, once the pain is gone, the trigger to use the technique disappears as well. I am keen to identify and/or develop a longer-term desire, so that as things improve, we are working toward something positive. In our work and play, we can always relate what we are doing directly and indirectly to their expressed desire.

This is my first opportunity to recognize and celebrate something the student is doing that is effective and constructive. This rightly helps them trust that they have the resources to respond to their goals and curiosity—and are in fact already doing so.

Do an Activity They Wish to Work With

This could be anything, but if they are a performer I usually ask them to start there. Seeing them do what they most care about is the best way for me to get to know them, to see how I can be most helpful. I appreciate what they are doing, often explicitly, as well as their willingness to share what they do. I observe their overall quality of coordination, how they respond to internal and external stimuli, and their current processes and strategies. I use all my senses in this process.

Identify What Works About Their Current Process

We do this together, but I ask them to lead the discussion by asking, "What did you like about that? What are you doing that's working?" It is crucial to recognize and celebrate what is working. Performers must know that they can be trusted, and that what they want and can recognize matters. (If they are unable to initially recognize or articulate something about this, we play with ways to do this until they can do it successfully.) It is as important to assess what is working and give it due value without being reductive or dismissive as it is to be able to accurately discern what is not working and when additional skills are required. This recognition is key to being able to accurately observe and analyze the quality of coordination, and it is essential to using AT in life and performing.

This is my second opportunity to recognize and celebrate something effective and constructive they are doing, to help them realize that they have the resources to respond to their goals and curiosity, are already doing so, and can themselves recognize some of the qualities and effects of that process.

Discuss Their Strategies

After they have performed and identified what's working, I investigate further by asking, "How did you do what you did? How do you know it's working? What are your metrics for success? Are they effective? Is your process sustainable? Joyful?" This inquiry helps me learn how much they are doing consciously to reach their ends, how specifically they can analyze and articulate their own process, and how accurate their perception of the processes and outcomes is. I ask them to identify what they feel works for them about the current strategy and how it addresses their goals. All of this helps me prioritize giving design information and devise appropriate experiments. It also renews their own constructive thinking: As they articulate what works, the good coordination they already use is reinforced—they teach themselves what to do to get what they want. It develops clear thinking, planning, and articulation as an integrated part of the process. They likely notice also some of the limitations of their strategies. With musicians, I learn about their current ideas of how their instrument works, as well as other relevant ideas about elements relating to their activity such as resonance, tuning, readiness, precision, and expression. I learn about what they value and how they give themselves feedback. At this time we often distinguish the difference between a fact (for example, the anatomical design of the pelvis) and a technique (something they may have learned to do with their pelvis at some point).

This discussion develops skills of observing, analyzing, and understanding the quality of coordination in themselves and others. Articulating what they are doing is a way of gaining understanding, discovering inconsistencies or incomplete steps in their processes, and developing a repeatable process and feedback loops they can use to teach themselves in the future.

Experiment and Elaborate

Next, I often introduce relevant information about design, or bring in additional information that reinforces someone's existing skills and strategies while adding more detail and fullness to the process. For example, this might be when I explain and demonstrate the head/spine relationship and its organization of our overall movement pattern. This is a collaborative process where we exchange ideas and delight in new discoveries. We find ways to approach what they do differently, in service of the things the student values, integrating strategies that already work with new information and perspective. In this process, they develop a more reliable feedback system, including finely tuned sensory awareness and more skillful motor planning.

As we proceed through their repertoire or piece (or shift into a different activity), I ask them what strategy they might use; if they have an idea, we do that and see what happens. If they don't have an idea, I suggest one. After using a strategy, we talk about how it went, what they noticed, and if they achieved their desired result (or beyond!). I have them lead this analysis, elaborating on what they've already noticed by offering additional details related to principles of coordination, physics, aerodynamics, and so forth. Along the way, we recognize and celebrate what they did that they intended to, how the new approach changed things at that moment, and what bearing this may have on their overall performance. Then we may go on to another part of a piece, or I may illuminate how these strategies can be used elsewhere for future experimentation.

This is also where I might use an affinity as a pathway. For example, when working with a violinist on a demanding concerto, I asked if he had any hobbies or other interests outside music. He said that years ago he used to skateboard pretty seriously. I asked him to imagine he was on a skateboard. His entire movement pattern changed; he was more flexible and lively. I asked him to play like that and observe himself. Then I asked him to play again using what he considered his "violin posture." Comparing the two, he was able to observe multitudinous differences in how his thinking and internal rule-set was affecting his desired outcome. In this case, I worked from the direction of a pre-existing affinity, using that to guide the student to play in a more coordinated way, then discussing and explaining the details and substantive differences. One of the many benefits in this approach is that the student discovers a meaningful resource they already have and can use immediately. They then gain additional context and data about why it works so well.

At this point, the student has used the technique to respond to their desires and curiosity. They have made changes on their own, are keenly aware of how they did that, and recognize that it was they who did it. This is a key time for establishing creativity as a necessary part of the process, of understanding and innovation. It also underscores the importance of understanding a system in order to guide the system in a particular way. By illuminating underlying principles of human design and movement, structure, and functioning, then linking that to a conscious, constructive process, the student is empowered to know why and how things work. This fosters self-reliance and creativity. They can invent their own plans and experiments based on their understanding of the reasoning behind them.

Engage in Rehearsals and Variations

When we've found a strategy that is constructive, cooperates with design, and serves the performer's desire, we repeat and vary it. This reveals any vagueness in the plan, tests its strength and adaptability, and allows us to riff on the ideas therein for other purposes. Becoming fluent in the process requires rehearsal: doing the constructive process repeatedly and in a flexible way. This also allows us to appreciate the work as a deeply creative process, marveling at how powerfully and dimensionally small adjustments can affect the overall result.

We frequently link the coordination across activities, sometimes improvising a procedure or having them do so. I may suggest, "Let's try that idea with walking, singing…" so that there is an immediate cross-pollination, making clear the essence of the coordination. The student can immediately use the new approach for multiple activities, thus strengthening the pathway. The message is that the strategy and underlying design information can be used and adapted to whatever they wish to do. Doing this jointly during a lesson helps them experience such a process, ideally sparking curiosity in other areas of their life. Engaging in rehearsal and variation develops and reinforces perception and planning as a blended process—action and intention become unified.

When performers can call up a plan to use in performance that serves their own desires, they are using the technique as it was designed—a tool to use when they wish to do something with quality.

Lively and Evolving Work

> In the study I found the things which I had "known"—
> in the sense of theoretical belief—in philosophy and
> psychology, changed into vital experiences which gave a
> new meaning to knowledge of them.
>
> John Dewey (Alexander 1984 [1932], p.11)

Using AT is a creative act. It can be used at will, to do with quality anything we wish to do. It is an invaluable tool we can use to open doors to a reliable, adaptable process calling up technical and performance skills. In this chapter I have explored what is needed to help highly skilled performers: recognition of what is working, keen discernment of what could use improvement, discipline to celebrate both a performer's current abilities and their desire to transcend them, and strategies to help performers do these things for themselves. It is my assertion that being skilled in performance oneself matters greatly in the pursuit of helping other performers. It is how we learn to synthesize our own skills and coordination, how we know how to help others do so as well. Using AT to teach highly skilled performers is an exciting, emerging field. By recognizing this field and the specificity of this work, we give full value to the skills of the people who have cultivated it as an area of expertise. We celebrate bringing all our resources, our whole selves, to bear in a glorious act of creation.

Notes

1   I began using the term *design* after starting to work with Cathy Madden a few years ago. I adopted it, using it the way she uses it, because it is a holistic, elegant way to express complex systems.

2   They include light, color, hearing, smell, taste, touch, pain, balance, proprioception, kinesthesis, heat, cold, blood pressure, blood oxygen content, cerebrospinal fluid pH, thirst, and hunger.

References

Alexander, F.M. (1984) *The Use of the Self.* Downey, CA: Centerline Press. (Original work published 1932.)

Blakeslee, S. and Blakeslee, M. (2007) *The Body Has a Mind of Its Own: How Body Maps in Your Brain Help You Do (Almost) Everything Better.* New York: Random House.

Capra, F. (1996) *The Web of Life: A New Scientific Understanding of Living Systems.* New York: Random House.

Feldman, M. (1969) "Between categories." *The Composer 1*, 2, 73–77.

Online Oxford English Dictionary (2017) Oxford: Oxford University Press. Available at www.oed.com (accessed on June 8, 2017).

A Mirror, a Mask, and an Actor

Julianne Eveleigh and Paul Hampton

AT Perspective

Our understanding of the Alexander Technique is strongly associated with the teaching of "neutrality" or "disponibilité": "an experiential condition...*centred* (in oneself) and balanced, ready to go in any appropriate direction. ...*poised* between all possibilities" (Frost and Yarrow 2007, p.197).

We interpret this state as congruent with Pierce Jones's "unified field of awareness": "attention...is expanded to take in certain key relations in the body as well as the activity on which attention is focussed" (Jones 1997, p.176).

Though just described as a "state," it is more accurately understood as a vigorous, multidimensional activity or dance calling for decisions regarding intention in space (*direction*), coordination in order to facilitate freedom of the head/spine relationship (*primary control*), and ongoing choice in the face of stimuli from both outside and inside (*inhibition*).

The Federation University Australia Arts Academy Performing Arts Program runs a three-year undergraduate Bachelor of Arts (Acting) degree. The integrating practice of our first-semester acting course is "neutrality" derived from the interplay between the Alexander Technique and the Neutral Mask (NM).

The key lesson that initiates this exchange is the class early in the first semester in which each student receives an AT lesson, in front of a mirror, while wearing the Neutral Mask. We have found that this class galvanizes many of the key skills we think are vital to the development of each new acting ensemble: mind/body coordination, playfulness, and freedom of choice. The mask–mirror class usually takes place in the third week of the new student's course.

Large parts of this chapter consist of passages from student journals. They have an authenticity that we think enriches and supports our story. Their inclusion is also an acknowledgment that student observation and reflection, no matter how awkward or naive, is a major part of their learning, and that the journey undertaken each year is a partnership. We learn a great deal from them and thank them for their generous contribution.

Neutral Mask History

When he set up a training school in Paris in 1921, French actor, director, and teacher Jacques Copeau was struck by the "excessive awkwardness" of his students, a "veritable corporeal impotence" that "the most assiduous gymnastic training could not overcome" (Copeau 1990, p.50). He identified a "disease" he called "*cabotinage*":

> a malady of insincerity, or rather of falseness. He who suffers from it ceases to be authentic, to be human. He is discredited, unnatural. Outer reality no longer reaches him. He is no longer aware of his feelings. Whenever they arise, somehow they become detached from his personality... I am speaking of the...total mechanisation of the person, of the absolute lack of profound intelligence and true spirituality. (Copeau 1990, p.253)

Copeau's first mask was a mere handkerchief covering the face of an actress who found herself unable to move:

I masked them. Immediately, I was able to observe a transformation…
You understand that the face for us is tormenting: the mask saves
our dignity, our freedom. The mask protects the soul from grimaces.
Thence, by a series of very explainable consequences, the wearer
acutely feels his possibilities of corporeal expression. (Copeau 1990,
p.50)

Copeau's students developed masks with the aim of removing
individual facial characteristics and regularizing their features. The
result was called the "noble" mask. In this new mask, his students were
able to achieve a quality of action he described as *neutral*: "*The point of
departure of an expression.* The state of repose, of calm, of relaxation or
decontraction, of silence or simplicity" (Rudlin 2010, p.56).

What we now know as Neutral Mask evolved in the hands of
later theatre teachers, most notably Michel Saint-Denis (Copeau's
nephew), who introduced training in the mask in England and North
America, and Jacques Lecoq, who in partnership with the Italian
mask maker Amleto Sartori produced the best-known mask design
still used in many schools throughout the world (Frost and Yarrow
2007, p.233).

Neutral Mask is, in essence, a human face devoid of discernible
"character," emotion, or obvious psychological history. The face is
symmetrical, the eyes wide open, the jaw released, the lips slightly
parted: the very image of equanimity, receptivity, and lively calm.

Preliminary Classes

AT guides the work from the very beginning. In voice and acting
classes, there is an immediate introduction to AT through an
emphasis on anatomy and psychophysical connection: Body Mapping
activities, a rudimentary understanding of Alexander's concepts of
primary control and the head/spine relationship, and an introduction
to the concept of *inhibition* or freedom of choice. Students begin to
explore Alexander's *directions*, and the notion of an indirect approach
to "cooperating with their human design" (Madden 2014, p.285)
through thinking and moving.

AT teacher Cathy Madden suggests that "continually refining knowledge of anatomical information is necessary when the performer seeks to fine-tune skills and is an immense help when learning a new skill" (Madden 2014, p.37). Introducing anatomy and Body Mapping activities at this early stage helps to dispel personal myths that tend to "interfere with our effectiveness" (Madden 2014, p.36).

Meeting the Neutral Mask

The central aim of the first Neutral Mask class is to manifest a resonant image of the mask: to recognize NM. Part of the particular power of masking in theatre history is that the mask is normally grasped as one: The performer looks upon the mask, there is a process of recognition, the performer dons the mask, the performer sees the world through the eyes of the mask.

First Impressions

With NM, there is at first no obvious familiar human character to the mask, no visible history etched into the face, no obvious character to get to know. Many students initially find this intimidating and they cannot relate to it:

I found it quite difficult to look directly at the mask. Perhaps this is just because I found it confronting to not be able to see the person's face. Also in today's horror movies a lot of the villains wear masks to hide their identity or their misshaped faces. This was just my initial impression and it did fade away as the class progressed. (Student journal 2014)

I found it confronting to put such a thing to cover my face, which is unusual, as I cannot leave the house without mascara or foundation on an everyday basis. This make-up is a form of mask to hide imperfections and insecurities. The expressionless mask strips me of the face that I have created and designed in accordance to fashion and social constraints. (Student journal 2015)

The unavoidable reality at this moment is that perceptions of the mask will not change until the students find ways of bringing it to life. This is the chief objective of the first lesson.

Protocols

Students are informed of the protocols and procedures for wearing the mask: always turning the back when putting it on and taking it off, never speaking in the mask, and so forth. They practice putting the mask on, walking in the mask, taking it off. Pragmatic issues of comfort/discomfort are dealt with at this stage.

What Is "Neutral"?

As a whole group, they practice carrying the mask in one hand at head height, walking in a "neutral" manner, and watching to see if the face lends them any clues as to its identity or purpose. Then in small groups, students put on the mask, turn toward the class, walk forward, pause, and take off the mask. Discussion and learning through observation begins:

Each step into the exercises involved self-evaluation. My first attempt to wear the mask was interesting as I found a change within myself as soon as it was on. I realized that the mask teaches you to rely only on your body and its movement; there is no other way of communicating. (Student journal 2014)

I know that the best way for me to show the mask would be to work on the tensions in my body, and to contain my habits/tics. (Student journal 2015)

Practicing with the Whole Body

Without the mask, the students practice going in and out of the floor, from lying to standing and back to lying. We observe coordination and flow. This is repeated with AT directions (head leads, body follows).

I immediately noticed little habits that I needed to get rid of just from this exercise. I love how the neutral mask teaches you to strip everything back. I think it is so important to learn to be minimal because it is harder than I originally thought. (Student journal 2014)

Creating and Following Images

The students are asked to call up a vast, uncluttered horizon with themselves at the center. A "whole," global space: Earth beneath, sky above, horizon in all directions. They practice going into and out of the floor and walking the room connected to and guided by this global image. They are coached to stay at the center of things at all times, to listen on all sides, to see rather than search, to receive the images on the breath.

Some students struggle initially with imagining on a three-dimensional, epic scale. It is common to find that their imagining is limited to the two-dimensional picture frame: the screen. Others may have real-life memories, but they are cluttered by too much personal detail. The sort of horizon needed to support NM is an austere place: a desert or plain that evokes limitless time and space. The horizon needs to be vivid and glowing with potential; a place of limitless probability—a call to adventure. All is new, as if for the first time.

We are creating the circumstances of "wholeness." It is an acknowledgment that NM only appears as a figure fully integrated in its world. AT teacher Tommy Thompson describes this as "ecological awareness." He argues that when we lose our connection with the *support* that the environment (social and natural) offers, "we define ourselves apart from mutual existence." The alternative, he maintains, is inventing support based on an unconnected "habit of identity" that leads to reliance on muscular effort: "Movement, though purposeful, is strained. If all is effort, then where is the simple joy of being alive, of moving mutually in this perpetual dance of life?" (Thompson 1995).

First Scenarios

Solo performances:

- Scenario #1: The mask sleeps, wakes, sees the horizon, stands, walks forwards toward the horizon (Lecoq 2002, p.39).

- Scenario #2: The mask sleeps, wakes, sees a mountain, and becomes one with the mountain (Lecoq 2002, p.39).

The teaching moves into a style that can be roughly described as "via negativa": saying "yes," hearing "no" (Frost and Yarrow 2016, p.244). The student is encouraged to keep saying "yes" to the work, to perform with commitment, without knowing precisely what is likely to manifest NM. The observers are encouraged to acknowledge what doesn't appear to work as well as what does. They are urged to watch each solo closely and use their observations to gather data for their own turn. "It is frequently only possible to say what is not working, rather than specify what is required" (Murray 2003, p.143, quoted in Frost and Yarrow 2016, p.244).

The students are coached to encompass the whole shape rather than getting caught up in detail; to capture "the function of action, life, or expression—…gesture" (Nicolaides 1941, p.15).

> To be able to see the gesture, you must be able to feel it in your own body…you feel the movement of the whole form in your whole body…focus should be on the entire figure and you should keep the whole thing going at once. (Nicolaides 1941, p.16)

Gestural perception is regarded as a characteristic of the right hemisphere:

> The right hemisphere, with its greater integrative power, is constantly searching for patterns in things… The process is not a gradual putting together of bits of information, but an "aha" phenomenon—it all comes at once. (McGilchrist 2009, p.47)

In this initial class we exercise the right hemisphere and watch out for a moment of recognition, the "aha" event.

Summary

The first NM class aims to achieve three things:

- The student has glimpsed NM.

- They have begun to deduce the sort of mind/body organization that manifests its appearance.

- They want to see NM realized and to develop the personal skills to make it happen.

Student journals show that they have begun to work out some important things:

- The whole body must be engaged:

I realized that the mask teaches you to only rely on your body and its movement; there is no other way of communicating. (Student journal 2014)

- Many have defined some essentials of neutrality: a unified self, openness, balance, detachment, control:

I felt comfortable inside the mask as if all my own personal judgments stopped and I had an open mind to anything that was going to happen. (Student journal 2014)

I felt that using our horizons led to people coming closer to achieving the state of neutrality. (Student journal 2015)

When the activity ended I looked at one of my classmates and we were both in awe about how much the mountain and mask activity had put us at rest but also made us feel very alive at the same time. (Student journal 2014)

- Many have begun to perceive embodiment in the work of others:

People who were completely connected and embodied the mask were: showing simplicity, moved with ease, their whole body was engaged, they were fully committed to the activity. People who were demonstrating were: off center, adding unnecessary movements or ideas, abrupt, hesitant. (Student journal 2013)

- Some are quite sure that they have been in the presence of NM:

The mask showed a pure form of human life, I felt so anyway. (Student journal 2015)

Although the student understanding is uneven at this stage, we have set up the pre-conditions to take the next step: the mask–mirror class.

The Mask–Mirror Class

Acknowledgment of Conditions Present

The mask and mirror session takes place in a studio with a full-length mirror on one side.

We all gather in a circle at the center of the room. As it is only their third week, there is a wide range of stance, posture, and attitude in evidence. We ask the students to pay attention to themselves:

"Where is the weight distributed over your feet? Are your feet close together or far apart? Do your toes point inward or outward? Are your knees locked? Where are your arms and hands in relation to the rest of the body? Where are your shoulders in relation to your ears? Where are you looking? What do you see?"

I discovered that my head was in a lowered position, vision was directed toward the ground, and shoulders were raised. (Student journal 2015)

My arms were crossed and my feet were together. (Student journal 2015)

My right foot has most weight on it so leaning to the side. (Student journal 2015)

"In what parts of your body can you observe tension?"

I automatically tense my abdominal muscles. (Student journal 2015)

Tension in my jaw and upper body. (Student journal 2015)

"Are there thoughts that you associate with this tension?"

I was trying hard to stand up straight because I have scoliosis and I'm used to setting my chest out and shoulders back to make my posture better. (Student journal 2015)

I tensed up, stressing about getting the exercise right, despite knowing that there is no right. This is really a large inner struggle for me. (Student journal 2015)

When this brief body-thought scan is complete we tell them they can walk around the room and let go of the things they have observed. We then request that they return to the circle and re-create the position they began with, exaggerate it a little, and then look around at their classmates.

The one constant I found throughout the group was that many of our habitual poses were closed, moving back and away from the space, or having arms crossed in front of the body defensively. (Student journal 2015)

Diagnosis—That's Me?

The opening circle disperses and the students take their places on chairs at one end of the room. When invited, each student steps up, walks to the center of the room, turns away from the group, and puts on the mask. They turn to face the class. They are alongside the mirror. The rest of the class can clearly see the mask wearer in the center of the room, but not the image in the mirror, which is viewable only by the wearer and teacher.

"Re-create, as accurately as possible, the position that you remember from the circle. Now turn to face the mirror."

When looking in the mirror at myself I saw someone who was closed off to others. With the mask off, however, I wouldn't have noticed all of these things, because I find that personally, the first thing I'm drawn to when looking in a mirror is my face, and often my facial expression won't actually reflect my body language. (Student journal 2013)

Looking in the mirror, I realized that by wearing the mask, it took away my face, the part of the body we all use as our "go to" point. It's how we recognize people; it's where we look at someone. It really stripped away my external personality and forced me to concentrate on my body's habits. (Student journal 2014)

Some AT teachers work with individual students in front of a mirror. They are, we assume, reproducing F.M. Alexander's initial, pioneering diagnostic process. In his isolated experiment in Melbourne in the late 19th century, Alexander decided that "when I wished *to make certain* of what I was doing with myself…[I] derived invaluable help from the use of a mirror" (Alexander 1984 [1932], p.16). He acknowledged that at first he was not practiced at discerning in the mirror the "slight" changes that were causing his problems: "I then lacked experience in *the kind of observation* necessary to enable me to detect anything wrong in the way I used myself when speaking" (Alexander 1984 [1932], p.10; our italics).

As a species our history of relations with the mirror is not simple. Some historians argue that the invention of the clear, glass mirror allowed us to see ourselves clearly for the first time. But the proliferation of "mirrors" (such as photography and video) has also led to acute self-consciousness, introspection, and endless variations of "mirror conversation."

It is possible to look without seeing, and to hear without listening… To look and see you need to be attentive, dispassionate, interested yet disinterested, inquisitive yet accepting, critical yet non-judgemental… Faulty sensory awareness pervades all our actions, including watching and listening. The use of visual or aural aids does not guarantee accuracy of perceptions. (de Alcantara 2013, p.165)

Judith Leibowitz, however, argues that the image in the mirror is already at one remove from ourselves and can be observed dispassionately: "See it in the mirror. See, if you deal with that image in the mirror, it's a little easier because you can see *that image doing it* and your body maybe will translate" (Miranda 2007, p.75).

The key to achieving this relatively detached state of observation is largely the coaching skill of the AT teacher. However, we also have found that the skill to use the mirror productively/constructively is infinitely enhanced by the presence of NM in the process:

When I turned to see myself in the mirror, I felt no connection to the person that was in the mirror. Seeing myself with a neutral mask on allowed me to detach my emotions from the person in the mirror, and just see them as a body. I felt as though I was correcting someone else's stance. (Student journal 2015)

The mask allows you to observe someone else (you). (Student journal 2014)

Desire for Change

"Is that what you want?"

I immediately shook my head, as the person I looked at looked as though they were too tired to give anyone the time of day, let alone be ready to do anything. My interpretation of someone calm, strong and balanced, however, actually made me create tension in my shoulders trying to stand up so straight. (Student journal 2013)

We ask the student to experiment with what they want. To construct a new pathway. They see their image and are surprised by what they see because it doesn't reflect who they are.

"So do what you need to do to get what you want."

I realized I was trying too hard to be this strong focused acting student. I had an image of what I wanted and struggled to materialize that, so I felt frustrated. (Student journal 2015)

I saw that my energy was travelling backwards and seemed very disjointed, with my upper body retreating backwards and my hips wanting to lead and push forwards. In adjusting myself, I first made sure I was connecting through the points of balance in my feet and made sure I was not locking my knees. I then looked side on in the mirror and tried to come into my height by lengthening my spine. (Student journal 2014)

Observing themselves in the mirror, the student begins the process of what Madden calls "wanting, recognizing, deciding, asking and experimenting" (Madden 2014, p.107). We invite them to look at themselves and make a choice about what they want. They then recognize that they can do something that will improve their coordination and decide to change.

An AT Lesson in the Mask

"Turn away from the mirror toward the class."

It is at this point that we call on AT, place hands on, and coach the student into an alternative coordination. The student is no longer observing the mirror/mask image but responding to sensory and verbal cues provided by the teacher. In effect, each student receives a short AT lesson. In keeping with AT tradition, the detail and tenor of each lesson is tailored to individual circumstances, so the range of procedures varies throughout the session. However, these are the central themes:

- The head/spine relationship is key to your organization and coordination, and its location is deep in the center of the head.

- The front of the spine is weight bearing.

- The torso begins at the atlanto-occipital joint (where the skull meets the spine) and continues along the length of the spine to include the shoulder girdle, ribs, and pelvic girdle, ending at the ischial tuberosity (sit bones), so it includes the hip joints.

- There is a balanced distribution of weight through the ball and heel of each foot.

- Locking the knees interferes with balance and coordination.

- Include the curves of the spine in your thinking.

- Allow the breath to be three-dimensional.

We verbally and visually reinforce accurate anatomy of joints, ribs, pelvis, breathing, and so forth. Depending on what presents itself to us, we go on to explore ways to:

- integrate the physical structure of the back in their thinking in order to release the shoulders so that arms come to life and are included in the whole self

- lead with the eyes or the bridge of the nose so that as the students turn in space they notice the habit of leading from the chin, shoulder, hip, leg, foot, or any other of the thousands of combinations that manifest.

This is what the students notice:

- -

In my new position my back was lengthened, arms loose by my sides, my knees were bent evenly, balancing my weight between my heels and the balls of my feet, lowered chin, open chest, and my hips back. (Student journal 2015)

I felt as though I was leaning forward a bit, but when I saw myself in the mirror, I looked completely straight and I felt really good about myself. (Student journal 2015)

I was able to feel much more length through my spine. I hadn't, before this class, realized how much I seemed to hold myself in a backward direction. (Student journal 2014)

I was learning that it wasn't about lifting up my body, but it was about which parts to engage and what parts to release. I was making a conscious effort to use the earth underneath me and balance through the balls of my feet. (Student journal 2013)

A number of key things were said to students that I found to be very helpful: to invite a sense of breath, eyes lead and the body follows, release the knees, redirect your energy, keep inviting freedom into your body, lead with the bridge of your nose. It's not about changing who you are, it's about becoming more of who you are. (Student journal 2015)

- -

An Alternative Self in the Mirror

"Turn back and look again in the mirror."

Although the image the student now sees in the mirror is still wearing the mask, they primarily see themselves. And the "self" they see is a revelation:

- -

I was so happy and so shocked because I never thought I could look like that. The person in the mask looked so comfortable and at ease with their height. (Student journal 2015)

- -

For many, this is a major shift in self-perception or self-image:

When I was asked to look in the mirror again I can only describe it as jaw dropping, to see myself not looking ridiculous but actually connected, as if I belonged in my own skin. (Student journal 2015)

I found that after being adjusted I felt as though I was too far forward but when I looked in the mirror my posture looked really natural and neutral! (Student journal 2014)

Some comprehend a synthesis between themselves and NM:

Upon looking in the mirror a second time, I immediately saw a different person. It seemed that I no longer noticed the mask and then me as separate entities, but rather myself as a whole being with the mask. I am not sure if I quite understand yet how I could so instantly become the person wearing the mask, but for now I am willing to accept the fact that the neutral mask can influence me to have the power to be whom I want. (Student journal 2013)

This particular and unusual AT lesson, therefore, culminates in a crowning image of unity: The student returns to the mirror to see a vivid, striking image of togetherness. This image of the coordinated self is startling, memorable—iconic.

The student perception of the mask has also changed; it is no longer a mysterious, distant "other":

The biggest change that I noticed in myself after working one on one was the dramatic shift in my attitude and feelings toward the actual mask. There is always talk about letting the mask take over you and to let it lead you and initially I was actually quite afraid of losing myself behind the mask. The physical appearance of the mask frightened me in a way as I saw it to be very intimidating and threatening. However, after looking at myself in the mirror whilst wearing it, I am no longer afraid. After my turn was over I took the opportunity to really look at my mask and I can now say that I am comfortable and confident in saying yes and being open to its impulses. (Student journal 2015)

Incorporating the Horizon

"Locate your horizon and let it turn you toward the class. Let the eyes lead."

It is at this point that NM becomes fully present. While looking in the mirror, the student has essentially seen themselves. When they reconnect with the horizon and enlist its support, NM is fully manifest. NM is only fully realized when it is fully integrated in its world. This is particularly clear to those watching:

After people had made their adjustments, the mask that they wore almost started to look like their face. But the thing that I found most fascinating was the fact that the mask smiled. The mask smiled when [the students] found their horizon. It was as though the mask had come to life. (Student journal 2016)

For those wearing the mask, this step offers another revelation: When they find this alternative coordination, informed by the ecological connection, seeing this imagined world becomes simple and easy.

It was at that point, when I was in the most comfortable position I could be, that the mask truly started to take hold. It was at that moment I no longer felt I had an agenda or something to achieve. I was no longer looking. I was seeing. (Student journal 2013)

When I had the neutral mask on, it was easier to imagine a horizon. (Student journal 2013)

The Room Again: Holistic Awareness

"Turn away, remove the mask, now turn toward the class, follow the horizon, and let the eyes lead."

At this point in the sequence, a new and central aspect of "neutrality" kicks in, although it has been implicit in the previous stage. They encounter a new and powerful condition, that of simultaneously being organized in themselves and also fully alive to the world outside: inside and outside coordinated.

I felt open to everything, but not defenseless! I was able to say yes with my whole body that let me…to feel powerful in my own stance, taking control over the space that was there around me. (Student journal 2013)

It has given me a new expanded sense of self-awareness, being able to adopt soft focus and be aware of myself, physically, mentally, and aware of the space and people in it. (Student journal 2016)

AT teachers understand this condition as a *unified field of awareness*: "attention instead of being narrowed is expanded to take in certain key relations in the body as well as the activity on which the attention is focused" (Jones 1997, p.176). Creating a unified field of awareness could be regarded as a good working definition of *neutrality*. It also corresponds closely with Jacques Lecoq's *disponibilité à l'événement*: "open to what is happening."

In their book *Improvisation in Drama, Theatre and Performance*, Frost and Yarrow argue that the term *neutrality* has unhelpful connotations in English and evokes "asensuality," "disengagement." They describe *disponibilité* as:

> an experiential condition; a way of being which can be sought and found. It is a condition of being centred (in oneself) and balanced, ready to go in any appropriate direction… In this state the actor is inhabiting the world outside and the world within his body. He is "neutral" only in the sense that he is poised between all possibilities. (Frost and Yarrow 2007, p.197)

The energy I felt from the room and the self was very powerful, I felt ready to leap into action in any dimension, I was ready to engage. (Student journal 2014)

What spoke out to me was seeing the transformation of everyone in our class, owning themselves in the space and standing, ready to say YES to anything. (Student journal 2013)

We do not use the terms *disponibilité* or *unified field of awareness* in class. In our situation the terms can feel pretentious or intimidating. However, throughout the semester, the students develop a collection of simpler terms and practices that stimulate the much desired state: place of possibility, availability, open, saying "yes," listening on all sides, "extraordinary listening." These terms become the daily currency of their classes.

The body "says yes" with better posture; looks more open and ready. This posture is called neutral which is absolute readiness. (Student journal 2013)

Our whole being and body become neutral, we change into a state of readiness where we are saying yes to the world…we move into a "place of possibility." (Student journal 2013)

Growing Up

Another important insight at this stage in the class is the shift in their view of each other. They observe that some of their friends "grow up" and mature, in the space of a few minutes:

The difference was such a shock to me. [He] appeared to grow a few inches higher and was now ready for movement and inviting his audience to see him. It had the effect of an adolescent transitioning into a man. (Student journal 2015)

After watching my classmates' adjustments, I noticed that they all looked very open and mature. Their stance gave them power yet they were unintimidating and I felt they all really came into their own. (Student journal 2013)

For many, this is a radical shift in their attitude to their peers. One of the mottos of the school is "unconditional positive regard." This moment early in their training creates a firm ground for this ethic. They have glimpsed the potential in themselves and their peers and have seen that unambiguous personal change is within reach of all. This understanding elicits empathy and respect. They are more likely to be both generous and skilled in their dealings with each other from this point on.

Moving On

"See your chair and go there. Or go for a run, or..."

I was asked to incorporate moving hands and swinging my arms naturally as I walked, letting the energy flow through them, and invite cooperation with movement from my whole body. (Student journal 2014)

Working It Out Later: Journals

I found the exercise so rewarding that it was hard to put it into words once I took the mask off. I guess that's why we have these journals. (Student journal 2013)

Iconic NM

The great value we have found with the mask–mirror class is that the students acquire an iconic image of NM: *iconic* in that it accumulates meaning through continued contemplation and use. The image of the NM is more than a symbol. It becomes a vehicle of self-discovery, knowledge, attitude, action, and skill. Moreover, a glimpse of the self-potential is folded into the image. It is a potent new "self-image."

The vivid memory of this singular appearance of NM integrated with AT from the mask–mirror class reverberates through all their work from this point onward. Furthermore, there is a powerful kinesthetic memory of ease, energy, and graceful aliveness associated with the image, and this points the way to new pathways to action in the world.

I perceived the mask as a symbol of acceptance toward finding my true self. I had never felt so comfortable and beautiful in my own body. (Student journal 2013)

I began to feel in a whole new place of possibility. I wasn't doing anything drastically different; I was just being there in space. I could feel this thought up my entire back. I felt ready to go. I suddenly felt more mature; I wasn't hiding or apologizing with my childish stance anymore. (Student journal 2013)

I feel that every time I have put on the mask I make a new discovery for myself about my own body and extraordinary listening skills. (Student journal 2015)

Above all, the image of the self—carrying NM with ease and grace—releases the student from the tyranny of unnecessary striving for effect.

I am so glad we all got the opportunity to do this exercise because it's helped me to let go of my warped idea of what a neutral stance should be like… [It] seems to be about being connected with your own body in order to invite the audience in so they can then receive you. It's not about trying to be some super strong intense figure. (Student journal 2015)

I think that trusting the fact that we can just simply be in a physical space without trying or feeling the need to prove ourselves is a very important step. (Student journal 2015)

Pragmatic AT

After the mask–mirror class the students are in no doubt that AT coordination is an effective means not only to attaining NM but also a default state of lively composure appropriate for any performance task.

Choice

They now have *choice*. They have a clear sense of their habitual use, a vivid image of improved coordination, and convincing proof of the result. They can decide to reject this offer or accept the challenge to invite conscious change.

When the mask is removed you can "go home" (physically) but don't have to. I've got to be aware of what "home" is for me so that I can make an informed decision in terms of how I present myself. So that I have options, and make a choice to stand the way I do. (Student journal 2013)

I found that I can make a conscious decision to invite my body to come into alignment and invite the energy to spring up from my heels, through my whole body and up to the head! (Student journal 2015)

AT is about choices, thinking rather than making a habitual action or false overcompensation. Confidence is key. Primary control. Lightness, ease, release. (Student journal 2016)

Trying

Students begin to learn what it is to release, rather than push into action. They begin to practice "not trying."

I found this lesson very enlightening because it taught me that I don't have to use a lot of effort and I don't have to strain myself to stand up straight. If I relax my shoulders and knees and just focus on the spine-releasing muscle shift through the entire length of my body, it can become a very easy thing to do. (Student journal 2015)

This whole experience has really been a lesson in how to return to the simplest versions of ourselves—listening, engaging, committing, and genuinely responding to our stimulus, and allowing beautiful work to come as a result of that. (Student journal 2016)

Detachment and Play

Michel Saint-Denis puts it well when he argues that:

> Mask work is central to training precisely because it enables the student to warm his feelings and cool his head; at the same time it permits him to experience, in its most startling form, the chemistry of acting. At the very moment when the actor's feelings are at their height, the urgent necessity to control his physical actions compels him to detachment and lucidity. (Saint-Denis 1982, p.170)

The mask–mirror class creates the ground for this sophisticated relation with the self and the self as student-in-training and performer. Detachment implies a gap, a pause, a space to make a choice. AT asks the student to take time to observe and try out new possibilities, to experiment.

In the mask one "plays" at being the horizon or the mountain. One experiments simultaneously with being in, and playing with, the mask. With the "external object on one's face, one will actually feel possessed by a foreign presence, without, however, being dispossessed of one's own self" (Saint-Denis 1982, p.171). In both NM and AT, one has space or freedom to play with identity. We have found that the ability to use AT and NM to learn to play is central to consistent success in all aspects of the course.

Altogether Now

We have concluded that the values and skills required to carry NM and the aims and methods of AT are largely congruent. The fusion of the two forms sparked by the mask–mirror class promotes self-awareness, clarifies the sorts of skills necessary to embrace personal change, and releases the student into the space of choice and play. The students are encouraged to experiment and explore with the means afforded by the integrated form AT/NM in all their acting, voice, and theatre practice classes.

At the end of the semester, they are asked to list the most important things they have learned about acting and themselves.

The most common include take time, cultivate and respond within a unified field of awareness, exercise compassion toward oneself and others, accept the privilege of choice, seek simplicity, observe oneself calmly and learn from others, and bring the whole self to the work. They have discovered that there is no simple definition of "neutrality." However, they have discovered that it is a fertile and productive field of play.

One student summed up the situation eloquently:

It all comes back to The Neutral Mask. Looking in that mirror, without the "distraction" of judgment on my face, I saw, simply, a body. I was not a patched-together collection of good and bad bits—but a whole, full, working, expressive, front-to-back, beautiful body.

[This] realization is a personal achievement. When I removed the mask, this notion of "the whole" remained, and months later I still regard myself with the respect and appreciation I found in that reflection. (Student journal 2016)

References

Alexander, F.M. (1984) *The Use of the Self.* Downey, CA: Centerline Press. (Original work published 1932.)

Copeau, J. (1990) *Texts on Theatre.* London: Routledge.

de Alcantara, P. (2013) *Indirect Procedures: A Musician's Guide to the Alexander Technique.* New York: Oxford University Press.

Frost, A. and Yarrow, R. (2007) *Improvisation in Drama, Theatre and Performance: History, Practice, Theory* (1st edition). Basingstoke: Palgrave Macmillan.

Frost, A. and Yarrow, R. (2016) *Improvisation in Drama, Theatre and Performance: History, Practice, Theory* (3rd edition). Basingstoke: Palgrave Macmillan.

Jones, F.P. (1997) *Freedom to Change.* London: Mouritz.

Lecoq, J. (2002) *The Moving Body.* London: Methuen.

Madden, C. (2014) *Integrative Alexander Practice for Performing Arts: Onstage Synergy.* Chicago, IL: Intellect, University of Chicago Press.

McGilchrist, I. (2009) *The Master and His Emissary: The Divided Brain and the Making of the Western World.* New Haven and London: Yale University Press.

Miranda, K. (ed.) (2007) *Dare to be Wrong: The Teaching of Judith Leibowitz*. New York: American Center for the Alexander Technique.

Nicolaides, K. (1941) *The Natural Way to Draw*. Boston, MA: Houghton Mifflin.

Rudlin, J. (2010) "Jacques Copeau: The Quest for Sincerity." In A. Hodge (ed.) *Actor Training*. Abingdon: Routledge.

Saint-Denis, M. (1982) *Training for the Theatre*. New York: Theatre Arts Books.

Thompson, T. (1995) "Moving from the still point of support." Alexander Technique International. Accessed on November 7, 2006 at www.ati-net.com/articles/thompson.php

To Learn or to Un-Learn— That Is the Question

Collegiate Performers and End-Gaining

Julia Guichard and Harvey Thurmer

AT Perspective

As we have taught together over the past seven years, several themes have emerged that are central to our thinking and teaching of the Alexander Technique. We are both influenced primarily by the teaching of Marjorie Barstow, with whom all of our major teachers studied. Therefore, the following ideas are not unique to us, but are shaped by AT educators who emphasize the same concepts in their own teaching. It is in the realization of these concepts in our teaching that we may have individual perspectives to offer.

We are psychophysical unities. Teaching AT, therefore, involves accessing nonverbal means of learning. In our own training there were frustrating stages, for example when a teacher would refuse to "explain" an "aha!" moment when it occurred in a lesson. We know now that only by starving the cognitive mind of its insatiable need to understand can the corporate mind be given the chance to fully develop and come to life. This is kinesthetic learning, something we all experienced while learning to ride a bike, but gradually relegated to a forgotten shelf as we went on to learn "more important" things. This mindset implies a hierarchy that always sets up the cognitive mind to win, to be the most important, to become the bully on the playground.

Because the division of mind and body as a principle has shaped our education system for centuries, the reality that the mind and body are really one emerges time and again as "new" thinking. AT teachers are inventors and entrepreneurs—we experiment no less earnestly than Thomas Edison. We are all engaged in creating new "light bulbs" for our students. For this to happen, we employ multiple modalities to create new neural pathways so thinking and moving may be altered. This is what we define as *process*. F.M. Alexander's term for this process was *means-whereby*. This attention to process is in opposition to focusing on the pursuit of an outcome directly, a principle that Alexander defined as *end-gaining*.

We introduce AT to performers who have been fully indoctrinated by the mind/body split. Like an "ice breaker," at times we meet with great resistance in students whose commitment to cognitive supremacy has resulted in great success. One's first AT lesson or class is therefore often bewildering and confusing. Only through continued engagement with AT principles and whole-self integration are our efforts as teachers realized. It was out of our own desire to assess whether our teaching had made a lasting impact that we undertook the study described in our chapter.

Teaching the Alexander Technique at a liberal arts university with strong departments of music and theatre has its challenges. Miami University has an outstanding reputation as a "public ivy," attracting high-achieving students with an excellent academic record and high scores on college entrance exams. Students continue pursuing this academic excellence in college, focusing on extrinsic validation including instructor approval and a high grade point average. Unlike students who choose conservatory training, our students tend to have multiple interests, often completing double majors or minors. They also need to balance dedication to their art with the demands of a hefty liberal arts curriculum. Our students are well versed in how to play the academic "game." This game tends to instill certain habits, both mental and physical, which when reinforced by achievement and social approval become deeply ingrained.

Most college coursework rewards the continued practice of these mental and physical habits. Students see in their syllabi the dates of their exams, group projects to be completed, what writing assignments will cover, and learning outcomes that must be demonstrated. In this context, what is valued are those activities that are graded. Rubrics explain what is expected of student "deliverables" in great detail. This academic structure is a fertile breeding ground for end-gaining, a principle central to AT.

> Alexander always emphasized the process of attaining his goal, rather than the narrow focus on the goal itself, an approach which differs from that ordinarily taken in dealing with the material world. We all know that the way to drive a nail into a piece of wood is to hit it directly on the head. The problem starts when we apply this kind of thinking to ourselves, particularly if we are trying to bring about some kind of change. The kind of approach characterized by a dance teacher who pushes down on a pupil's raised shoulder, or a drill sergeant who shouts "chin in, chest up," is of limited value and will probably produce compensatory maladjustment elsewhere.
>
> Each of us is so complex that we must carefully reason the means we employ to reach any goal. Alexander found that most of us let our immediate goals dominate the field of our attention; he called this "end-gaining" or the "one track brain method." (Gelb 1995, p.80)

In the academy, the concept of end-gaining may become a dangerous concept to challenge. After all, end-gaining seems to be what the whole education system encourages and propagates. End-gaining has allowed these elite students to succeed and excel through their high school years, or so it seems to them. Yet it is the first concept our introductory AT class seeks to disrupt.

Dubbing our AT course at Miami University the *un-class*, we have created it to eliminate traditional ends as much as possible. The actual day-to-day activities of the class are typical of a group lesson as taught by a teacher certified by Alexander Technique International: Students are taught in a group format, the AT principles are applied to activities brought in by the students (often with "hands-on" by the teacher), and peer feedback is fundamental to learning. Our experiment with this class has been to frame *explicitly* for the student an experience that contradicts the constant pursuit of grades and rewarding of results. We consistently reinforce the notion of process rather than results throughout the course: in the syllabus, in class discussions, and by modeling process in all our interactions with students. Additionally, the design of the class itself removes the typical reward system and formal evaluation methods imposed by the pedagogy of higher education. We offer choice, process, and kinesthetic awareness as an alternative to end-gaining. For example, the course fulfills no requirements in either the theatre or music department curriculums; it is offered credit/no credit only, eliminating the need to pursue a grade. Readings are optional; the only assignment is a reflection paper at the end (although students are encouraged to journal throughout the semester). The paper has no minimum length or format requirement; we provide only questions/prompts. In class sessions, students are allowed maximum autonomy, deciding when (or if) they wish to have a lesson and what activity they wish to explore. The only real requirement for credit is to show up to class. This course design confronts the student with their own desire to learn, making this the primary focus.

Students initially haven't known how to respond to this model of learning: It is contrary to the predominant thinking at the university, as well as the educational culture out of which these millennial students have emerged. The very structure of our course takes most of our students a while to grasp and embrace. It is no less a struggle for us, the instructors, as we have debated back and forth about whether our un-class model creates enough motivation and structure to promote learning—particularly as students prioritize work in classes that "count." How can we know if the students are actually learning?

The Study

Reflecting upon the past five years of team teaching our un-class at Miami University, we have anecdotal evidence that students are in fact changing some of their long-standing patterns of learning and performing, at least while *in* the class. We were curious about the extent, if any, to which our students were able to apply those new patterns of process (rather than end-gaining) as they returned to the traditional and product-driven academic environment and/or as they entered the professional world beyond the academy.

To investigate this question, we designed a study to collect and analyze qualitative evidence from former students. We contacted all of the students who had enrolled in our class each spring from 2010 to 2014, a total of 59 students. They were invited to participate in the study[1] by completing an interview either in person or via Skype. Twenty students responded and agreed to participate: 11 theatre majors and 9 music majors. The interviews took 15 to 30 minutes each. Participants were encouraged to use our questions as prompts but also welcomed to go off on tangents. We stressed that we were not looking for particular answers but were open to whatever themes emerged over the course of the study. Once completed, interviews were transcribed to facilitate close examination. We also reviewed reflection papers that these students had submitted as a final assignment in the course. All quotations in this chapter are student comments from reflection papers or interview transcripts unless otherwise noted. Each student has been assigned a fictitious name to protect anonymity.

The Monkey Trap

> It is said that a simple way to trap a monkey is to present him with a nut in a bottle. The monkey puts his paw through the bottle's narrow mouth, grasps the nut, then cannot withdraw his paw because he will not (and hence cannot) let go of the nut. Most people are caught in monkey traps of unconscious habit. They cannot escape because they do not perceive what they are doing while they are doing it. (Jones 1979, p.4)

The metaphor of the monkey trap provides an excellent framework for our discussion of how college performers experience end-gaining. As we have taught actors and musicians over the last five years, one thing is clear—the varied cultures that have developed around teaching actors and musicians are a breeding ground for developing habits of end-gaining. Although the ends or "nuts" are defined differently in music than in theatre, the mechanism of the monkey trap—the principle of end-gaining—is identical. The way out of the monkey trap of such habits can also be identical—the application of fundamental principles of AT. Since we are particularly interested in how the principle of end-gaining affects performers, it is helpful to compare and contrast the cultures surrounding teaching in music versus theatre in order to understand how end-gaining develops differently in each discipline.

The Culture of Music

The culture of learning a musical instrument, as well as singing, typically involves passing down time-honored skills, rather like an apprentice who aligns himself with a master craftsman. Reading the biographies of performers often reveals a genealogical history of that performer's lineage, connecting them to established stars who achieved fame and fortune. The general assumption is that given the success of the mentor, similar qualities are passed along to the apprentice. This might include quality of sound, affects of gesture, or interpretation. Aside from the sheer technical skills required to play an instrument, careful attention is given to tempo fluctuations, interpretive choices, varieties of tonal color, and dynamic ranges. The "good" student mimics as closely as possible the exact directions of the mentor. The more quickly the student can reproduce the qualities demonstrated by the mentor, the more "talented" they are declared to be.

Similarly, the mentor himself achieves fame as a pedagogue by his quick, adept, and confident assessment of problems and ability to get to their roots with the precision of a surgeon. If a student were to hear words that hinted at doubt about how to "fix" a problem, it certainly would not be considered an asset. Rather than inviting an apprentice into a mutual journey of exploration to discover solutions together, the culture that develops is one of rigid conformity. The more quickly the certain quality being taught can be reproduced, even once during a lesson, the more "successful" the student is deemed by both mentor and apprentice. After years of this sort of training, musicians become astute observers of physical habits and mannerisms. Success is achieved by the rapid absorption of these habits. These quickly become cemented into a student's psychophysical toolkit, akin to a collection of magical talismans that, it is hoped, ward off "failure."

So in the case of musicians, the nut in the monkey trap typically includes striving for flawless intonation (a combination of training the ear and the movement needed to play or sing), beautifully produced sound, thorough understanding of the composer's musical intent, stylistic considerations involved with interpretation, and the ultimate goal of presenting all of these things in an emotionally convincing performance. These attributes are admittedly important and crucial to the development of a musical artist. Depending on the particular instrument or vocal type, as well as the background of the mentor, each of these aspects is specifically addressed and trained by whatever methods the mentor might employ. "Methods" of teaching have been written since the time of Mozart for the violin, and I am sure the same is true for other instruments as well. These methods explore every aspect of how an instrument is held, the physical movements associated with playing the instrument, how to stand, how to sit, how to balance weight, and how to breathe.

The plethora of highly refined recording techniques in today's musical market adds to the list of demands with which a musician must now contend. The assumption is that an audience expects to hear a flawless reproduction of their favorite recording of any particular work. Musical competitions that weed out all but the most flawless technician add to the stress of "making it" as a performer. Individual interpretation that might depart from the currently accepted standards of performance practice are encouraged perhaps only after a student has mastered the art of faithful reproduction of the standard practices, ensuring their success.

So initially, the habits formed around all the specific aspects of developing technical skill and interpretive nuance create a strong commitment to following the "rules" imposed by the mentor. The idea that one might actually improve by attending to anything other than those cardinal rules meets with great resistance, if not outright rejection. Typical music students at the college level bring with them deeply embedded psychophysical habits linked with their concept of what it means to be a performer.

Within this predominantly accepted culture for music training, the AT teacher must help the student unravel layers of habit that have usually resulted in success for the performer. Not only that, the student is dutifully following the exact advice of mentors they have come to revere and love. Some of this instruction is excellent and needs to be revered and continued! Other aspects need to be critically examined to determine if they are truly useful for a performer's ongoing journey.

I have only just begun to understand what AT is about and why it is so terribly difficult to find words to describe it, because in explaining the parts, the quality of the whole concept seems discounted. It is adding levels of consciousness to take layers of doing away. It is trusting yourself to allow things to fail. It is understanding your body structure so that you can move as one entity. It is inhibition and allowance. It is consciousness of what we thought was instinctive. It challenges thought and affects movement. (Adele)

The Culture of Theatre

While student actors also bring strong psychophysical habits to college with them, they are formed by a rather different culture. Historically, much of actor training in the 20th century has been influenced by the work of Constantin Stanislavski and the Moscow Art Theatre. Their US tour from 1922 to 1923 had a powerful and lasting impact on American theatre and actor training. Stanislavski's theories were adopted, interpreted, and developed by many of the most important acting teachers of the century. Some of these, such as Stella Adler, Lee Strasberg, and Sanford Meisner, developed studio approaches to acting that, while based upon the Stanislavski system, differed in their understanding and application. Arguably the most influential of these on the zeitgeist surrounding American actor training in the 20th century was Strasberg's "Method"—a psychological approach to acting that relies heavily on the experience of the individual actor. Method actors are encouraged to remember circumstances in their lives and the accompanying emotion, then substitute these for the circumstances found in the play. Fundamentally embedded in the psychology of acting to this day, the Method has promoted the actor's individual experiences, humanity, and emotional life as the source for highly original interpretation and "truthful behavior" in a role.

High school students may or may not have been exposed directly to the legacy of the Method, but they are certainly influenced by it at least indirectly. As consumers of acting all their lives (through film, television, and, for some, the stage), they see acting as a business in which the personality of the actor leads. Additionally, young actors in high school and well into their college years equate emotional output with good acting—"Can I make myself cry?" Thus, while both actors and musicians end-gain, the specific nature of their ends is different. The student actor typically substitutes personal habit for the "truthful behavior" in the Stanislavski system; their nut in the monkey trap is often their own experience of emotion, a feeling of connection to a role, and what feels natural to them in any given moment. These feelings are inevitably tied to habits of thinking, moving, and behaving that are a product of long-standing patterns that feel "right" to the student actor—in other words, what fits their personality. They carry with them experiences from high school in which they were rewarded for the successful (and sometimes quite skilled) presentation of their personality onstage. While acting students, particularly those who choose to study in a BA program, have typically not practiced their craft for as many years as music students, they too have developed psychophysical habits linked with the concept of performance. As with musicians, actors often follow the advice of high school drama teachers whom they admire and love.

When I first started acting, I was very insecure with myself and every role that I portrayed tended to be forced. I had my idea of what I wanted the character to behave like and there was absolutely no deviation, which severely limited my abilities. Yet I thought that because I kept getting cast, I must have been doing something correctly. (George)

End-Gaining

The idea of AT doesn't go with what a college class is, to begin with, which is "Do this my way, turn it in, and then go do your thing and never think about this again." (Jane)

While keeping these differing cultures in mind, we also have found an overriding similarity in our students that transcends disciplinary specifics. We have come face to face with the consequences of the limitations of the "no child left behind" era—an era in which tests, quizzes, right answers, and accountability have largely superseded imagination, critical thinking, problem solving, and process. In designing our interdisciplinary course in AT, we deliberately created a structure that contradicts the educational system through which our students have progressed. We fashioned the course to confront the students with their own assumptions, removing the "carrot at the end of the stick": being taught the right answers—the *end* that all students are supposed to *gain*. Their realization that there are choices to make is the first concept that challenges the end-gaining system they have long been practicing. In some cases, particularly for musicians, this AT class may be the first time they have encountered a college course where their own opinions, feelings, sensations, and observations mattered to the outcome of a course. It is easy to see how a young musician could look at accomplished performers and assume that they were given the right set of answers by their teachers. And so that is the primary task in their performance studies: Find the right answers!

Acting students are much more likely to have encountered college courses in which their own sensory and emotional experiences are central to learning, but they still want the validation of the instructor (or director), while also believing there is a right answer for creative choices. This is particularly apparent in their fear of taking risks, making it difficult for them to explore the possibilities for truthful behavior that lie outside the borders of their narrowly defined personalities.

Before [AT] when I would end-gain, I didn't know that I was end-gaining. I thought I was trying to do exactly what I was told when I was told. (Max)

For both music and theatre students, the concept that they are not locked into gaining a particular end but can focus on the process can be threatening, or at least require more of them than they have ever expected.

I think it takes a lot of courage to be able to let go of something that you've always done and try something new that seems like "There's no way it's going to work." (Jane)

There were times I tried to fight [the process]. I was set in my ways because they were working for me (I say "working" in air quotes). They got me to where I wanted to be, but if I wanted to improve beyond that, I needed to do something else. And so committing to a process that was going to take more work and more time was a difficult choice. (Natalie)

160

Although these students, after emerging from the university and being out in the world, might feel liberated by this concept (as our interviews indicate), at the moment of discovery, it seemed quite challenging for many of them. With such a strong focus on the principle of end-gaining in our course design, we were gratified to note in conducting the interviews that the vast majority of former students identified end-gaining as the most, or one of the most, important and lasting concepts from their class experience.

Usually if it gets really bad for me, where I'm just feeling overwhelmed, usually [end-gaining] is the root of it. I'm reaching for something that I haven't quite grown to reach yet. It's crazy. It's like I'm trying to bloom before I'm ready. (Rosanna)

AT has entirely revolutionized my way of thinking. I had always been so destination oriented before; I would end-gain when thinking about major life decisions. I would try to plan my life out for the next 30 years, and in a field like ours, we won't be working at a firm for the rest of our lives with insurance and job security. (Natalie)

By just letting things happen and not predicting how they were going to end, they always ended better than I could have ever imagined. (Eva)

I think the class definitely impacted me because trying to go back to what my mindset was before—it's difficult. But I do know that I was probably more concerned with the final result of anything, whatever that was. Before the class not so much about process, more about the result. I think after the class [I am] a little bit more centered and in the moment and trying to be present throughout, not just reflecting at the end. I definitely end-gain, but the class and what I've learned has informed me what I can do instead of that. The biggest thing, honestly, is just being in the moment. It's all about the process; all the stress, all the worry, all the tension isn't going to get me some great result. (Mandy)

The Concept of Choice

Fundamentally tied to the principle of end-gaining is the concept of choice. When one is not locked into immediate gaining of an end but focuses on the process, then choices and the accompanying sense of freedom are suddenly available. Given an education system that emphasizes doing what must be done to get the right answer, the idea that what they choose to think matters at all is a revolutionary concept for both music and theatre majors.

I don't think I really realized I had so many choices prior to taking the class. Now I think, "I have the choice to wake up in the morning. I have the choice to do this homework. I have the choice to perform when I want to, or whenever I feel like it." So that in and of itself was powerful. (Maeve)

I didn't even think about [choice] before taking the class. You never really think about making choices—the way you handle yourself, the way you take care of yourself both mentally and physically, you have to make very big choices in that. (Rosanna)

That said, there are differences in the way that music and theatre majors think about choice, dictated by the variable cultures surrounding each discipline.

MUSIC MAJORS AND CHOICE

It takes a lot of hard work to learn any instrument or sing well enough to be admitted to any music school as a performer. Up to this point in their training, the main objective is the technical training needed to advance to this level. This is where musical training relies heavily on observation and mimicking of the mentor. This technical training may not have engaged the student in much exploration of their individual choices. Interpretive choices come later in a student's training, once the technique is more fully developed. Whether thinking about technique or interpretation, a student is careful to replicate their mentor's admonitions, which often ring inside the head of the student for years like a second personality, or the Ghost of Mentors Past!

Before I was exposed to the Alexander Technique, really the only question that I ever found myself asking was, "Is this right or wrong? So is it the right intonation? Is it the right rhythm? Is it the right kind of sound?" Looking back on it, I was locked into that one way of thinking. (Max)

In this culture of learning, thought processes behind physical movement choices are often not investigated. The division of mind and body is furthered by this learning culture. The self-talk of most students consists of a laundry list of commands. The focus is narrow, and broadening the "field of awareness" to include how one feels while playing the instrument is rarely addressed.

After having the Alexander Technique, I appreciate that I have the awareness to begin to ask myself those questions. To make the choices for how I want to feel, and how I want to sound when I'm performing. Not just "Is this correct or incorrect?" (Max)

Even to entertain one's right to make a choice caused some disruption for the music students. Students expect to be told exactly what to do by their teachers. This eliminates the responsibility of making choices or working to understand a technical principle, then arriving at a personal solution.

I would say before exposure to AT, it wasn't just a matter of me not making choices. It was a matter of not knowing that I could make choices. I didn't know that the questions existed for me to ask. I didn't know that I had the ability to choose to do things a different way. (Max)

I came to pride myself on the ability to control, exhibiting discipline by forcing myself to do things that I did not want to do. This whole idea of "choice" is a little uncomfortable for me, because I sort of thought it showed lack of dedication when people considered their daily pursuit of their art as a "choice." I realized recently that giving yourself choice is discipline, and actually can be more scary and difficult than the alternative. This is ground-breaking for me. (Jane)

THEATRE MAJORS AND CHOICE

Unlike musicians, theatre majors—particularly upperclass students who have a few years of studio classes under their belts—are aware of the need to make choices. Acting teachers stress the importance of making strong choices for character, objective, and action. Those choices, however, when pursued within a habitual pattern of end-gaining, can create a need to make the "right" choice. Students tend to latch onto these choices as ends to be decided upon and pursued, rather than as points of departure for exploration.

I have struggled with getting a picture of what the character is, in my head, and then striving to embody that instead of experiencing being there in the moment. That would make me judge a character for what they're doing or why they're making this choice. It pulls you straight out [of the moment].

I've been able to notice when I do that and when other people do that. You can tell then they've got an idea of what their character should be. (George)

Former theatre students report that after studying AT, they have more freedom to see creative choices for character and action as living and changing moment to moment through the rehearsal process. AT appears to foster an attitude of experimentation and flexibility—"What happens if...?" becomes a coordinating principle within which specific artistic choices can be made and remade.

[In rehearsal] I was using a lot more of "I have the choice to move here. I have the choice to say this, this way, with using this emotion or this intention." [AT] allows performance-wise for you to live in the moment and make each performance a little different because you have that freeing ability to do so. (Maeve)

In New York, I was auditioning like two or three times a week. It became really static, I would say, and nerve-wracking. So [AT] helped to relax my body, think about that I had a choice to go in [to the audition] and see whatever was going to come out of me. It made it more fun, and I didn't feel as nervous or that something specific needed to happen in the room. (Mandy)

In the rehearsal process, you have to choose to be there every day, which is a commitment. You choose different tactics to affect your partner—character choices. But I think the most important [choice] is your mindset when you enter the space to work that day. You have to be open to what can happen. You can't have a plan for what you think needs to happen that day. You can't end-gain the rehearsal. The work will happen; you just have to let it. (Natalie)

Impact

Of particular interest to us in reviewing papers and transcripts were the ways in which former students articulated their perceptions about the impact of AT on their lives.

The Paradigm Shift

In a recent interview, Pedro de Alcantara—cellist, AT teacher, and author of several books on AT—described the difficulty of defining the technique. He conceptualizes AT as a paradigm; he defines paradigm as a "collection of concepts, tools, filters, priorities…a way of thinking and a way of living in the world" (Moore 2016). He suggests that studying AT is a paradigm shift that can be compared to learning a new computer operating system when switching from a PC to a Mac. A shift in how one receives and responds to incoming data is a wonderful way to describe what happens to students of AT. No matter what initial issue brought a student into our class, it soon became clear that a whole new way of thinking was what was really at stake. In assessing the impact of AT on these former students, we noted a self-described paradigm shift in their approach to rehearsal/performance/life. Students used words like "revolutionary," "awakening," and "complete change" to describe the shift in their thinking.

[AT] has completely changed my way of thinking, and my path, and the way I do everything. (Holly)

[AT] has revolutionized the way that I look at life. Life isn't linear. When it comes to a career in the arts, it's not about where you want to end up, but rather what you want to do next. You can go all kinds of different places instead of just thinking about going in one direction, so there's a little bit more freedom. (Natalie)

I think my approach to performing totally changed when I was in undergrad, in that I let go of my perfectionism, and gained a much deeper appreciation for the process. That enabled me to start enjoying performing, instead of being totally wracked with fear and anxiety. (Lydia)

I realize now that I have a good amount of potential that I am not fully utilizing. When Julia said the process is ongoing and who would want it to end, I did a double take. I would love for the process to end. The end is the goal, right? Who wants to never reach their goals? That kind of thinking is crazy. But I am realizing that the process does not mean lack of progress or lack of success, it is just a means to embrace growing in grace and knowledge. Self-awareness allows one to live fully and grow continuously. Who wants to stop learning? Who wants to quit seeing and experiencing more? (Shelly)

Within the overarching concept of a paradigm shift, several specific themes emerged in student comments: an experience of freedom and allowing, a journey of personal growth, improved ability to carry out tasks, and improved physical well-being.

A Sense of Freedom

Students unanimously spoke about the freedom the new way of thinking opened to them in both personal and professional pursuits.

AT makes it seem like there's never a perfect ending; you keep working on it. Which is nice and also freeing. You have a lot of freedom to play around and trust that it's going to where it is and where it needs to be. I also think a part of you always wants it to be perfect again. But it's nice to know that perhaps it doesn't matter. The [AT] class specifically was like "Are you ready to perform? How do you feel about it? Are you going to make this next choice?" That's really great, especially for a perfectionist. (Maeve)

The first time that I really felt a breakthrough in class was toward the middle of the semester when I played the Bach Sonata No. 1 Adagio. Something happened that I couldn't explain, where I gave up control but still remained totally present. It also did not become "out of control"—I was not helping or forcing, but allowing. (Jane)

A Personal Journey

Many students spoke explicitly or implicitly about the impact of AT on their personal growth and journey. AT takes all who engage with its principles on a journey into physical habits, taking the risk along the way of abandoning trusted solutions for an outcome that cannot be predicted. Students described their emotional and physical experiences in a variety of ways:

I'm aware of the fact that when I get excited about something, my body goes "WAH," like turns into a little ball—my shoulders go up to my ears. [AT helps because] I feel less nervous when I'm not in a crazy, excited ball. I feel just more comfortable in my own skin. It just feels a little bit more comfortable to be onstage when you're not jumping into that ball. (Karen)

[AT] is like a springboard that gave me experiential knowledge to take risks, and to understand that the best way to be effective as a performer is to let go of control. I'm experiencing a physical approach to performance that's not so cognitive and not so micromanaged. (Adele)

I am learning to see beauty in process and to find enjoyment in questions. I have learned an invaluable life skill. For the first time in my life I play because I want to. Not because it will make me a better teacher or because I need to put my time in or because I have a lesson on Thursday. (Shelly)

Improved Performance

Students also observed improvement in their ability to effectively carry out a variety of tasks, including writing papers for other classes, paying attention in class, taking auditions, making presentations, and performing.

By giving myself the option of speaking or not speaking, I realized that I had a choice. For the first time in my entire theatre career, I gave myself the choice of not performing, and it was awesome. I have serious stage fright when it comes to presenting in classes (especially classes that aren't full of theatre majors), and when I started giving myself the option of not performing or presenting, I suddenly became aware of what I was doing physically, and I was able to open up and deliver a clear presentation without feeling anxious or mumbling. (Rosanna)

I learned in AT that when I do allow more space [in my hip] and I'm working on elongating that leg, I can actually get my leg higher and I like that. (Natalie)

AT helped me gain the confidence physically that I needed to stand up and speak. How do I stand up on stage and give a TED talk to people who are twice my age who've done way more in their lifetimes than I will ever hope to do? AT helped me have the ease to do that. It gave me the confidence to operate my body, and just move. (Eva)

Physical Improvement

Finally, many students talked about changes in their physical well-being as an absence or decrease of pain and a greater sense of physical ease.

Definitely, the way that I walk has changed. I know particularly around my pelvis things have totally rearranged. I used to have a really accentuated lumbar curve that I don't think is quite as accentuated anymore. I never really have lower back pain anymore, which I used to get just from daily activities. (Lydia)

I have become much more effortless in the way that I move about the world, and not necessarily forceful in the way I move about the world, which is what I used to be. I was just punching or sledging my weight through the world instead of becoming a human and walking through the world. (Donald)

I've realized my knees aren't hurting as much. My spine is more in line. Being more aware of that has helped me a lot with back pain getting out of the car, and pain in general. (Albert)

Conclusions

We began the journey of this study with a question—to what extent, if any, have our students been able to apply the new patterns of process (rather than end-gaining) to the traditional and product-driven academic environment and/or the professional world beyond the academy? Although we too felt the urge to end-gain and "find the right answer" as we conducted the numerous interviews, we inhibited this urge. What has resulted is a deepening of our interdisciplinary conversation as teachers about who our students are, what they value, and how we might best structure our AT class to offer an effective alternative model of learning within the traditional structure of the academy.

Impact of Class Structure

It is clear from student responses that the structure of the class is, in and of itself, a significant factor in enabling students to make a paradigm shift in their thinking. While they may have initially expressed discomfort about the un-class structure, they were overwhelmingly positive about it in retrospect. Freedom from the pressure of grades and an end product allowed them to focus on learning and experiment with new ideas.

To me, requirements probably put a tight hold on, I don't know, something in your brain where you can... You're too focused on "I have to write this paper. I have to do this, I have to do that." You probably wouldn't be able to access the things that you really need us to be able to access in order to experience these new things. (Tom)

I was always the student who would do everything. I couldn't not try my hardest, and so for me, that's presented a freedom. You don't have to get an A. It doesn't matter. This isn't a grade, it's not about succeeding. It's about learning. I had all these ideas of what it meant to be a classical musician, and how much work I needed to do. That was very freeing for me to realize, it's not always about the grade. (Holly)

I believe we should abolish grades because that becomes so much of a student's focus. We talk a lot [in education] about meeting a standard. So having a class where it's like you figure out what you need, and you work toward that, and you do it when you're ready, you're still pushing yourself because there's no pressure from other people. I wish all classes worked that way. (Maeve)

I didn't get credit for the [AT] course, and yet I have absolutely fallen in love with [AT]. I think that was a turning point too, because typically I would freak out, "Oh my gosh, I didn't get credit for this." Then I was like "Wait, I learned so much the credit doesn't matter, and I found something I want to do, and found something that I really enjoy doing, and that I enjoy learning." (Eva)

I really actually enjoyed [the class structure]. I feel it's a more relaxed setting. I feel like people are more willing to open up in that kind of setting because when something is for a grade immediately you start thinking about end-gaining. I didn't think of it as a class. I just thought of it as AT. I'm going to AT. That's what you do Fridays at 4 p.m. (Rosanna)

It is important to note that not all pressure is lifted from students in the un-class. Many students are intrinsically motivated by the need to get it right whether or not there is a grade attached. And one student noted that the pressure of performing in front of his peers was still strong:

I thought [the class structure] made the learning experience slightly richer in that I was able to rely more on the professors to give information rather than to force information down my throat as if I was preparing for a quiz or something. That said, there was still pressure in the class, mostly social pressure that just comes with the nature of being in a group of other people. Effectively, when one person is being "Alexandered," everyone else is watching and judging for their own educational benefit: "How will this work for me?" The judging adds a little bit more pressure to make [me] want to succeed. Therefore, even though we're not end-gaining, because there were people observing us, I was still end-gaining. (Albert)

The risk in allowing such freedom from ends is that the traditional academic structure that holds students "accountable" for demonstrating learning outcomes is removed. We observed that students did not always complete readings, write consistent journal entries, or use the final paper as an opportunity for deep, personal reflection.

I felt like if I had other reading to do, I always put that other stuff before AT; if we had to read the text [for AT class] that was my last priority on the list, in all honesty. (Karen)

We were willing, and remain willing, to take this risk, even if it means that students don't prioritize the reading and reflective writing we value and encourage. However, we continue to look for pedagogical techniques that will maximize student engagement: Would a group wiki work better than individual journals? Should we focus part of the semester on a performance project, or just allow students to bring in activities as they arise? How can we structure readings to be as relevant as possible?

Several students noted that the structure of the class worked because we were "practicing what we preach." They were not trying to learn a new paradigm within an old existing pedagogical model. The *way* in which they were learning reinforced *what* they were learning.

If you're standing up there saying, "You have a choice to come to this class," but then say, "but there's an attendance grade, dadadadada, you'll lose a thousand points if you don't show up or something," if you want students to understand this principle of "I really and truly have a choice," [then] it's important for the class to be formatted that way because it speaks volumes to what you're trying to portray. It was a way to understand that it was basically putting what you were saying about choice into practice, that says a lot. The buy-in for students is a lot higher if you're practicing what you're preaching. (Tom)

Impact of Interdisciplinarity

Not surprisingly, the interdisciplinary nature of the class was also of great benefit to both music and theatre majors. At Miami, the departments are quite separate and students have limited opportunities to cross the disciplinary divide. Musicians were generally happy that actors were in the class, because their viewpoint was so different from the feedback they get from other musicians. Rather than the usual listing of technical issues relative to a performance, the actors could focus and provide feedback on broader aspects of a performance and its overall impact on them. A completely disastrous performance in the eyes of the music student might meet with affirmation from an actor. Again, this can be traced back to the varied cultures of these disciplines and what they value. Musicians value perfect execution over connection to an audience. If connection is made despite faulty execution, it is usually a complete surprise! On the other hand, actors are more accustomed to feedback from their peers in a classroom setting. Since they learn and rehearse collaboratively rather than in a solo practice room, actors look to others for information about the impact of their choices on an audience. The theatre majors really appreciated seeing AT applied to a different discipline. In music, application of AT principles often resulted in improved sound quality and expression/connection to the music. Theatre students could easily hear/see/feel these changes, which then enabled them to see the immediate transferable benefit to acting.

- -

I found that having both music and theatre majors in the class offered a chance to see how AT can be applied to another field of study. Seeing AT applied from the different perspectives of instrumentalists, vocalists, and thespians enhanced my own understanding. (Tom)

Having theatre majors in the class provided a different perspective into how AT can be useful for anyone. When a student practiced the tools we learned in class before she delivered her line, I could feel the difference in impact. (Holly)

Thinking back, I remember feeling at the start of the class like there might be a kind of divide between the theatre majors and the music majors. Not due to any feelings of animosity, but because there was a comfortable familiarity with the students I had taken several classes with, and the music majors were coming from a different program altogether. I think it may have been the first physical exercise when it became clear that it didn't really matter what the focus of study was, and that the principles of AT can apply to anyone. It was helpful and eye-opening to see that in practice. For me on a more personal level, I particularly enjoyed having the music majors in the class, because I had a background in music and I think there's a lot of crossover. I could relate to the different issues or moments of discovery that they brought to the classroom, and that's probably something I wouldn't have otherwise experienced in other theatre classes that focused solely on the actor. (Mandy)

What Does This Mean for the Future?

Our choice to structure our class without formal assignments, requirements, or assessments has challenged us as well as the students. We are also products of and participants in the educational system. There is a certain comfort in creating lesson plans, quizzes, projects, and assignments. We have struggled over the last five years with how to emphasize the AT principles while engaging the students in an individual process that confronts them with their own desire to learn. We have debated back and forth about whether our un-class creates an environment that effectively models the principles we desire to teach. And since we have removed the typical ways in which progress through a course is normally evaluated, how do we assess if our learning outcomes are achieved? How can we defend the value of this course without the traditional "evidence" provided by formal assessment? These interviews with former students have reinforced our observations that students are able to apply principles of AT beyond the AT classroom to make positive changes in their lives. The principles are indeed staying with them long after the course concludes, and they recognize the value in what they have learned.

When does performance begin or end? As we have read and collated student responses, it is clear that the impact of the class has been quite broad, on stage and off. Learning the principles of AT starts with awareness in everyday activities, then expands to encompass all that one does, including performing. In the end, all of life becomes galvanized, including the part we share with an audience as performers. This inclusion of performance as part of a life that is aware—that integrates mind, body, and emotion—is the result our students have reported experiencing. It is also what we as teachers of the technique continue to enjoy. The process once begun can broaden to include more and more of life.

A century ago, John Dewey, noted American philosopher, psychologist, and educational reformer, called for the inclusion of AT in our educational system. In his introduction to Alexander's text *Constructive Conscious Control of the Individual*, he wrote:

> The method is not one of remedy, it is one of constructive education... Its proper field of application is with the young, with the growing generation, in order that they may come to possess as early as possible in life a correct standard of sensory appreciation and self judgement. When once a reasonably adequate part of a new generation has become properly coordinated, we shall have assurance for the first time that men and women in the future will be able to stand on their own feet, equipped with satisfactory psycho-physical equilibrium, to meet with readiness, confidence, and happiness instead of with fear, confusion, and discontent, the buffetings and contingencies of their surroundings. (Alexander 1985 [1923], xxxiii)

Today, unfortunately, we still struggle with an educational system that runs counter to the principles of AT, a system that encourages— actually demands—end-gaining, a system that fosters the continuation of habitual miscoordination. The un-class presents a model that can build a bridge for students in the academy, offering them freedom and choice, enabling them to function with awareness, joy, and ease in life, on stage and off. It is not enough to tell students to change. Imagine that a student is standing on the other side of a great chasm with a narrow, precarious rope bridge spanning the space between you. Does calling out to them "Come on—cross that bridge!" from the relative safety of your side of the divide stand the best chance of getting them to move? No—you must cross the bridge yourself, meet them on their side of the chasm, and show them how to take the first step of the journey across. Using this metaphor, we must not simply abandon existing educational structures, telling students there is now a better way to learn. We must meet them where they are, create a learning environment that acknowledges traditional pedagogical structures, then help them begin the journey toward a paradigm shift in their thinking about learning and performance.

Before AT, I was just acting in pursuit of my destination and I wasn't really thinking about what I was doing. I was just going for it and hoping for the best. What good does that do? What's the success rate of that? I think AT, the emphasis on process, has a more consistent success rate, a more consistent outcome. The product is important, but in order to create a consistent product, you have to be confident in your process. Nothing I've experienced—other classes, other techniques—nothing has put this into perspective for me other than AT. (Natalie)

Note

1   This study was conducted with approval from the Institutional Research Board (IRB) that regulates research with human subjects. All participants signed consent forms. Project # 01644e.

References

Alexander, F.M. (1985) *Constructive Conscious Control of the Individual.* Downey, CA: Centerline Press. (Original work published 1923.)

Gelb, M.J. (1995) *Body Learning: An Introduction to the Alexander Technique.* New York: Henry Holt and Company.

Jones, F.P. (1979) *Body Awareness in Action.* New York: Schocken Books.

Moore, K. (2016, December 30) Pedro de Alcantara interview: The real truth behind Alexander Technique [Video file]. Dailymotion. Accessed on June 8, 2017 at www.dailymotion.com/video/x3k4qdo_pedro-de-alcantara-interview-the-real-truth-behind-alexander-technique_creation

Alexander Technique Interventions for Stage Fright

An Interview with Michael Frederick and Elaine Williams

Kathleen Juhl

AT Perspective

Michael Frederick

A lot is written about the Alexander Technique these days: lots of blogs and Facebook posts, various introductions to journals focused on the technique, articles in newsletters, and complete books. There is a lot of information from AT teachers who have widely varying and often incomplete training in the work. There are so many perspectives on the technique that it is overwhelming and can be inaccurate and confusing.

My perspective is that AT is simple and straightforward. The renowned British author Aldous Huxley (a student of AT) said, "Our business is to wake up!" AT teaches you to do just that—to wake up to the ordinary and make it extraordinary. It is a psychophysical approach to learning that I call "Western Zen."

The whole essence of F.M. Alexander's work is based on the understanding of non-doing. This does not mean "doing nothing," but rather creating right action within the immediacy of this particular moment, seeing that the mind and conditioned self are simply a repetition of one's past conditioning and cannot operate within the present moment with anything new and fresh, only offering secondhand reactive thinking. One has to create a space between our habitual stimulus-and-response patterning, allowing for something original to enter in. If we do not, we are simply the ball in a pinball machine bouncing off the bumpers before disappearing down the rabbit hole.

As you are reading this, ask yourself, "Am I really here? Am I aware of my habits mentally, emotionally, and physically? Am I reading with any sense of inner awareness about the quality of the 'use of the self' as Alexander intended? Am I actually thinking about lunch or the important phone call I need to make, or an issue that occurred earlier this morning? Am I skimming over this reading, but really thinking about today's to-do list?" It is said that the great Buddhist teacher Thích Nhất Hạnh was once asked the question, "Why do you wash dishes?" His answer was quite simple: "I wash dishes to wash dishes."

One of my favorite aphorisms attributed to F.M. Alexander is "People do not decide their futures. They decide their habits, and their habits decide their future." The discoveries that he made, the principles that govern his work, are as valid today as they were back in the 1890s when as a young actor he learned how to regain his voice. I had my first AT lessons almost 50 years ago following my actor training at the Bristol Old Vic Theatre School in England. A lot has happened in my life since then. The swing of the pendulum from birth to death and back. AT is the one constant that has served me well over the decades while experiencing the unforeseen changes of life and the fear that so often accompanies these changes. AT works. It is not a panacea or quick fix, but nothing of importance is.

AT Perspective

Elaine Williams

Sanford Meisner offered a simple definition of acting: "Acting is living truthfully under imaginary circumstances" (Meisner 1987, p.15).

Actors are storytellers whose prime directive is to create and experience intimacy. To create this non-self-conscious "public solitude," the actor cannot succumb to tension or stressors that inhibit relaxation and ease. For the actor, the use of body, mind, spirit, and emotion is athletic in nature. A relaxed connection to focus and concentration is a necessity.

The Alexander Technique, established by F.M. Alexander, offers a solution for performers who deal with physical tension, anxiety, or stage fright. AT suggests that performers exercise a subtle pivot and redirection of their attention and physical energy—a return to the awareness of their own breath, a lengthening and widening of the muscles, and a return to presence in the moment. Actors become firmly rooted in the "now"—able to live fully and naturally through the given imaginary circumstances of a play. Actors are their own instruments; they must be finely tuned to enable listening, reacting, and moving without inhibition, using their entire instrument in playing a scene.

My goal in teaching and coaching actors is to guide them to an alive, aware connection to their imagination and help them to express their impulses naturally and organically in relaxed, effortless movement. The difference in poise, vocal vitality, and imaginative connection in actors whose consciousness has been shaped by AT can be astounding. Voices deepen with richer tone, bodies relax into their natural alignment, and relaxed emotional connection reveals presence and power. Suddenly, the audience is exposed to the full humanity of the actor and transported into the full reality of the story.

For actors to fully engage their imagination and play pretend with childlike abandon, they must remain relaxed.

The tools of AT may not be literal magic—but they can help the actor build a bridge into the relaxed ownership of their talent.

Reference

Meisner, Sanford (1987) *Sanford Meisner on Acting*. New York: Vintage Books.

Michael: Elaine Williams is one of the premier Meisner technique teachers in LA. She's on faculty at the Baron Brown Studio in Santa Monica, a Meisner-based actor training studio started in the early 1980s by Joanne Baron. Elaine is one of the senior teachers at the studio. How many years have you been teaching there, Elaine?

Elaine: I think it's 20.

Michael: I started teaching at the Baron Brown Studio in 1984 and took the two-year Meisner training program at the same time. Elaine is very supportive of the Alexander Technique as is the whole faculty at the Baron Brown Studio. But Elaine really steps up to the mark.

Elaine: Stand-up comedy and acting have always been my passions, and both can foster tremendous anxiety. When I was a student at the Baron Brown Studio before I became an acting teacher, I listened when Joanne Baron said how many artists leaned on relaxation and breathing techniques as a way to stop the fight-or-flight response so they could avoid stage fright and be more aware and more adjusted and more open and relaxed when they performed. I listened to that, and I heard it immediately. When I was an acting student, I had a partner in my acting class who was interested in AT. He and I worked together quite closely, and he encouraged me to join him in AT classes. After I had taken several AT classes he said to me, "You don't seem to appear visibly nervous at all." And I said, "Well, it seems to make everybody better no matter what they're aware of or what unconscious patterns they have." So as a student, I found AT very useful. And then, a few years later, I carried that into my teaching. I found students who held their shoulders up to their ears. They had tremendous anxiety and experienced near-panic attacks. Their desire to push toward results made them nervous and self-conscious in front of audiences. AT helped these students to relieve the tension almost immediately and understand what not to do in order to accomplish that. I also came to understand a very important thing for an acting instructor to share with students, and that is where students can most effectively place their attention. I am a great fan of AT because when my students are using the technique, I see such quick shifts in them in terms of being effective on stage and in their lives, and in my personal experience with the technique, I have benefitted in similar ways. When I started to take classes with Michael, I found AT to be simply fascinating. Intellectually and with performance, it was so helpful. But the real response came from people watching my work. People would approach me and say, "I didn't think you had any nerves at all. I see an even richer performance since you've done AT." What goes on inside of me because of AT is a simple, relaxed, easy shift of awareness. So when I simply knew where to place my attention, I felt little to no anxiety or stress, and I also understood it in a simple way that didn't take effort or tension to execute. I think what was happening inside of me was joy that I didn't have to defend or resist or anything else. Because of the way AT has helped me address my own anxieties about performing, I know it helps my students who have stage fright.

Michael: I received my Bachelor of Science degree in Speech and Theater in 1968. After graduation, I moved to Minneapolis, Minnesota, where eventually I became an apprentice at the Tyrone Guthrie Theater under artistic director Michael Langham. I was also assistant to the founder and director, John Donahue, of the Children's Theatre Company in Minneapolis. Later, in the early 1970s, with the help and support of Langham, I moved to England where I trained as an actor at the Bristol Old Vic Theatre School.

I lived there for ten years and also trained over a four-year period with master Alexander teachers Walter and Dilys Carrington and was certified as an AT teacher in the spring of 1978. I then moved to Southern California and began teaching actors in Los Angeles. As I said, I also studied Meisner acting work with Joanne Baron and was fascinated by that.

However, when I was acting during my university years, I was always petrified inside. In the summer of 1967, I was doing summer stock theatre, and I was playing Damis, the young son, in Molière's *Tartuffe*. During the production, I had to sneak across the stage and hide in a cupboard. I was overhearing Tartuffe talk to my mother, and at one moment I was supposed to burst out of the cupboard. It was hot and I was sweating. It's a little buggy. And I could see through the slats of this cupboard. The audience was literally less than a foot away from me on either side, and it was very claustrophobic, and I was always insecure with my lines. So I burst out of the cupboard when I was supposed to, and I started the speech, something like "No, madam, no! This news must be reported! But heaven's favor..." and I forgot my lines completely in front of the audience, God, and everyone. I took the palm of my right hand, tapped my forehead, and said, "Oh shit, I forgot my lines." But the thing that happened was that, kinesthetically, I felt like I had shrunk to about four feet tall. It was the most extraordinary experience! Then, very quickly, within a matter of moments, I regained my composure and cut to the end of a long speech, and the poor actor who had to make the entrance on my exit was scrambling to get on stage in time as I exited.

I went on to finish the run of *Tartuffe*, and I did other plays that summer, and I've done a lot of plays since then. However, my experience as Damis always stayed with me. That fear of forgetting my lines was pervasive, so I used to carry a script in my back pocket just for emotional security when I went on stage. Right before I went off to the Bristol Old Vic Theatre School when I was still an apprentice at the Guthrie Theatre in Minneapolis,

Fran Bennett, the voice and movement teacher there, led me to a better solution. Fran was a wonderful lady who had been trained by Kristin Linklater, author of *Freeing the Natural Voice*. Fran was the first person to tell me about AT. I said, "What is it?" And Fran said, "Well, it's an approach to movement where the actor learns to deal with fear and stage fright." And my gut experience was, "Oh my God, Fran, how could I study this?" No one had ever told me there was something that could help me with my own stage fright. And Fran said, "Well, there are no teachers in Minneapolis–St. Paul, only one in Chicago, and a handful in New York." But she knew I was going off to England to further my acting training, so she said, "There are lots of AT teachers in England. Find someone and just trust it."

And she was correct. And I did, and I lived there ten years and studied the technique, and it was the first time I ever had any legitimate freeing control over stage fright. It was not an easy journey, but it worked. And when I trained as an AT teacher in London with the Old Guard, people who had trained directly with F.M. Alexander, I really got a clear understanding of what the technique was. And I saw that most of my life, all the self-help approaches I had done to overcome stage fright had been processes of accumulation. And this was the first time it dawned on me that AT was a process of deconstruction and subtraction through mindful awareness. It was not trying to get a feeling like those other approaches had been. It was not even trying to get it right. It was simply watching like a hawk, watching one's conditioned mental, emotional, and physical behavior. AT is psychophysical, emotional reeducation. Being able to observe the fight, flight, freeze response or, as the Buddhists would say, the "monkey brain," and creating a space between the stimulus and response, and expanding awareness, allowing freedom to occur, was incredible.

And so, to me, that's what it was all about. You can see that it has a therapeutic side-effect, but it's not therapy. You could say that it helps your back problem, or your voice improves, or your breathing frees up, all sorts of good things may happen with improved coordination, but that's just the byproduct. The technique, really, is a process of observing the primary habit pattern that is "me," my conditioned self, and one can observe that in a variety of ways. We differentiate between the process of thought, which is a function of our central nervous system just like our eyes dilating to the sun, the digestive juices in our stomachs digesting our food, the pulse rate, and all the synchronicity of the circulatory and nervous systems. All that is a function, and thought is no more than that. AT does not exist in thought, even though we use thought as a tool. AT, in reality, in Buddhist terms, is a form of mindful awareness where you have a center of gravity, your attention in your senses, an integration of mind, emotions, and body in a psychophysical balance.

One of my dearest friends for over a quarter of a century was Laura Huxley, whose husband was Aldous Huxley, the great British writer who wrote *Brave New World* and *The Doors of Perception*. This is what I'm talking about—our "doors of perception." Our senses only exist within this present moment and this is where the AT work resides. You only see now, you only hear now, you only taste now, you only sense movement within this present moment. If you can bring your awareness into the present moment without any history, without filtering through comparison, you enter a different world. A world that is not "time bound" by thought.

Thought has its place, however. Thought in its right place has a future and a past. You know where your car's parked, you know a task you have to do later today. The architect can build a building through imagination, which resides in thought, and the actor can visualize the play and his or her various actions within the play through thought. What I teach my actors is how "thought in its wrong place" interferes when you allow fear to enter into the performance. The actor can simply learn to move their attention away from a fear response into a mindful awareness. That's what I teach my actors because when they go to an audition, and a big audition, with Steven Spielberg or George Lucas or Quentin Tarantino, what happens is they start mind-fucking themselves:

"Am I going to be good?" or "Look at that person in the audition room…they look just like me, and I thought I was the only one in LA." All these reactions are simply "stage fright" manifesting. Virtually all actors go through this fear reaction. Through AT, I teach them to observe and to change their state by initiating a change in their coordination, re-creating a delicate movement by lengthening and widening, head leading and body following, letting go of unnecessary downward pressure and, more importantly, to simply let go of the emotional feeling of desperately needing to be right. This delicate movement of lengthening and widening allows the actor to move from a "fear-based reaction" to a more conscious mindful awareness that allows inner freedom and creativity. Don't judge it as negative, don't try to change it, simply stop inside and observe like a hawk watching. I want them to come back to the basic "Alexander directions" of delicately allowing their heads to lead and their bodies to follow and coming back to a lengthening and widening throughout their whole selves. I call this "smart relaxation," coming back to good posture. However, it is not a holding position. It is all a process of allowing and letting go into upright length. And when my students do that, their breathing frees up. I encourage them to free their voices through free breathing and to learn dialogue without unnecessary tension and stress. I teach my actors to free the breath in the waiting room before they go into an audition. I tell them point-blank, "All those other actors are so freaked out that they're not paying any attention to you. Do what you need to do. Work on yourself. It's like having your own personal mindfulness practice."

Alexander never called it AT. He only called it psychophysical reeducation. Or better yet, the "Work." So I tell my actors, "Don't be lazy—wake up and apply this work! Use the tools you're learning with me to rise above and alleviate your stage fright."

Elaine: Right, there we go. One thing that came to me as I was listening to you and thinking about what my students go through when they are trying to function in a scene, be responsive, and remain relaxed and aware is that they focus on surface attempts at perfection. Which means they're trying to look like swans while, underneath, their feet are going madly and wildly at warp speed. I mean, that's the thing I tell my students because I experience it constantly still in my own performance, teaching, and life. There are moments when I can literally feel my face getting flushed, my ears getting hot, my breath becoming more rapid. And sometimes when I am super-aware, I can feel that I'm not even breathing at all. I'm holding my breath, and that stops any ability to experience because I'm in every past moment and every future fear, and I'm trying like the dickens to get it right. For me, that is the definition of stage fright. In that state, there's no way to get it right. There's also no way you can put your attention on what you really want.

In teaching my actors and directing scenes or improvisations, I may bring them back to an awareness of their breath. I get them to stop their habit pattern within the moment by directing them verbally to place their attention back on their breath and on lengthening and widening. Whether I am helping a student or working on a scene myself, my goal is to remove "the stuff" that creates stage fright. I do this by focusing on the tools of AT that specifically bring me back to physical poise, breath, and presence. So I'm reflecting on what Michael said in terms of how much all work, especially for performers, is about "smart relaxation," is about mindful presence, and is about being able to see the opening to freedom. In acting, it is seeing and experiencing what is actually happening and being open and available to react and seize the moment. Whether you're a painter or a musician, an actor, or a singer, you've got to be able to relax. They talk so much about this in athletics. You see the opening and you have to be able to run through it. As a teacher, I can absolutely see and identify moments when my student's bodies tense and their brains begin trying to micromanage their responses. I say to them, "Can you feel your neck tightening, your shoulders tightening, and your brain trying to figure out how to maneuver the situation?" When the student is judgmental and self-critical or compares herself to another actor, she is not in any state to be open and authentically reactive and available.

Michael: In order to get students to what Elaine is talking about and to how AT teachers actually interact with students, hands-on and otherwise, you have to watch their thinking. You watch where they are physically as they enter the classroom. I never arrive to class with a predetermined "lesson plan." Maybe I have a general sense of what I wish to teach. But I'm interested in where my students are in the moment because you're waking them up to a different way of perception. They come in with their whole worlds bouncing around in their minds, but that's not the world I want them to act and perform in. I want them to be in a different world, and that different world is one where they're not trying to go for an end result. Obviously, there are end results that one wants, but that doesn't mean that one creates force and pushes for this end result in a negative way. You can learn to watch your fear reactions. So I get them to wake up to their habit patterns, the way they think, feel, and move.

Now, using one's hands to delicately suggest to students to release into movement is something AT is famous for. But hands-on work is so often misunderstood. You know, a lot of Alexander teachers will use the phrase, "Well, you gotta get your hands on them right away." And I think that that is not quite correct because then the new Alexander student thinks that AT is the teacher's hands doing something to them and it's not. The Alexander teacher's hands are useful in an inhibitory way that gives students a sense of "not this and not that" as far as their head/neck/back coordination is concerned. And the hands-on work has to be married to the way students are perceiving the work in the present moment and the way they're feeling. It has to be a psychophysical, emotional way of teaching. Alexander never had anyone work with him directly. He figured this out through his own inner work.

During the 1980s and early 1990s, I spent well over a decade studying with Marj Barstow in Lincoln, Nebraska. I consider her to be one of the greatest Alexander teachers, on the level with any of the first-generation teachers in England. Except for her original teacher training in London with F.M. Alexander in the 1930s, she very rarely allowed anyone to touch her. She may have shared lessons with a few of the "oldies but goodies" early teachers, but she always manifested a great pioneer spirit of self-reliance. After all, she was born in 1899. Later in her life Marj never had anyone give her "an Alexander turn" as it were. I clearly remember asking her, "Marj, here you are, you went off in 1929, 1930 to study AT in London. You completed the original three-year teacher training with F.M. Alexander. You came back to the States and did some training with F.M.'s brother A.R. Alexander in Boston and Frank Pierce Jones, both your dear friends. But then you went back to Lincoln, Nebraska. There wasn't another Alexander teacher for 3,000 miles. What did you do?"

She paused and looked me in the eye and said, "Well, Michael, I just got tough with myself." And that's how AT works. If you're always relying on the teacher's hands-on work, you're not getting in touch with yourself. And it's easy to become an Alexander junky. It feels good, but that's not the work. That has a slight payoff. I mean I put hands on in the first class, but they have to earn it. I'm not giving it to them as a treat or to make them feel good so they'll stay in the class.

Elaine: Because I don't teach AT, I can only share my experiences with my students and point them toward Michael, but because I don't teach it, I am so aware of the things that I've learned and seen in the work, so what I find is that if I just simply stop the student and say, "Wait a moment, I can see that you're not breathing," then I stop the whole scene, and as I stand beside the actor and I say, "There's such a concept as your head leading your body, allowing a sense of lengthening and widening," suddenly I notice the student shifting into better posture in a gentle easy way when they don't feel like they're on display. It seems to be reminding them of something they already know, and I think that's the genius of AT. It seems to be able to point to the literal things you can already do, and it reawakens an awareness that you already have instinctively and it seems to stick with you.

Michael: I agree with you. You're absolutely correct, Elaine. It takes away the interfering patterns, allowing you to be authentic, to be balanced in the way nature's taken 3.5 million years to sort out upright posture.

Elaine: Yes, I see them empowered when they discover that upright posture. Empowered by their discovering it within the moment.

Michael: Sure. Exactly. I agree.

Elaine: And it's fantastic! So when you add the experience of the Alexander teacher using hands-on work to gently guide the actor into better coordination and balance, the actor experiences a gentle yet profound sense of self where there is less fear. That's how I experience it physically and emotionally. I find it to be such a noninvasive process even though someone is using their hands directly to guide me. I don't feel any invasion and suddenly it feels so empowering. It's as if I am doing it.

Let me tell you about a student of mine who had a deep stutter. His wife had taken the Baron Brown Studio's actor training, and she wanted him to do it because it had been so transformative for her. He had an interest in being a teacher of health and nutrition, but he was too frightened to do it because of his stutter. So I met with him. He wanted to meet the teacher before the class. Typically we don't do that. However, in this case I went in to meet him, and immediately he said, "Elaine, I don't know if I'll be able to do this because of my profound stutter." And I said, "You can stop right there because you don't have any bigger blocks than anyone else studying acting. There are going to be people in class who have far more profound stage fright and fear than you have. I'll see you in class!"

We get to the first day of class, and he does the same thing. "Please let me apologize to anyone if I have problems." I said, "Sit down! People have more problems than you and no one is noticing." Literally, that's what I said. He got up and began to act and was suddenly seized by fear. To relieve his anxiety I gently brought his awareness to the application of AT. For him, this was simply placing his attention outside of himself and onto his acting partner, being aware of his breath and creating an interruptive pattern that allowed him to be more aware and mindful. Suddenly there was no stutter. He had a pattern of apology and shame, if you want an "armchair therapy assessment." He had a pattern of tension that would occur and exacerbate the stammer. It was similar to the way singers with a similar vocal problem perform and the problem disappears because their attention is outside of themselves. Through applying the principles of AT, he was able to replace his fear reaction and "stage fright" with conscious attention. Through his training to be an actor and overcoming his stutter, he was able to accomplish his dream of teaching health and nutrition. He was taking acting classes along with AT, and the combination of both disciplines helped him to reach his goals. So that was huge.

I very often have experiences in the beginning of the work where people are so emotional that they can barely stand on stage, they're literally shaking. They are distracted from their acting partners' behavior by falling back into their fear patterns—from laughter to anger, from politeness to sarcasm, going straight to fighting or freezing, any myriad of things. And students sometimes literally have so much emotion that they stand and have tears release in front of me throughout their critique. They're not looking for attention. It's just the fear. And when those people go to Michael and take Alexander lessons, they return to me with a completely different physical and emotional availability. They become grounded, simple, relaxed beings. It's amazing. The anxiety will dissipate and disappear. Now they may still have the typical excitements and enthusiasms and fears, but they no longer are controlled by it. They now have the tools to create balance and overcome the major blocks that have kept them from exploring the imaginative circumstances within their acting. And that's a radical shift.

Michael: I have a couple of examples too. There's a through line in these examples I will relate. If you don't have a strong will to change, nothing's going to happen. You can dream about change until the proverbial cows come home, and all it will create is a dream, not a reality. Of course, dreams and creative imagination are important, but I'm not talking about that. You have to visualize what you want and actualize what you visualize and embody into reality. People do not decide their futures. They decide their habits, and their habits decide their futures.

I got a phone call from a guy named Luna, and it turned out he's homeless. For some reason he hears about AT, and he calls up and inquires about it and I had this feeling that I should listen to this guy. He's staying in some shelter in downtown LA. So I invite him to the Saturday morning AT classes. To my surprise he actually shows up. He's a little bit overweight, and he's at a place in his life that's pretty rough, but he has a really good heart. So he joins the Alexander class and it was like that old cliché, fish to water. He ate it up. The work starts changing his life. Turns out that he's a hair cutter, and through gaining confidence while studying AT, he gets a job at a reputable salon in LA, allowing his self-worth and esteem to soar. While cutting hair people tell him how good he is, and it completely changes his self-image. He finds a place to live because he's saving money. On top of all this, he really falls in love with training to be an actor. So he's saving money to attend the Baron Brown Studio and study the Meisner work.

This is a clear example of how AT completely changed someone's self-image and gave him a new constructive path in life. At some point, I'm going to bring it up with Joanne Baron that this guy deserves a shot at being part of the studio because of his hard work and discipline. He is also quite interesting. He's not like the generic "actor type" you meet in Hollywood.

Now another person is Phil, who is a real businessman. This guy lives in Brentwood, but he flies to New York constantly. Has a real job in insurance in New York, wears a suit in Manhattan in one of those mammoth skyscrapers, and makes much, much more than a six-figure income. He's been studying with me for years, and is absolutely consistent in how he approaches the Alexander work. Phil, because of his maturity, understands that nothing comes easily. He has a high level of tenacity. He understands the value of honoring the process that unfolds in small steps as he pursues acting in a very real and practical way.

Phil's success doesn't happen all at once. He understands the importance of applying AT to ordinary daily activities. He understands that his instrument as an actor is the same instrument that accomplishes the small tasks of everyday life. As result, he's out there performing in and directing plays in LA. Most of it, mind you, is in community theatre; however, the thing about Los Angeles is most of this community theatre is virtually professional standard. And he's really applying the technique to that process. So you can talk about people who have big fear reactions and AT chills them out, but it also gives people like Phil who already have their life together a competitive edge and through line for how to approach acting, which is his love.

And then I've got another guy, Ryan, who is an exceptional human being, and he's a young man in his early twenties and good looking and tall and from South Carolina. He is so dedicated to AT, I cannot tell you. He has no money. He's even been losing weight because he said he only has money for ramen noodles to eat. I let him come to study for free because I want to support him.

The thing about the technique is that it gives inner support to people whenever they feel life is falling apart around them, whenever they go through that "dark night of the soul." And it happens because of an integration in a psychophysical emotional way. They're not discouraging themselves worrying about if they're going to be a successful actor. What they're doing is balancing out the immense stress and strains of trying to get a career going in LA, which is not an easy task by any means. Yet in a harmonious light, I teach them that it is you who are making the choices. No one is making you do this. You are in control. AT gives you that inner control, that gravitas of substance. Whenever you're in Los Angeles and you go to Starbucks with other young actors and they're all bemoaning the fact that they don't have any work, I teach my students to apply the technique, come back to length and width at that moment, don't get into a negative mindset by pulling their inner selves down. And above all, learn to work from inside out. Don't simply be like a pinball machine where the pinball bounces off the bumpers. What you're doing is you're in control, you're working from inside out. Most people are on automatic pilot and are simply reacting to what is happening around them, to outside stimuli. There's not much consciousness there.

What makes actors interesting is when they have an inner core that is not dependent on an audience's positive or negative response. In other words, stuff happens that we like and don't like all the time, and it will continue to happen. The traffic jam on the PCH or the 10 or the 405 will occur tomorrow, but if you know how to rise above it and change your state by using AT, then you have a shot of being a success. You're no longer controlled by fear. It doesn't mean that fear doesn't exist, it just means that the tail isn't wagging the dog.

Elaine: I agree, Michael. Now, what if we walk into an imaginary classroom where we are teaching a class together?

Michael: Okay, so the first thing is that I respect and understand your approach to actor training and I absolutely do not interfere with it. I want to be supportive of you, Elaine. So that's one thing. So the students view us as a harmonious twosome who are there to make their lives easier. That's how I frame the very first beat. And then, how to do it? I would talk to Elaine way in advance and sketch out a plan to have them prepare some scenes at the very beginning when they don't know much about AT. This will let all their habitual fear reactions start to pop out. And then, once people start to see that, then they can describe it, describe their shoulders coming up to their ears or their heads being pulled back and down or gasping air in on the phrase or getting sweaty palms or pushing for emotion, whatever interfering pattern it might be.

Once they start to see this I say, "Okay, now what we're going to do is we're going to shift the focus into AT work."

It would be very hard for me to give them, while co-teaching with Elaine, any depth of what I wish them to understand unless they have in their hip pockets some experiential practical knowledge of the technique. Without this, their learning would be very shallow—the Alexander part of it. So let's say then that I give, over an extended period of time, a basic understanding of the Alexander principles so they learn to think on their own. And then, working with Elaine, we would apply what they thought to their scenes. So, if Elaine was teaching them in this next level, they would be doing scenes, and Elaine would be giving them critique, and then I would give critique from an Alexander viewpoint. Because they would then have a detailed understanding of the Alexander principles kinesthetically as compared to a cerebral way, I would say to them, "So let's do the scene again, and when you pulled down on that line and you noticed your brain going wacko with fear and your breath became shallow and you were worried about getting it right, I want you instead to come back to length and width in that moment, in a nanosecond. Letting your head lead and your whole body follow will have a positive effect on your breathing and posture. No one knows it except you, and it will change your state mentally, emotionally, and physically. Don't hang out in that downslide."

So that's the way I would work with Elaine. She and I have such a deep understanding of the Meisner work and AT that we could go in this afternoon and teach a class together. For the students to really apply the technique, they have to really have a visceral practical understanding of the work, more than simply asking "Where's the bathroom?" and "Where do I order a taxi?" in French. What so often happens in Alexander classes where the people aren't trained properly, the teacher just steps in and gives them a "little sugar treat" of an experience. Master teacher Marj Barstow, for example, did not want to give "experiences." She encouraged people to learn how to work on themselves using

Alexander's principles so that the student's experience would be born out of their own inner experiences and desires.

Elaine: I've had the pleasure of having Michael visit my classes, and it's transformational. For the students to be in the middle of the work and in the middle of feeling all their fears and emotions—there is a shift from a distracted state into more awareness of what is happening in front of them that is making them more aware of their scene partners and connecting with them in the space they're in. Allowing them to see their unconscious habits and where they're not paying attention. To simply have the actors experience Michael using his hands on their tense shoulders, allowing their necks to be free so they can release into overall lengthening and widening, is wonderful. I watch people literally shift emotion effortlessly and release tears right in front of everyone. Gaining an inch or two of height. Creating a powerful presence on stage. Beginning to see and hear things that they had avoided or simply didn't notice before. Their senses become more alert. They are waking up inside—it's amazing. When they are in the middle of a monologue, it feels like the molecules change in the room.

Michael: I would say that's true. What happens is that the atmosphere does change because when people move out of fear and when they become more balanced within themselves, they feel better primarily because the breathing rhythm changes. We're all just picking up people's breathing rhythms, and when someone has anxiety onstage, that affects the audience's breathing rhythm. But if the actor can come back to length and width and free up the breath, taking the pressure off the breathing mechanism, everyone feels better in the room. I would say that, for stage fright, AT is helpful all the time. The essence of what Alexander discovered was that his fear affected his posture and his breathing, causing downward pressure that restricted his breathing and subsequently affected his voice.

But the one thing I might mention: I consider talent about 80 percent good coordination. And then you have about 20 percent super smart or genius or whatever creativity happening, but basic talent; if you look at the "stars" out there, most of them are pretty coordinated. When we allow healthy coordination, it affects the overall quality of the ways we think, feel, and move, creating an integrated balance because we don't interfere with the natural human processes of living.

Now I'll give you a really interesting example. I taught at the Old Globe Theater down in San Diego in their MFA program, and one day—this was before he became super famous—one day Ian McKellen came to do his one-man Shakespeare show. And I asked him if he wanted Alexander lessons and he said sure. So I ended up giving him four or five lessons. When I first put hands on Ian McKellen, I put hands on his head and neck, and I thought, "Holy shit, this man is like a thoroughbred race horse." That was my reaction. The coordination he had was amazing. So I sometimes tell that story to students because the thing is they all have talent but often they're covering it up through interfering with their birthright of good coordination. They try and try, and it's not going to shift anything. They've got to move out of the interfering habit patterns into basic healthy coordination.

Then the final thing I want to say is that living in England for a decade in the 1970s, I saw all the great actors live on stage—Paul Scofield, John Gielgud, Judi Dench, Maggie Smith, Alan Bates, Peggy Ashcroft, Sir Laurence Olivier, Glenda Jackson, I mean on and on. You can name them and I saw them all. And the most exciting of any of them hands down was Paul Scofield. He was dangerous, and I wanted to find out what made him dangerous. You knew he was a consummate actor. He had integrity, he wasn't hot-dogging it, but he was dangerous. He created a situation where audiences were literally on the edge of their seats not knowing what would happen next. And I met an actor once, Johnny McDonald, who was in a production of *The Tempest* where Scofield was playing Prospero, and I asked Johnny, "What is his process?" He paused and said, "Well, it's like this. When Scofield approaches acting, he's going down the path and in front of him are two doors. Inside the right-hand door, if you walk through it, all your skill comes to the forefront, all your life experience—you do a magical job and everyone pats you on the back and says how great you are. But Scofield doesn't walk through that door. He walks through the door on the left. That's where all of his fear, insecurity, sense of not knowing, all of that exists. And because that is what he constantly does, that's where that sense of danger comes from. He is working on a very deep level of internally facing his personal fear." And when you have the courage to do that, you can be awarded a PhD in acting. There's a great quote I love by a guy named George Addair: "Everything you've ever wanted is on the other side of fear." Scofield moved toward the other side where his fear existed. And that's what I teach my students. We're all afraid. It's healthy. There's nothing wrong with fear. So you can think of stage fright as a positive reaction that sharpens our senses. The problem is that it often gets out of control.

Elaine: That's the truth. That's something. We think that fear is wrong, and it's not.

Michael: You're right. So I expand the phrase. I say, "Everything you ever wanted *in acting* is on the other side of fear." That's what I teach. It's how to go there. Because if you lengthen when you encounter stage fright, you can walk through "that left-hand door," and you're not going to be controlled from the outside in, you'll be working from the inside out. You won't be worried about what the audience thinks. You will be working from a place of inner knowledge and confidence. When you face your fear, you'll transform from a reactive pattern of avoidance into something creative that comes from inside.

Elaine: Yes, and going further, I think anyone who is trying to have an accomplishment, anyone who is trying to share a gift or a passion, experiences this. Anyone who, like Luna, was drawn to AT "like a duck to water" has been helped to get around natural barriers of preciousness, fear, disappointment, not wanting to be judged, so that they have the courage to be more transparent. Actors must get beyond simply moving mechanically through life without any internal change occurring. I teach my actors to get behind their fear responses using AT. I mean to get beyond the barriers that pop up for people when they have so much to contribute in a simple joyful way, which can be addressed so profoundly through AT in a nonintrusive way. To see young people blossoming from it and working through the stress created by competition and rejection, I find amazing. To be able to transform their world by encouraging them not to be controlled through knee-jerk reactions is just fantastic. It's about getting students to pull back from habitual responses based on fear and creating joy in their acting. They find something that none of us knew in advance. Something pure. Something that is authentically theirs, and that fosters incredible confidence, incredible empathy with other people.

Michael: And it really helps them deal with the industry, the business side of acting. The work of being an actor is difficult. It creates lots of pressure. What I call "I gotta get it right" type of thinking. You know when they go out there and they only look for end results, missing out on the creative process that leads to a great performance, they literally can't move through fear responses.

Elaine: Right. This Alexander principle of end-gaining prevents them from being able to deal with the rejection that they will inevitably face. Not only in the execution, but to deal with the aftermath as it were, which has nothing to do with anything. It's all made up. It's all speculative. But that is the thing that can stop you from ever beginning the pursuit of a creative life.

Michael: You're making a choice to enter a profession where, almost more than any other, you're constantly rejected on a daily basis. However, the thing about it is that you're choosing to be in this "business of acting." No one is making you do it. If you learn how to stop, look, and listen, coming back to a sense of lengthening and widening, freeing up your mind, your feelings, and your body through re-creating an intentional movement, balance happens. There is a psychophysical emotional shift that leads to an inner harmony when actors learn to create what I call a "delicate movement out of fear." I mean it gives them such a practical tool, such a feeling of inner freedom, they absolutely love it and become better actors for it, unhampered by stage fright.

Mindful Bananas and the Alexander Technique

Kathleen Juhl

AT Perspective

I am happiest and feel most helpful offering my skills as an Alexander Technique teacher when I am working amid actors, singers, and instrumentalists as they engage in rehearsal or classroom activities. I circulate among actors in classes and rehearsals, offering hands-on work. I sit onstage in a voice studio class and provide AT support to individual singers as they rehearse their songs and arias. I collaborate with the voice teachers to suggest ways to improve. I work similarly for groups of instrumentalists. Hands-on offerings in the moment of activity are effective for supporting young artists as they develop their performance skills. I move *among* students; I work *with* them.

Through an activities-based approach, AT offers opportunities for collaborative, egalitarian relationships with young artists. Mindful processes are central to developing these relationships. The rehearsal and classroom processes I have developed encourage students to move intentionally forward through time, moment to moment, and I move with them. In acting classes, for example, students explore short bits of play texts in turn, gently interrupting one another. They create a continuous flow of activity, always focusing on the present moment as I move quietly among them, offering my hands to encourage coordination.

This approach discourages what F.M. Alexander called *end-gaining*, and I enhance this by approaching the students playfully, unexpectedly, surprising them so they slip into the present moment. When that happens, end-gaining stops and my hands can successfully support them toward thoughtful and nuanced rehearsal of their performance texts. When I work onstage as actors and musicians rehearse, my hands are always a surprise because I consciously approach them from as many directions as I can manage in the midst of their movement. This process encourages them to open to their fellow performers and environment so they coordinate and move and speak in relation to what they must accomplish— pursuing objectives in order to create compelling moments that tell stories in captivating ways. My perspective on engaging AT with performers is to inspire mindfulness and playfulness as I offer my hands to support them as they invite audiences to go with them on exciting theatrical and musical journeys.

I sit in the director's chair watching student actors "play to make a play." They move up delicately as they play—prancing and preening and puzzling and practicing. They pull down when they slip into work mode—concentrating, questioning, and mischievously complaining about everything I ask them to do. They run circles around me and sometimes leap lightly, celebrating moments when they figure out the best way to deliver a line or negotiate a complicated bit of staging. As part of celebrating their discoveries, I ask them to think about character interactions with a clear purpose in mind. How will they pursue their desires with expectation and determination? Ah! There's the rub! Pursue, expectation, determination—strong words that can imply pull-down, tension, un-easy habits, and end-gaining. As they think about chasing after the elusive desires of characters, their voices are often frayed and their breathing forced as their limbs flail about searching for success—focused voices and movement and gesture, dreams fulfilled in playful moments that slip easily forward...telling a story.

I encourage them to check the relationship between their heads, necks, and spines so they coordinate themselves. I help with gentle hands that communicate AT ideas. I want students to explore and discover new and elegant ways of following those dramatic dreams. My desire is for resonance and depth in their voices and concise and precise movement as they strut the stage and clarify their characters. But how are they living in the bodies of the characters they are imagining and creating and embodying? Are those bodies spacious and coordinated? Have their characters been created with courage, embracing the dangers, the pratfalls, of playfulness as inevitabilities that will allow them to dip their toes into the unpredictable present moment? Do they know what that means? This chapter is a meditation on the ways playfulness can connect AT principles and practices with mindful rehearsal processes that encourage performance students to stay both coordinated and centered as they explore and discover avenues toward accomplishing artistry and excellence.

Mindfulness is a practice and an approach to life that engages deeply with each present moment as it happens and is perceived. Mindfulness, says Jon Kabat-Zinn, who originated the Mindfulness-Based Stress Reduction Program at the University of Massachusetts Medical Center, is "the awareness that arises by paying attention on purpose, in the present moment, and non-judgmentally" (2013, xxxv). When I watch students parading and posturing on stage or in rehearsal rooms more focused on the end product than on the process in the present moment, I am concerned. Instead of rehearsing and practicing with ease, they lean forward into the future, voices pushing, muscles working, and for what? To gain an end: applause! We need remedies for what F.M. Alexander called *end-gaining*, something AT teachers are concerned about. For when performers are pushing toward an end, their movement is most often inefficient and un-easy because their heads are pushing ahead of their spines. This pushing often disappears when students engage mindfulness and stay in the present moment where they can effectively move their head delicately up from the top of their spine, initiating coordination throughout their body.

Mindfulness practice has been meandering its dreamy way through our culture for decades. If actors, singers, instrumentalists, and dancers used mindfulness in performance preparation and practice, there would be less end-gaining. One way to help performers work in the present moment is to engage them in activities involving "play." I begin my thoughts here by invoking play as inherent in theatre rehearsal practices and processes: "We play to make a play." It is also productive to use playful practices with musicians and dancers to encourage productive and fruitful fun. It is delightful to witness the ways lightness and ease *play out* as young artists explore and discover centers of gravity and creativity in the present moment through a synthesis of mindful, playful activities and AT.

Play theorists Johan Huizinga and Richard Schechner both believe in the necessity and productivity of play in human activities. Huizinga says that play is "a *significant* function—that is to say, there is some sense to it. In play there is something 'at play' which transcends the immediate needs of life and imparts meaning to the action. All play means something" (1950, p.1). In fact, Huizinga says that play "is one of the main bases of civilization" (1950, p.5). Similarly, Richard Schechner says that playing is:

> the underlying, always-there continuum of experience... Ordinary life is netted out of playing but playing continuously squeezes through even the smallest holes of the worknet... No matter how hard people try, play finds its way through—banana time is always with us. (1993, p.42)

Thus the presence of playfulness, of banana time, in the creative processes of performers moves their activities inevitably forward because rehearsals and practice operate in the flow of life where play, according to both Huizinga and Schechner, thrives. We *play around* in rehearsals and practice in order to be productive and discover riches as we engage the ingredients of our ingenuity. We play and sing notes using a whole host of tantalizing techniques to make music. We play with new combinations of steps and rhythms as we create a dance. We play around with vocal textures and movement vocabularies as we create characters for the stage. And when "banana time is always with us," there is always a chance that, as we play, we will slip on a proverbial peel. And slipping on that peel, according to Schechner, makes for dangerous, precarious, off balance, and exciting artistic processes and performances (1993). I would add that slipping on a banana peel must always happen in the present moment and is always a surprise and an opportunity to engage AT.

As I ask students to dabble in playfulness that will move them toward daring performances, I tread carefully. I encourage them to center and coordinate themselves as they playfully explore the skills they need to perform well. Play can be rowdy and raucous and potentially tight, stiff, and uncoordinated. But play also can be the light and supple bridge through which mindfulness practices and AT become a dynamic duo, essential to artistic processes. As AT teachers, we, like Jon Kabat-Zinn, teach our students to "pay attention on purpose" in order to make new choices nonjudgmentally and in the moment of activity. Building mindfulness into rehearsals and practice, in combination with the openness that is necessary for engaging AT effectively, can be accomplished through laying a foundation of playfulness that pulls performers into the present moment.

Habits are done "mindlessly." We often don't notice how we are moving when we walk across a stage or dance or sing or play an instrument. As AT teachers, we work (and play) with students to help them identify habits that prevent them from becoming effective, poised, and elegant young artists. We inspire them to move toward new and well-coordinated habits. To make new choices, we encourage students to be conscious, mindful. According to F.M. Alexander, the conscious mind must be "quickened," made more alive (1910). When we are conscious of the present moment as we work with students, we can approach them exactly where they are without judgment. Understanding play processes can "quicken" and enliven our teaching. When students unexpectedly slip on Schechner's banana peels, their minds quicken and enliven so that they can center and coordinate themselves by engaging AT as a way of mindfully "paying attention on purpose." AT can help them do this with ease and efficiency. They can ask themselves or work with a teacher to engage a process of allowing their heads to move so their whole bodies become coordinated and they can move toward accomplishing their artistic activities in balanced and effective ways. To facilitate mindful artistic practices including AT, my students and I set up "play spaces" that are suitable for activities I call *Core Practice*, a concept I borrowed and modified based on the pedagogy of Matthew Shaver, a teacher who works and plays in Boston, weaving mindfulness practice into his work with middle school students (personal communication with Bayla McDougal, 2016).

The play spaces my students and I create for Core Practice and our subsequent artistic work are designed to foster the peace, calm, and safety necessary for mindfulness activities. They easily transform into vibrant and energized environments ripe for "banana time," where slipping on peels and wiggling through Schechner's "work net" foster imbalance and mistakes that lead to artistically productive explorations and effective physical coordination and ease. Students are often off balance and slip on handy banana peels, reminding them that AT processes will help them move toward a free open space between the head and spine that leads to coordination. Mindful performance practices engaged with coordination help students appreciate imbalances and blunders as phenomena that move them toward artistry because creativity flourishes in the present moment. For example, actors who interact on stage moment to moment, watching and listening with curiosity as they strategize ways to pursue and attain their characters' desires, tell stories in compelling ways. Effective dancers are compelling when they execute choreography in the present moment, one step at a time, so their movement is synchronous with the performance environment and other dancers. Musicians who understand that they cannot play or sing effectively if they are pushing notes too quickly or determinedly toward audiences discover that musicality emerges when they stay present with the musical line as they play or sing. When artists push toward results, they often leap past the present moment, engendering tension in both their muscles and minds. End-gaining and uncoordinated movement is the result. AT operates best when a coordinated teacher works or *plays around* with students in the present moment, and I have found that what I call *play environments* are wonderful places for exploring effective AT work.

To lay the ground for that work, I use Core Practice activities in play environments to prepare students for performance work and teach them mindfulness. First, I help students understand that I teach by suggestion rather than by leading or managing. I introduce them to specific Core Practice activities that include an amalgam of all the practices I engage in a well-designed performance warm-up: vocal and physical explorations, text work, free writing, imaginative investigations, and, of course, mindfulness meditations and AT considerations. I lay out a basic protocol and suggest activities, but students design and lead Core Practice so the discoveries they make are their own. I play the part of subtext—I gently poke and pry a bit here and a bit there. I add ingredients: a note I sing or play on a piano, a costume piece, a prop, an inspirational do-si-do and, of course, a soft hand at the nape of a neck or a finger lightly touching a shoulder or hip to encourage lightness and ease. I mindfully maintain a meditative approach to my attentive but discreet interventions.

Core Practice might begin like this for young singers, actors, instrumentalists, or dancers in a rehearsal or studio class: Everyone sits facing one another on chairs in a circle, eyes closed, feet flat on the floor. One student leads the group toward ease and mindfulness by asking his colleagues to release their head up and away from their spine so their body follows gently toward coordination. A second student asks everyone to keep their eyes open for a few moments and plays soft, recorded music chosen by the group. The students and I listen. Core Practice moves slowly and mindfully, so enjoying the music can last from a few moments to ten minutes. After the music has relaxed and enlivened them, another student quietly asks the group to scan their bodies: "Picture where your joints are located anatomically," she says. "Move slowly from head and neck, shoulders, hips, knees, ankles.

Imagine your joints vividly." Another student takes over: "Now take time to scan your body for muscular tension. Slowly notice from your feet through your limbs and out through the top of your head. Do you notice any discomfort in your body right now, in this moment? Release the discomfort if you can, but please make no judgments. Just notice. You are fine just as you are." Another pipes up: "Close your eyes now. Notice your breath. Don't change it, just notice. Is it moving your chest more or moving your belly?" Another continues: "Count your breaths—in one, out two, in three, out four until you reach ten. Then start over. If thoughts distract you, simply notice them gently as they cross your mind, let them pass, and focus once again on counting your breaths. We'll engage this process quietly for ten minutes. Enjoy!" And they do enjoy! After ten minutes, a new voice begins: "Imagine yourself performing for us. Picture all the details in the scene. Where are you? Who is there? What are you wearing? How do your clothes feel against your skin? How does the air feel around your body? What are you doing? What do you hear? What do you see? How does it feel to be doing what you are doing? Are you moving? How does it feel to move? Are you making sounds? What do you notice as they move through your body?" Another student takes over: "Okay, stop performing in your imagination. Take a moment to appreciate how amazing you were on your imaginary stage and the thunderous applause you received from your imaginary audience. Where do you perceive muscular tension now? Has your breathing changed? How do you feel in general? Are you living in the present moment? Can you stay there while we move to more physical work and play? What are you noticing?" A brief discussion about the process ensues. Then the students lead each other in more traditional vocal and physical warm-ups along with free writing and games, anything they deem important and appropriate for the performance they are working on.

During this student-led mindfulness practice, I move quietly from student to student making suggestions verbally and through hands-on encouragement using AT ideas. I have them walk around the space while they listen to music or scan their joints, for example. I gently and discreetly touch ribs, bellies, and hips to remind students to breathe fully and effortlessly. I touch arms and legs to encourage ease of movement. If I can get away with it, I quietly whisper silliness into their ears, trying to tickle their fancies and make them giggle. I add in this dose of playfulness in order to distract them from their thoughts, judgments, ruminations. I maintain my own good use as I do this and, of course, a meditative, present moment, and playful attitude. I purposefully encourage them to mess up so they can stay in the present moment and keep a playful attitude throughout the practice. We don't worry if someone cannot stifle a guffaw when I tickle his fancy whispering a good joke in his ear during the music or formal mindfulness practice. It is okay if someone cheers because the performance she imagined was so incredible she cannot help herself. We don't mind if some prankster purposely trips and yells in "pain" during the body scan. Silliness in small doses is part of the game because we know it ultimately prepares us for productive creative work.

In the play spaces where my students and I engage Core Practice as well as explore and practice and create performances together, banana time flourishes. When performers slip on imaginary peels for one reason or another and trip over their feet a bit or mess up a line, imbalance is the inevitably playful and productive result. When musicians play or sing a wrong note, dancers miss a step, or actors struggle with a costume, they inevitably leap into the present moment where, if they maintain a playful approach to their work, they can right themselves, coordinate themselves, and laugh at themselves. They can choose to stop pushing, end-gaining into the future, with all their fears and insecurities intact. End-gaining toward the future, determined to reach or accomplish a goal, causes muscular, mental, and emotional tension and pulls students out of the present moment. A singer pushing sound toward an audience will probably move off his center and out of the present moment. He may pull his head back and down and push his chin forward in an inefficient effort to make a connection with the audience. An AT teacher, using her hands or words, can gently encourage the singer to move into a coordinated position in the present moment. If I do this in a good-humored or perhaps mischievously playful way that engenders a giggle or a guffaw, students respond and accomplish coordination more quickly.

Core Practice, including both my serious interventions and silly pranks, is designed to discourage end-gaining and encourage students to engage in the moment-to-moment movement of performance practices as they emerge in silly or playful ways. End-gaining is endemic in rehearsal processes because rehearsals are, by definition, about moving forward into the future. We assume that we need to move ahead toward perfection. But perfection is impossible, as an understanding of play makes vividly clear. The metaphor I use for my work with play is, again, Schechner's "banana time." Slipping on a banana peel is always an accident or mistake: "Whoops!" The rug is pulled out from under us. Play in the context of banana time is, ultimately, about the "power of mistakes," about giving mistakes or "slip-ups" an honored place in creative work. Mistakes are decidedly productive. Stephen Nachmanovitch, in his book *Free Play: Improvisation in Life and Art* (1990), says, "The unconscious is the very bread and butter of the artist, so mistakes and slips of all kinds are to be treasured as priceless information from beyond and within" (p.89). Nachmanovitch is an improvisational string player who honors mistakes as an important and productive part of his artistic work. He describes playing an evening, outdoor concert in high humidity that causes the violin's bottom string to loosen and go out of tune. Instead of tuning the string, he worked with it, discovering a "new and interesting harmonic relation with the other strings" (p.91).

Jessica Johnson, in "The self-compassionate musician" (2016), is interested in how artists can approach their own shortcomings: "When we view our flaws with compassion we begin to realize they don't define us" (p.20). And yet, they do. They play out in inevitable, productive, and exciting ways as Huizinga, Schechner, and Nachmanovitch describe. Mistakes and slip-ups, which can lead to happily playful performances, are not flaws but rather opportunities to discover the present moment where surprising artistic insights can emerge. Audiences relish moments when they can watch performers regain their balance, remember a line they lost, or find the notes they forgot. Humans are, for the most part, kind and compassionate, even humored, by performers who recover from mistakes playfully and in the present moment. Part of the reason for this phenomenon is that mistakes suddenly swoop audiences into the present moment, right along with the performers. Heightened attention and delight ensue. Core Practice is not performance. It is not rehearsal. It exists in a liminal space where mistakes and slip-ups are the heart of the game.

Subsequent to Core Practice, my theatre students and I engage another activity that is deeply dependent on play: I call it Round Robin Improvisation. This activity is performed in an environment or landscape where we explore playful work with play texts, props, costumes, and rehearsal furniture. Similar work can be done with horns, pianos, flutes, drums, and oboes for instrumentalists; songs and arias for singers; and creative movement vocabularies for dancers. When I developed this activity, my primary objective was to teach and honor mindfulness and playfulness in theatre performance processes. I later learned that I could effectively weave AT into the practice.

Lesa Lockford and Ronald Pelias's approach to theatre improvisation inspired the structure of Round Robin Improvisation. In "Bodily poeticizing in theatrical improvisation: A Typology of performative knowledge" (2004), Lockford and Pelias say that, "no matter the form or aim of the improv, the performer's work requires a communicative connection." They describe improvisation as simple human interaction:

> Improvisational moments are engaged through an ongoing process of negotiation and coordination, through a positioning and repositioning of performers and their characters, which is done in an instant. Adapting to emergent circumstances, these performers are called to be aware communicators who can draw upon their cognitive, affective, and intuitive abilities—sometimes with great urgency—in order to absorb interactional details, create characters, and establish characters. (p.434)

Round Robin Improvisation features communicative connections and encourages students to draw on "emergent circumstances" as they come up in the work. Using the students' understanding of basic everyday interpersonal encounters, the activity encourages them to move forward through improvisational play, using the specifics of those circumstances by "absorbing interactional details" as they make discoveries.

To set the stage for the activity, I ask students to arrange the rehearsal furniture in our classroom in a rough circular formation so they can sit on or stand near a variety of levels and surfaces and easily see each other. They have square boxes and rectangular pylons of various sizes, platforms of varying heights, a doorframe, and sturdy chairs and tables to create an "environment" that forms the landscape for the playful work to come. I ask them to sit in this landscape aware of interesting sitting postures as raw material for the improvised "characters" they will create.

The action begins when the students identify a partner and, based on their sitting or standing positions in relation to their created landscape, partners, and others around them, improvise conversations inspired by their current experiences and interests. They come prepared with short memorized monologues and/or brief dialogues they are working on. When it seems appropriate, I ask them to interrupt conversations in progress either by beginning a new conversation or interjecting material from the texts they have prepared. I keep things moving by engaging in conversations and interjecting short monologues myself. I also play the role of subtext, handing out costume pieces and props, snacks, and bottles of water. I offer soft and delicate touch to encourage coordination. As in Core Practice, I whisper silly nothings into their ears to distract them and encourage giggles, keep them on their toes, and provoke productive, enlightening mistakes—slipping on banana peels, of course! Everyone tunes into the conversations that unfold around them. I ask them to respond richly to everything that is happening in every moment. I often tell them to work with folks across the space instead of those sitting near them. I ask them to move, sit, or stand next to new partners and start new conversations. I encourage them to move when they speak or stand or walk across the space. I suggest they use whatever they are experiencing in the present moment as well as what they experienced in Core Practice when they scanned their joints and whole bodies and imagined themselves performing. I quietly prompt the students to see, hear, taste, touch, and smell. I play music and sound effects. I change the lighting in the room.

They watch and listen attentively, senses on high alert, waiting for an opening to interrupt, using everything in the environment to color and texture their perceptions and performances. I ask them to listen for moments when they can easily pick up and expand on a conversation in process. I suggest they interrupt when the topic of an improvised conversation seems connected to the topic or emotional quality of the memorized text they have prepared. Inspiration for moving from one improvised conversation to another or weaving in the words from play texts can take many forms. The key is that the spoken words, rhythm and gesture, nuance, and movement from actor to actor, from couple to couple, never stop.

I want the students to move toward what the psychologist Mihaly Csikszentmihalyi called "flow." In his seminal work, *Flow: The Psychology of Optimal Experience* (1990), Csikszentmihalyi says that flow happens "when individuals are immersed in their activities to such an extent that they are completely absorbed and in the moment and nothing else seems to matter" (p.4). The students and I experience "flow" after a few awkward moments of Round Robin Improvisation when students drop lines in monologues and scenes or hesitate to join improvised conversations. Once we get into the "groove," my students and I move forward with only a rare hiccup along the way. We often sustain our states of Round Robin improvisational "flow" for 50 minutes or more. Merging mindful work in the present moment with AT ideas and interventions while traveling on a slippery trail of playfulness is fun and fruitful for young actors. They become completely immersed in the moment of activity, experiencing focus and spontaneity. During subsequent classes when monologue or scene work is on the docket, I continue to provide appropriate costumes and props, food and drink, silly whisperings, and AT interventions with hands and words. I disrupt, interrupt, needle, and provoke. They learn that they must always stay on their toes, always ready for a pratfall, a slip, a slide—an encounter with a banana peel that will shoot them without warning into the present moment.

We often work on monologues and scenes in our "environments" until formal scene or monologue showings loom. When the students perform, their bodies are easy and lively. Performances are nuanced and textured physically, vocally, and emotionally. Objectives are clear and students pursue them with energy and a determination to see their desires fulfilled! I teach acting theory, and we work on voice and movement skills before tackling Round Robin Improvisation and scene and monologue work. Skills and understanding solidify within our improvisational process. Students are relaxed and confident. They dabble in details because they have worked through a process of flow in a lush landscape of sensory, intellectual, and emotional richness and, most importantly, artistic discoveries.

These discoveries are made primarily through the improvised conversations that emerge along with material from play texts and my insistent and liberal sprinkling of proverbial "banana peels" throughout the rehearsal space. I engage my own playful activities and sneaky interventions to egg the students on, leading them toward discoveries I see or sense are lurking seductively in the environment we have created. In the process of either dodging or slipping on the "peels" I toss around through my silly and willy-nilly interventions, students enter the present moment and effortlessly calm their nervous energy. Stage fright dissipates, and the students can focus on the task at hand: pursuing objectives toward successfully performing monologues and dialogues more formally for scene showings.

In his article "Mindfulness: An operational definition" in *Clinical Psychology: Science and Practice* (2004), Scott Bishop describes:

> the moment when mindfulness begins bringing awareness to current experience—[participants are] observing and attending to the changing field of thoughts, feelings, and sensations from moment to moment—by regulating the focus of attention. This leads to a feeling of being very alert in the here-and-now. It is often described as being fully present and alive in the moment. (p.232)

Bishop's description of mindfulness is more intense than I have described it: It is "being *very* alert" and "present *and alive* in the moment." This is the experience my students and I have during

Round Robin Improvisation. It is intense and alive because our landscape is so rich with sensory and interactional details. It is also like the experience Virginia Woolf describes when she theorizes about the importance of the "shocks" that pulled her free from what she called the "cotton wool of daily life" and drew her—almost violently, as she describes it—toward artistic insights. Woolf's intuition can be usefully, albeit anachronistically, linked to Bishop's penetrating description of mindfulness. In her memoir *Moments of Being* (1985), Woolf says that we all tend to perceive the world through opaque "cotton wool" that makes it difficult for us to see beauty clearly. But, she says, "Behind the cotton wool is hidden a pattern; that we—I mean all human beings—are connected to this; that the whole world is a work of art; that we are parts of the work of art" (p.72). As an AT teacher, I am interested in subtle patterns of movement like the patterns beneath the "cotton wool" Woolf describes, which underlie and make performance activities possible. I am also interested in patterns of movement and sound that make what audiences see and hear beautiful.

Performers create from both internal and external patterns. Creating vivid and compelling characters involves strong and efficient breathing, rich gesture, and vocal texture. Creating vibrant music involves technical prowess, focus, and flair. Creating beautiful dance involves strength, flexibility, grace, elegance, and style. Behind the "cotton wool" of an artist's bodily surfaces lie the power and patterns that make performance possible. When those patterns emerge, artistry, or in Woolf's case, writing, flourishes. The artist is a specialist in a world where, as Woolf would have it, all of us are "parts of the work of art."

Woolf is not by any means a play theorist, but I want to suggest that she has a profound understanding of "banana time," of the ways human beings can discover the present moment through a playful phenomenon she calls a "shock." She describes having long periods of "non-being" in childhood:

Then, for no reason that I know about, there was a sudden violent shock; something happened so violently that I have remembered it all my life… [For instance,] I was looking at the flowerbed by the front door; "That is the whole," I said. I was looking at a plant with a spread of leaves; and it seemed suddenly plain that the flower itself was a part of the earth; that a ring enclosed what was the flower; and that was the real flower; part earth; part flower… I still have the peculiarity that when I receive these sudden shocks they are now always welcome; after the first surprise, I always feel instantly that they are particularly valuable. And so I go on to suppose that the shock-receiving capacity is what makes me a writer. I hazard the explanation that a shock is at once in my case followed by the desire to explain it. I feel that I have had a blow; but it is not, as I thought as a child, simply a blow from an enemy hidden behind the cotton wool of daily life; it is or will become a revelation of some order; it is a token of some real thing behind appearances; and I make it real by putting it into words. It is only by putting it into words that I make it whole. (Woolf 1985, pp.71–72)

The "revelations" of performers become something very different but no less "whole" than Woolf's "words." Her words appear on a page and move through storytelling brought to life in the imaginations of readers. Performers' revelations are brought to life through the surfaces of their bodies, inspiring imaginative reflection in the minds of audiences that experience and are engaged in communion with them in real time and space. It is useful to think about complex and often chaotic rehearsal processes as the "cotton wool" through which embodied artistry emerges. Round Robin Improvisation is designed to pull actors through the cotton wool and toward artistic prowess. When performing artists playfully slip on their banana peels and are transported into the present moment, something closely akin to Woolf's "shock" is the result.

It is also useful, I think, to conceptualize work with AT as analogous to Woolf's close exploration of the plant in her flowerbed. Having been transported into the present moment when receiving a shock, her insight is that the plant represents "the whole" because it is "part earth, part flower." The earth nourishes the plant, and the plant nourishes the earth. When we work as AT teachers, we nourish students with insights about the potential of a process that just might lead toward coordination and enrich their performances. As students become coordinated and their artistry appears on the scene to delight us, we are nourished. This process is "whole" in a way as profound as the beautiful whole Woolf reveals through the shock of her revelation in the flower garden.

In her book *Integrative Alexander Technique Practice for Performing Artists: Onstage Synergy* (2014), Cathy Madden implicitly invokes F.M. Alexander's psychophysical unity when she speaks of the "whole" from an AT teacher's and performer's perspective:

> When performers use the Alexander Technique, they consciously cooperate with the wholeness of our design in a way that allows all parts of the design (which includes new techniques and skills) to integrate in the service of the performance. The "complex association" of all these elements intentionally "working together" transforms the artist, and in turn the audience, in ways that go beyond what is possible if the person, techniques and performance skills are treated as separate parts. (p.304)

Playful processes in my pedagogies are the wiggly glue that allows AT and mindful performance practices to support coordination as my students and I work and play productively together—because we very seriously believe in and are devoted to "banana time"!

References

Alexander, F.M. (1910) *Man's Supreme Inheritance.* New York: Paul R. Reynolds.

Bishop, S. (2004) "Mindfulness: An operational definition." *Clinical Psychology: Science and Practice 11*, 3, 230–241.

Csikszentmihalyi, M. (1990) *Flow: The Psychology of Optimal Experience.* New York: Harper & Row.

Huizinga, J. (1950) *Homo Ludens: A Study of the Play-Element in Culture.* Boston, MA: Beacon Press.

Johnson, J. (2016) "The self-compassionate musician." *American Music Teacher,* August/September 2016, 19–22.

Kabat-Zinn, J. (2013) *Full Catastrophe Living.* New York: Bantam Books Trade Paperbacks.

Lockford, L. and Pelias, R. (2004) "Bodily poeticizing in theatrical improvisation: A typology of performative knowledge." *Theatre Topics 14*, 2, 431–443.

Madden, C. (2014) *Integrative Alexander Technique Practice for Performing Artists: Onstage Synergy*. Chicago, IL: Intellect, University of Chicago Press.

Nachmanovitch, S. (1990) *Free Play: Improvisation in Life and Art*. New York: G.P. Putnam and Sons.

Schechner, R. (1993) *The Future of Ritual*. New York: Routledge.

Woolf, V. (1985) *Moments of Being*. Orlando, FL: Harcourt Brace & Company.

Report on a Five-Day Introductory Class for the University of Washington School of Drama

Cathy Madden

AT Perspective

Current Short Description of the Alexander Technique

> *Constructive Conscious Kindness to Yourself,*
> *Cooperating with Your Design,*
> *Supporting Your Desires and Dreams*

The Alexander Technique provides us with keys to cooperating with our magnificent design, beginning with a constructive process for cooperating with the relationship between head and spine that is inherent in vertebrate coordination. The process is initiated by a wish that invites whole-self response (psychophysical response). I believe that it is necessary for this process to be directly applied to a current task for it to be effective, sometimes emphasizing this by saying that I teach Integrative Alexander Technique Performance Practice.

This requires an investigative process to identify the wish and sequence of the current task, if necessary replacing any obstacles to success with constructive choices. All this is done in the context of freedom to choose, knowing that each of us is perfect. By this I mean that we do perfectly what we know, and as our knowledge grows, what is perfect evolves. The way I teach the investigative sequence is essentially the process that F.M. Alexander describes in the first chapter of his book *The Use of the Self* (1984 [1932]):

I want to do something

I recognize something about it (i.e. either that I care about its quality or that I am concerned about its quality)

I decide to investigate (F.M. wording: *"freedom to choose"*)

I gather information
(F.M. wording: *"analyzing the conditions of use present"*)

From the information I create a plan[1]
(F.M. wording: *"reasoning out a means whereby"*)

I use the plan to do what I want
(F.M. wording: *"using the directions to carry out the means whereby"*)

Always knowing I am free to choose.

Personal Terms

I do not use many of the terms F.M. Alexander used in his original descriptions. I find that they are not as clear as actually saying what you want to have happen. In the previous sequence, I indicated where what I wrote corresponds to one of Alexander's phrases. There is one word I did not include that I believe the Alexander community uses in many ways. (In editing this collection, whenever an author chose to use it, I asked them to define or clarify it.) The word is *inhibition*.

While I don't use this word directly in my teaching unless I am in what I call "Alexander Land"—the particular world of AT teachers—I describe inhibition as an end result: Inhibition occurs when the old idea is replaced by a new one.

COORDINATION

My use of the word *coordination* is idiosyncratic. I intend it to refer to how all aspects of who we are contribute to our accomplishing whatever we are doing. At the Performance School, a center for the study of AT that I co-founded in Seattle, our definition was emblazoned on one of our brochures: "Coordination is the ability to conceive of an idea and carry that idea out as conceived." The quality of our coordination is determined by many factors; AT seeks to optimize the factors facilitating our search for excellence.

The first step in using AT is to ask yourself to coordinate. The sense in which I mean "coordinate" is the second definition from the Online Oxford English Dictionary: "To place or arrange (things) in proper position relatively to each other and to the system of which they form parts; to bring into proper combined order as parts of a whole" (OED 2013).

DESIGN

My use of *design* is also idiosyncratic: I use it in the sense of the OED definition related to artistic design, applying it to our humanness:

7.

a. The art of drawing or sketching; (hence) the process, practice, or art of devising, planning, or constructing something (as a work of art, structure, device, etc.) according to aesthetic or functional criteria; (also) this as a subject of study or examination.

b. The completed product or result of this process; the arrangement of features in something planned or produced according to aesthetic or functional criteria; a particular shape, style, or model. (OED 2013)

References

Alexander, F.M. (1984) *The Use of the Self.* Downey, CA: Centerline Press. (Original work published 1932.)

Online Oxford English Dictionary (OED) (2013) Oxford: Oxford University Press. Available at www.oed.com

This story of the University of Washington (UW) School of Drama's summer 2016 introductory class is offered as a model for a short course in the Alexander Technique for a university. Each class I design is unique. This chapter provides ideas for AT teachers new to group teaching or who are considering adding group teaching to their practices, documents the effectiveness of group teaching, offers a brief glimpse of academic structures (such as syllabi and grading), illustrates how an AT class serves other performing arts classes, and demonstrates specific teaching ideas.

To place this class in context: My UW School of Drama classes include graduate and undergraduate classes. Most of my work is with the Professional Actor Training Program (MFA), where I design a three-year sequence specific to the students of each class. While there is an overall arc of instruction, it is idiosyncratic year by year. In the undergraduate program, I have taught full-term, half-term, two-week, and five-day introductions.

This summer term five-day class, Drama 455, is offered for two credits. Fifteen students registered for the course. Three people assisted me in the course: Carol Levin, an AT teacher who trained with me, and Diego de Acosta and Crispin Spaeth, who are learning to teach. We met in the evenings from 6:30 to 9:30 p.m. The enrollment was mostly drama students, with a few others taking it for schedule reasons.

Syllabus

As preparation, the students receive a syllabus a few weeks before the class.

Drama 455

The Alexander Technique

Summer Term 2016

> *Be patient, stick to principle,*
> *and it will all open up like a great cauliflower.*
> *A.R. Alexander*

Cathy Madden

cathmadden@uw.edu

Office hours by appointment. I am generally available 15 minutes before class.

Class Requirements

Participation is 70% of your grade.

Reading/class responses are 20% of your grade.

Daily out-of-class experiment and report are 10% of your grade.

Text

Integrative Alexander Technique Practice for Performing Artists: Onstage Synergy by Cathy Madden.

This book is available through Amazon in either hard copy ($50) or Kindle edition ($20) and is also available on Google Play ($10). The instructor has a limited number of hard copies available for $40 in class.

Participation

You learn AT by using it. Please come each day with at least one question or activity to explore during the class.

If you will be gone from class due to illness, please leave me an e-mail message. If I do not receive a message, you are considered absent. Note that because participation is 70% of your grade and this is a five-evening class, absences rapidly

---

affect your grade. Three days late for class will be counted as one full day's absence. (There is an extra-credit option if unforeseen circumstances affect participation.)

Reading and Class Responses

There will be readings assigned Monday to Friday. Before 5 p.m. the following day, please send a 10–15 sentence e-mail that includes:

- Your response to the reading
- Any response to the class the evening before
- At least one question
- A short report about your out-of-class experiment (described following and in class).

The class responses can be 10 to 15 sentences in length.

Late reports receive 75% credit. (No reports accepted after June 27.)

Daily Out-of-Class Experiment

Pick one thing you do each day.

At least once a day, use AT as a primary tool to explore it.

Include a short response to your exploration in your daily e-mail to me.

Teaching Assistants for the Course

Diego de Acosta, Carol Levin, Crispin Spaeth

Monday, June 20

WHAT IS THE ALEXANDER TECHNIQUE?

Assignment: Due by 5 p.m. on Tuesday, June 21

Read Chapters 1 and 2 *Onstage Synergy*

E-mail reading and class responses including out-of-class experiment.

Tuesday, June 21

HOW DO WE WORK? AT IN PRACTICE

Assignment: Due by 5 p.m. on Wednesday, June 22

Read Chapters 3 and 4 *Onstage Synergy*

E-mail reading and class responses including out-of-class experiment.

Color *Anatomy Coloring Book* pages (Kapit and Elson 1993).

Wednesday, June 22

MINKING AND THOVING: SOME BELIEF CHANGERS; AT IN PRACTICE

Assignment: Due by 5 p.m. on Thursday, June 23

Read Chapters 5 through 8 *Onstage Synergy*

E-mail reading and class responses including out-of-class experiment.

Thursday, June 23

CONSTRUCTIVE THINKING: THE PROCESS OF AT

Assignment: Due by 5 p.m. on Friday, June 24

Read Chapters 9 and 10 *Onstage Synergy*

E-mail reading and class responses including out-of-class experiment.

Friday, June 24

INTEGRATIVE PRACTICE, THE PATH AHEAD

Assignment: Due by 5 p.m. on Saturday, June 25

Read Chapter 13 *Onstage Synergy*

E-mail reading and class responses including out-of-class experiment.

Elements of the Syllabus

Grading

How do you grade an AT class? Since grading based on each individual's coordination would be inappropriate, what criteria serve the learning environment best? Active presence in the class has proved to be the key to students' success. Thus, for me, participation makes up 70 percent of the grade. Students can pass the class solely if they are active day to day. Punctuality is included in my syllabus because while I am able to "go with the flow" when people arrive late, students in former classes gave feedback that it affected their ability to learn. The response papers and daily project are part of my current curriculum because, in my experience, they are the most effective out-of-class assignments for supporting student learning.

Reading

For the first time my book *Integrative Alexander Technique Practice for Performing Artists: Onstage Synergy* was available as a text for this course. Part One, "Performing Artists' Foundation for Using the Alexander Technique," is written corresponding to the sequence of learning that has emerged from years of AT introductions for performers and others. I was curious to see if it functioned in practice as I had written it. And it did. The questions I received in class comments (see next section) often would point to the material in the next reading assignment. Many responses said things like:

First off, I would like to say I noticed how aligned our activities were with what you wrote in your book. (Ad)

---

or:

A lot of the concepts at the end of Chapter 9 related to my discoveries in class yesterday. (G)

Class Responses (Written Work)

Various forms of quizzes, journals, and papers have always been part of the undergraduate class. While these have all proved useful, the e-mailed daily responses are wonderfully effective. Responses to the reading and class, questions, and brief reports on out-of-class projects start filling my inbox just before the 5 p.m. deadline each day. Most receive a brief personal response. Using this information,

I review my class plan, noting themes and questions to clarify that evening. These short missives give me a window into the needs of individuals and the class as a whole. Many members of the class have given me permission to quote their responses, and you will read their words throughout the chapter, identified by initials only.

Daily Out-of-Class Experiment

Because the mission is to enable students to use this work on their own, the daily project sets up this expectation immediately. Students are asked to "Pick one thing you do each day. At least once a day, use AT as a primary tool to explore it." Asking them to write about the project in their daily responses makes it much more likely that they will do it—even if they haven't done it yet that day, they can quickly do it as they write their responses. Teaching intention accomplished!

Daily Reports

Each daily report includes a sketch of the class plan, followed by a chronicle, including a description of selected events as well as student impressions.

Class 1: What Is the Alexander Technique?

MONDAY PLAN

1. Tear out paper people, write why they are taking the class on one side of the paper person, put their name on the other side

2. Intro to AT via the purple papers; pick the invented word

3. Opening round of turns with purple people

4. Small breakout groups to discuss why they are there, noting F.M.'s wish quote

5. The "why" reports

6. Syllabus and project explanation

7. Small breakout groups to pick project

8. End of class: Walking to the Strawberry Moon

CLASS CHRONICLE

Unusual art activities often begin my classes. About five minutes before the scheduled starting time, I distribute the materials. The chosen activity needs to be easily joinable as new people arrive. With something to do, the awkward silence that can precede a first class is replaced by casual conversations among class members. Starting early encourages promptness. Indirectly, people receive the message that you honor their time. The art project already invites the class to see the world a little differently. Ideally, the project is impossible to do right, wrong, or "perfectly." It is fun and funny.

As this class assembled, I handed purple paper directly to each person arriving, providing an informal moment of greeting, inviting them into the world of the class. The instructions are to tear a person out of the sheet of paper. If they ask for more explanation, I say the same words again as I make one myself. Some people attempt to make it "right" by folding the paper in half so the two sides match—but since they are tearing, the resulting figure still has uneven edges. There may be other clues about how people think about themselves in how their purple people look. Once the students had their creations, they had a moment to reflect, writing their motivations for study on the back of their paper person, readying them for the ensuing introduction.

At the official start time, I guided the group through a multiple-style, many-layered introduction to AT. My goal is to present it in enough ways to "match" as many learning styles as possible. You can find virtually full texts of my introduction to AT in the 2011 Congress Papers (Madden 2012) and the second chapter in my book. (Some students commented that it was helpful to read the introduction in the book after experiencing the introduction in class.) Some of the specific variations for this class included:

Welcome to this introduction to the Alexander Technique. I am delighted to be able to offer you some information about this practical tool that you can use in your daily and professional lives. My current short description of this process is:

> constructive conscious kindness to yourself
> cooperating with your design
> supporting your desires and dreams.

In a moment, we'll be talking about heads and spines; note that it is in service of:

> constructive conscious kindness to yourself
> cooperating with your design
> supporting your desires and dreams.

Since many of you are performers, I'll also offer you a quote from A.R. Alexander (the brother of the man who originated this process—we'll talk about his story in a later class): "The hallmarks of the Alexander Technique are creativity, spontaneity, and adaptability to change."

Then I launched into the class content. Key elements included:

- Selecting an active, playful way to introduce the significance of the head/spine relationship in human behavior. I turn the lecture format around and create the lecture through leading the students through a discovery process.

- Guiding them through their first use of the sequence of the AT process so that their first experiments are without my direct help. I want them to be the leaders in their learning from their first encounter with the work. When they ask later, "How do I do this myself?" I want to be able to say honestly, "You already have."

The purple people returned as the "subjects" of the first experiments. First I asked the students to put the paper people somewhere nearby so they can pick them up off the floor. They picked them up as they usually do. Then I asked them to consciously introduce a scrunch between head and spine, and report how many other things are affected by that action. With this active approach, students discover for themselves that the dynamic relationship between head and spine is a key factor in vertebrate coordination. We are replicating in a condensed form Alexander's original discovery.

The experiment continued: "For the next experiment, please start out scrunching between head and spine as you pick up the object, and partway through picking it up change your mind and stop the extra scrunching." Each student—in varying degrees—replaced the interference in the relationship between their head and spine simply by choosing to "unscrunch."

Next came the explanation of the need for an *invented word*—a verb defined as the action of restoring the relationship between head and spine, cooperating with the design of human coordination. I briefly explained that in my experience this has worked well, because any word we already know carries our past meanings with it. "If we want to embrace learning something new, it works best to have a new word, one that has no previous associations with it, one that we create meaning for by our discoveries in class."

Offering the class choices for the invented word saves time. Noting that our class began on the night of the Strawberry Moon, my suggestions were based on Native American names for this lunar phenomenon. The class selected the Anishinaabe/Chippewa word for strawberry moon—*ode'imini-giizis*, which we shortened to *imini*. This name for the June moon contains a bit of learning poetry since it indicates the time to gather ripening fruit. The class repeated the task of reaching for the purple people with a bit of a squish between head and spine, speaking the word *imini* as they decided to "unsquish."

Following this introductory material was an opening round of individual turns within the group—using picking up the paper people as the task. One of the advantages of using the same activity, such as picking the paper person up off the floor, is that the class has already seen each other do this multiple times. When they do it individually, they tend not to be concerned that other people are watching them—it has become normal.

An important first step in moving to individual turns is a description of how touch, using my hands to teach, may be part of the lesson, while also noting that this teaching tool is optional. If anyone has concerns, I ask them to let me know; I tell them that I trust them to take care of themselves. My explanation for the use of touch in teaching is "My primary way to use my hands in teaching is to 'follow you as you change as a yes to the new idea.'" During the introduction, I told a story about how we perfectly do what we intend based on the information we have at this moment in time—including that our current information has perfectly led us to seek more information. "If I use my hands as part of the teaching process, it seems to help you stay with the new idea rather than the old 'perfect' idea for a split second longer so that you can experiment with a new option."

My whole introduction is designed so that everyone understands their agency in the lesson—I emphasize that they are the ones who can ask themselves to *imini* so that their heads can move so that all of them can follow so that they can do what they are doing.

In the class, I experienced some changes when I picked up the paper person and walked using the technique, and also saw some amazing changes in other classmates. When all the movement is following the head and spine relationship, it is almost effortless and gets rid of all unnecessary things. I am not going to pretend that I know all this, but it is a good experience. (Ju)

Following the opening round, we formed four discussion groups (each led by myself or one of my assistants). The topic was prefaced by a quote from F.M. Alexander: "It is the wish, the conscious desire to do a thing or think a thing which results in adequate performance" (Alexander 1995, p.81). Students talked about what brought them to the class and in the process began to know my assistants and each other more—beginning to develop a learning community.

As we came back together, I "read the room" and thought that, for this class, it seemed important to get in motion again. I invented a way for the students to share their goals with the whole class. Each person chose a spot in the room and walked to it while saying what they had said in the discussion group—continuing to build the constructive learning community. They had their first exploration of AT and walking while also metaphorically moving toward their desires.

Individual lessons began just before our break time (about 8 p.m.) and continued after the break, giving everyone a window into the process of a more detailed lesson. Many of the students were eager to start experimenting. Here is a pair of complementary student responses:

The evening class brought me a lot of different joy and knowledge, such as the performance from the students, picking up the paper person, and the walking around activity. It makes me understand how the spine and head work. The efficiency to use our whole body helps us to improve a lot of different movements. For example, the student who sang in the class found out something new from AT—it helps her voice get louder and clearer. It is really amazing to see how people improve their performance skills. (P)

My experience with singing in class yesterday was also phenomenal—I never thought about performance as an excited state, and that I had myself caught in a vicious cycle wanting to suppress the adrenaline. (A)

With an eye on the clock, I explained the details of the syllabus around 8:45 p.m., including an explanation of the daily project. Following that we returned to small groups (rotating to a new teacher) to discuss possible daily experiments. It was my hope that by selecting these before the class ended, I could ensure doable choices and clarify the assignment as necessary (see Exhibit 1, Daily Project Reports). This also facilitated immediate implementation. My plan for the end of class was walking to view the Strawberry Moon through the windows of the classroom.

My impressions after the first meeting: Surprise filled the room when they learned where the head sits on the spine and where the arm attaches to the body; breathing needed attention/information; a theme of being your own size emerged; the usual need to debunk posture, grounding, and so forth. As the learning community developed, the class started to participate with enthusiasm, asking and asking and asking!

In reading their response e-mails, the dominant issues—expectedly—were about how to know whether or not what they were doing was right; when could one use the process—all the time, sometimes, occasions that wouldn't work; and confusion in trying to get a specific feeling for the process itself.

I wonder if it is possible to make every position more comfortable just using *imini*? Or if there are occasions when one must change our physical environment so as to *imini* well? (A)

Additionally, I am curious whether a "master" of AT consciously employs it in ALL of their everyday activities (opening doors, picking things up off the ground), consciously or subconsciously. (T)

I addressed these issues in brief e-mail responses and planned to continue responding to their queries during Tuesday's class. What was very exciting to note was the abundant and enthusiastic experimentation that was going on: Between 9:30 p.m. Monday and 5 p.m. on Tuesday, AT had been applied to an interview class, basketball, jogging and walking, piano, Suzuki training, driving, dancing, sit-ups and sitting, guitar, drumming, and monologues. Some of these represented their out-of-class experiments, but many more were moments in life. They were doing the work to make the process their own:

I used AT today in playing a drumming exercise called 8/25. I played it three times, once without thinking of my head/spine/body, once scrunched, and once with AT. The first rep felt a little tense, the second rep felt especially tense in my shoulders, and I believe I lost concentration on the third rep, because it felt wonderful for the first half and then switched to restrictions halfway through. In any case, I did experience some sort of connection between my head/spine relationship and how my hands/wrists moved throughout the exercise. (T)

When I came home, I picked up my guitar and set up a video camera, attempting to use this technique. Granted, I only had one day under my belt of learning this technique. However, to my surprise, I noticed a change. When I played the guitar before, my body was uncomfortably hunched over the instrument as if I was hugging it. But when I straightened my back and moved only my head to look down at the guitar, it gave my arms more room to move and hit those chords correctly. (J)

Class 2: How Do We Work? AT in Practice
TUESDAY PLAN

1. Walks at 6:22 p.m.

2. Three turns using paper people to determine lesson order

3. Draw your skeleton

4. Breakout groups with skeleton

5. Walks

6. Three turns

7. Break

8. Breathing discussion and small groups with breath or sound focus

9. Three turns

10. Group juggling

11. Three turns

12. Walking with three foci

13. Four turns

14. Small groups with daily activity

15. Finish

CLASS CHRONICLE

My assistants greeted the students at the door with a sign-in sheet requesting both their name and what they wanted to explore in class that day. This sheet became my attendance/participation record and expedited the class by asking students to commit to an activity. I gave quick lessons in walking before the official start time. When people join a room that is already in motion, the message as they enter is about movement, change. These quick lessons also mirror how we use AT in life—quickly, simply, practically.

The central event of the night was the "draw your skeleton" event. I handed out a piece of paper—pre-graded with stars to assure them it is not a test, with the instructions to draw their skeleton (see Exhibit 2, Skeleton Drawing). I believe I first heard this idea from Barbara Conable. It is another version of discovery learning rather than lecture. The class exclaim and sometimes moan as they draw, discovering that they have some gaps in their conception of themselves. The skeleton drawing is a second-day class event because I want the first night's message to be clearly about whole self. We need the anatomy, though, because we are inevitably going to talk about our structure as we go through the week. Questions about structure were already present in the first day's class.

A full-size skeleton—"Skelly"—appeared in the classroom as the students finished their drawings. First, they simply looked at their drawing and the model to see what they saw as different—resisting any urge to correct their own drawing. We broke into groups to look at the drawings and discuss them. These small breakout groups gradually coalesced into a whole-group discussion of key points in our design.

Tuesday's class, when we looked at the skeleton, was fascinating. It's scary to think where we think our joints are, and find out where they actually are. It was also fascinating to see our body as not something that is in isolation from the different parts, and know that everything moves as a whole. This concept was demonstrated clearly when we stood on one foot and breathed in and out to see how our whole body moves together when we breathe. (A)

The evening class brought me a lot of different fun and enjoyment, such as the seeing our classmate using the AT to do performance and then drawing the skeleton. It is such a surprise to me that I have no clue about my own body. And when I drew the skeleton, I could see myself missing a lot of different parts. And, this makes me understand how important AT is. (P)

Individual turns ensued, the order determined by pulling a purple person out of the hat. This is faster than calling for volunteers, particularly the first time around, and establishes the classroom practice of turn taking. Using the playful element of chance uses time more effectively. Anyone can pass and put their purple person back in the hat for later—it is vital that everyone experiences freedom of choice throughout their learning.

After the class break and a few more turns, I introduced an exploration of breathing and we broke into small groups to experiment.

I also had a big moment when I was working on voice with Diego and he explained that the abdominal cavity curves like a kidney bean and goes deep into the pelvis. Then when I asked to coordinate and speak my monologue there were vibrations and engagement of sound happening in my pelvis which is the lowest I've ever felt my voice coming from in my body, but it had a much richer and smoother quality which was exciting. (G)

Here are some reports of the individual lessons that followed:

I tried to sing with your help of using AT and it came out beautifully. I felt more air coming in and out in a smooth fashion, and my voice sounded better. (J)

In class, when you taught us that the bend at the hip when sitting down was a leg movement, it completely changed the way I thought of sitting. (A)

My immediate answer to "Where does your breath/voice go?" is a clear example of how much perception can affect an individual's performance and coordination to the point where it can be crippling for a career. (D)

Everybody's activities were relevant to daily life, and it felt like there was much to gain from being omniservant [author's note: a play on *observant*, emphasizing all senses] in watching them. (A)

My assisting teachers offered quick turns as the students were observing lessons. These are like the quick walks—in-the-moment, real-time opportunities to cooperate with our design in service of our life. I explain that in class we slow our exploration of an activity down to examine the component parts, and ultimately, this is in service of making new choices at the pace of life. The assistants help me maximize every participant's opportunities for learning during every class. There are questions that the students ask the assistants that they are reluctant to ask me or ask in front of the whole group. The small groups give everyone discussion time and continue to build the learning community.

My questions to myself following the class were to consider ways to emphasize that AT can be used to enhance the ability to follow impulse, to continue looking for ways to coax a relationship to process rather than "getting it right," and *imini* endurance, what F.M. called "a wish you carry with you through activity" (Alexander and Fischer 1995, p.169).

Anatomy and breathing responses were the "a-has" of the e-mailed responses:

I have many memories of being told to try to bend in places that do not actually allow the body to bend, or to breathe into my arms. Both of these I was told with the intention of creating a graceful quality that I have seen a few of my classmates achieve through whole-body coordination instead of physically impossible analogies. (G)

Many questions about how to use AT for warm-ups of different kinds influenced my planning for the next night:

How can I use AT to warm up for a show/audition/performance? Even though I feel like I'm learning a lot,

I'm still unsure whether using it by myself will be effective. I'm guessing the answer is to keep doing what I was doing before, but with AT? Are there any particular warm-ups you have found useful for yourself before performances? I always feel warmed up after performances are over, which is quite useless. (A)

Class 3: Minking and Thoving: Some Belief Changers; AT in Practice

WEDNESDAY PLAN

1. Numbered papers: Write name and short definition of AT

2. Pre-warm-ups

3. Perhaps trio warm-ups

4. Groups; Crispin with the student who was sick last night for skeleton drawing

5. "This is my" game—with instructions for reaching

6. Then art gallery exchange with arms

7. Turns 1 to 5

8. Unified field of attention/group juggling

9. Small groups

10. Second group of five individual turns

11. Discussion on impulse

12. Third group of five individual turns

13. Review of steps wanting–recognizing–deciding–asking–experimenting, perhaps with the action of sitting (to address G's response)

CLASS CHRONICLE

The title for the class came from a former student whose conceptions of thought and movement were so separate from each other that, if you said one or the other word, he completely went out of coordination. For him, we invented some words—conflating thinking and moving into the new words *minking* and *thoving*. The plan for the third night was to practice mink and thove.

Quick walking turns began about five minutes before the class. As class members arrived, one of the assisting teachers asked each of them to pick randomly a small, already numbered, sheet of paper. Their instructions were to write their name and current definition of AT on the paper. The papers served as an attendance record, determined the order of individual turns, and provided me with a quick check to see if any ideas about AT could use more explication. Here are a few of the answers, noting that these came after two nights of class:

AT is a system of practice that seeks to bring the body/mind into more efficient and coordinated movement following the natural design of the body.

AT is everything or it is a part of our life. We can use AT to do anything, any time. I believe that everyone has their own AT, so I cannot say what AT is, but I would say it is part of our life.

Optimization through calibration.

The relationship with the head and spine to overall movement/coordination; working in accordance to the optimal design.

The skills to choose to act with your whole body when doing a task.

The ability to recognize and coordinate our body and mind to help us operate at our optimal, natural, and most efficient capacity.

About a third of the responses talked specifically about the body, while another third emphasized whole-selfness.

In the responses to Class 2, students indicated a high desire to integrate the process with what they were doing—particularly expressing a desire to know how to warm up using AT. While there are no AT warm-ups per se, I introduced a sequence of "pre-warm-ups" that I designed for the Professional Actor Training Program.

The first warm-up uses AT while looking at yourself doing a sequence of small movements from foot to head. "*Imini* so that your head can move so that all of you can follow so that you can look at and move your right foot—watch it moving, front side, back side, right side, left side, upside-down side, inside, outside, all sides, all ways." And so on, through left foot, right lower leg, left lower leg, and so forth. My prompts emphasize that we are waking up our instrument to ready ourselves for action. On this evening the warm-up also playfully reviewed the previous night's anatomy discoveries. The series creates an operational active definition of minking and thoving. The direct self-observation reinforces each person's image of themselves as a three-dimensional being.

A similar vocal series followed, using AT throughout a "breathing into humming with the intent to communicate" warm-up. This series emphasizes dimensionality by asking the group to hear the sounds all around them. Including the intent to communicate is important because connecting the sound-making to the reason you are doing it facilitates a cooperating coordination.

The intent of these pre-warm-ups is to consciously use AT to acknowledge, "wake up," our whole self, readying ourselves for ensuing tasks.

As we moved into the first round of individual turns, one of my teaching assistants took a student who had been sick on the second night aside and did the skeleton drawing with him. The e-mail responses contained a lot of anatomy questions, and throughout the evening, I answered those questions as we did individual turns.

The next integration project sprang from a practical need—returning the previous evening's skeleton drawing and collecting the coloring book pages that were their homework. The task was to replace their drawing of the skeleton with their coloring book page. We rehearsed the sequencing of the action using AT as the primary tool.

1. *Imini* so that your head moves so that all of you follows so that you look at your hands.

2. *Imini* so that your head moves so that all of you follows so that you lead with your fingers to your drawing, extending your elbow joint.

3. *Imini* so that your head moves so that all of you follows so that you move your fingers around the paper in such a way that you could pick it up.

4. *Imini* so that your head moves so that all of you follows so that you move your fingers toward the paper to hold it.

5. *Imini* so that your head moves so that all of you follows so that you flex at your elbow joint to bring the paper to you.

And then we rehearsed this in reverse—putting a paper back down.

Including AT at each change in action was systematically practiced. This led to the discussion of what I call *studied rehearsed plans*:

> *Studied rehearsed plans* are developed skills that serve the desired action. The primary studied rehearsed plan relates to the underlying coordination—"Ask myself to coordinate so that my head can move so that all of me can follow so that I can do what I am doing." The secondary studied rehearsed plans are those that include using the Alexander Technique for a specific skill or event. The primary studied rehearsed plan organizes your underlying coordination so that the secondary studied rehearsed plans can carry out your performance plan. (Madden 2014, p.295)

While initially studying AT seems to be more about restoring our ability to cooperate with our design, its ultimate value lies in its ability to assure a constantly evolving, usually pleasurable, efficient response to the tasks of our lives. We rehearsed this series of *studied rehearsed plans* together, then each individual carried through their own action and also watched 14 other people do it—reinforcing the sequence multiple times. My intent is to create an evolving plan for reaching for anything in life.

Individual lessons within the group made up the remainder of the class. Everyone witnessed one person's continually improving plank position. He had worked on it himself at home, had assistance in his small group, and took another step with a lesson in front of the whole group. I asked one young woman, who had told us on the first day that she was in significant pain every time she sat, "How is sitting going?" Her answer was a sudden joyful smile: "Sitting is fun!"

One student's turn in class began with the question "What is the right way to stand?" I took the opportunity to turn his question into a whole-class game. Each person in the class was invited to stand in a different way—and we used AT to stand efficiently in all these different ways, emphasizing that all the ways were right. The man who asked the question went last, using AT as he took an unusual pose. He seemed satisfied with the exploration. Throughout the lessons I was analyzing movement, emphasizing anatomy as necessary.

The next student got up for his turn and said, "But really, what is the right way?" I was so surprised, reminded again of the strength of rightness versus wrongness in many of our beliefs. This time I talked about how we are constantly in movement. While we could identify balance locales—the atlanto-occipital joint, center of the glenohumeral joint, spine as it comes into the pelvis, hip joint, center of the knee joint, and ankle joint—we are never exactly in the same spot. I used the word *hover* to continue emphasizing that there was not one right place. Since our balance changes every time we breathe, our ideal balance is hovering in relation to these balance references. I made a note to think of another way to approach these questions the next day. (Note: *hover* worked very well as a concept for this group, but in other groups, the word has not proved so useful. I wouldn't recommend it as a word/concept for all occasions.)

Throughout the night I verbalized the sequence of each lesson— they began with desire, recognized that there was something to explore, decided to explore it, and used AT to do it. My commentary was laying the foundation for introducing the full sequence in Class 4.

Some student responses to the night:

I discovered that thinking of my head/spine relationship with a floating indication of "center" helped me feel ready to move because it unlocked my knees when I stood there. It also improved my circulation. (G)

The practice of standing makes me understand the belief that I learned before is wrong. It is because our spine is not straight up. So, we should redefine the word "standing straight" because it is not accurate. (P)

When Ju practiced her sit-up in class yesterday, it surprised me. Because this allowed me to unlock more ways to use AT, especially in my own training. (Je)

What we learn in this class and in this book is really a belief change. (J)

We ended the evening with group juggling—a game I learned from *More New Games* (Fluegelman 1981, p.61). In it, the group creates a pattern to throw a ball. They started with one ball, then I added another ball to the pattern, then another, and another. They were juggling about seven balls at the end. This is a way to reinforce replacing old ideas of focus and concentration with minking and thoving. Indirectly, it offers an opportunity to practice responding to increasing challenges through asking to *imini* rather than tightening.

More and more questions about how to do specific things arrived in class and in my e-mail each day, including how to coordinate to the heightened energy of performance:

I would like to know how to maintain performance excitement without tightening or feeling like needing to calm down. (G)

In my mind (and body I guess), it's always a matter of either-or—I either am observing and interacting, or I am thinking. Similarly, I try to "suppress my nervousness" so that I can think, but I guess in trying to suppress my body I also stop/ignore thinking. Which altogether ruins my performances. (A)

Numerous e-mails talked about experiments they were doing on their own:

Something that happens once in a while is a small muscle soreness behind my right clavicle. Trying different arm movements, I could not seem to pinpoint which movement was causing the tightening of that particular muscle. I experimented with crossing my arms and putting my hands on my shoulder to release the pull-back tension. I noticed that instantly the cramp disappeared. I discovered that it was the constant pull-back posture that was causing fatigue in my right shoulder. (Jo)

Some of the questions pointed to the central topic of the next day's class: What is the process?

Despite the focus on the steps/process of the technique that we went over last night, I wonder if we could take a particular physical activity and clarify what we would say to ourselves with each step in order to fully use the technique? (TJ)

Class 4: Constructive Thinking: The Process of AT
THURSDAY PLAN

1. Sign-in sheet in order

2. Walks, turns into triangles

3. Small group (20 minutes)

4. Intro of the steps (30 minutes)

5. Feathers

6. More individual turns

7. End with progressive group

CLASS CHRONICLE

After two questions on Wednesday evening about the right way to stand, indirectly challenging the search for "the right way" was important. On Wednesday night as class began, everyone stood on a dense foam pad so that they could receive outside feedback that our balance changes throughout every breath.

I tried sitting on my bed for the out-of-class experiment, and found that like the blue mat, my body swayed with every breath I took. That way, I had an internal rhythm that I was subconsciously rocking to while sitting down. I used AT to cooperate with this internal rocking of my body so that I could curve my spine in a way that was more comfortable for sitting on a bed. (A)

Standing on the pad evolved into walks, then into a walking game: As everyone walks, each person has the intention of keeping two people in the group in their field of attention—secretly. I note that no one else knows if somebody has lost their people. Since I am playing too, I acknowledge when I lose my people—modeling process rather than rightness.

Small group sessions followed the warm-up to create a foundation for the explicit introduction of the AT process, providing "fresh" experiences to explicate the didactic information that was to follow. I wrote the sequence up on the board and we worked through all the ideas until the evening break:

Wanting
Recognizing
Deciding
Gathering information
Creating a plan
Inviting yourself
To action
Knowing you have freedom to choose.

(For a more complete discussion, see Madden 2014, Chapter 9.)

Following the break, I offered a game with peacock feathers I learned from AT teacher Wolfgang Weiser to further challenge the notion of one right way to stand. Simply balance a peacock feather on your finger. To accomplish the task you need to move with the feather. Each student got a peacock feather as we rejoined class. It worked:

The most amazing experience was the feather because I always have a hard time understanding the process of coordinating (your head can move so that all of you can follow so that you can do what you are doing). But the exercise helped me understand. When the feather went forward and backward, I could feel that my whole body was trying to coordinate. (P) (This comment was from the student who had asked, "What is the right way to stand?")

Individual turns emphasizing noting the steps of the process followed. We continued with a progressive series of lessons: One person has a short turn with an activity, then everyone does that activity. A second person has a short turn, then everyone does the first activity and the second activity. By the end of the progression, there are 15 activities everyone has done multiple times.

Two class responses directly related to the evening's focus on the AT process:

Last night, I got very clear about the sequence in the constructive plan to experiment with AT: wanting, recognizing, and deciding, creating a plan, gathering information, asking, to action. Actually it is very inspiring to me about the freedom of choice. Recently, I have been trying a new diet that is really hard for a person like me who really likes to eat. Last night, I really *wanted* to eat some unhealthy food such as burgers, but I *asked* myself if I really wanted to eat that or just had psychological hunger. Then I *recognized* that I don't really want to eat them now, it is that they look and smell so good. So I could still notice the smell and watch people eating on the street (*gathering information*), but not really having to eat them now (*deciding*). I *made a plan* to eat a burger tomorrow for lunch if I wanted to. This is really cool because I could never do this before. I used to eat whenever I wanted and not really be able to control myself when it comes to food. Sometimes I know I am not eating good things or in a healthy style. I realize that this is a funny way to use AT just to make a choice. This experience is somehow similar to the idea of constructive thinking in the book which guides my experiments and I can coordinate my body to do what I want it to do. (Ju)

In Chapter 9, I was inspired to really think about this when I did my task today. So I asked to *imini* so my head can move so the rest of me could follow so I could do my task after acknowledging my want (to stomp harder), my recognition that I wanted to improve the skill, and my goal to connect my foot to the ground. I gathered the information about the activity I needed to complete and how my body was fitting in the design that best suits itself, and created the plan, keeping in mind my body and the task at hand. And then I did the task using AT. Usually the first time I do it during the day, it really doesn't do much, which I think is because I'm remembering the feeling and not the technique, and without the feedback from the class it's a little bit harder for me to intellectualize in the moment. Then I gathered information by comparing my result with my goal, which was to stomp harder, which it was unclear if I did. So I created a new plan by filming my process with my computer to see if there was any change in case I didn't feel it in the moment or had difficulties reflecting afterward. So I experimented again and again, continually gathering information and creating a plan. And in that moment, I figured out how I can work with it on my own. Internalizing this structure and just keeping experimenting and assessing and recalibrating. I suppose it was my "a-ha" moment this week where I really felt like I "figured it out." (N)

Class 5: Integrative Practice: The Path Ahead

FRIDAY PLAN

1. Begin with walks

2. Three individual lessons from last night (we ran out of time!)

3. First small groups with process worksheets

4. Questions/turns

5. Relay change-of-thought game

6. Questions/turns

7. A bit on going forward from here…

8. Communication (Uta Hagen questions to walk across the room)

9. Questions/turns

10. Small groups

11. Games

- pick-up sticks

- "Tip the Waiter" game

- spring

- put a skeleton together

12. End with maze, then spring again

CLASS CHRONICLE

The last night of class provides a pathway for future exploration. We began with quick walks, noting the passive movement of the spine as people walked—reinforcing that this process is about movement rather than position. Then we caught up on some promised lessons from the night before. The overall plan was to alternate small groups and the whole group, give some structure to thinking about AT and communication, and end with a variety of games that playfully highlight the many ways this work can be used.

In the small groups, students were offered worksheets so that they could note the steps of the process for their own as well as someone else's turns (see Exhibit 3, AT Process Worksheet). In analyzing their own turns, they review how the process unfolds in their own work. By doing the same thing with someone else's lesson, they get a teacher's-eye view of the process. This in-class practice led to a discussion of how they carry out the work on their own, noting that the reading assignment for that night—deliberately an assignment given after the last class—tells F.M. Alexander's story and is a great guide for continuing self-learning. I always include some version of "The Evolution of a Technique" from *The Use of the Self* (Alexander 1984 [1932]) in the class reading assignments so that my students have a life-long guide to using AT on their own—even if they never take another class.

Lessons and small groups as well as two whole-group explorations alternated during the evening. A relay change-of-thought game looked at using a change in direction as a cue to renew *imini* so that you could walk another way. Several "teams" lined up opposite each other. The first person on one side walked to a person on the other side. As they arrived, the second person asked to *imini* to walk back to a person on the other side. It was simple and quick—not a race, just a practice at using external cues to facilitate a change process.

The second whole-group experiment used AT with a set of questions from Uta Hagen's *Respect for Acting* (Hagen with Frankel 1973), which could be used to prepare for an acting scene, meeting, audition, and so on.

After completing rounds of turns and small groups, the final series of AT and games occurred. Each of the assistants and I offered a game to use AT with—one group had giant pick-up sticks, one group had a "Tip the Waiter" balance game, one group had a giant spring to pass around arm to arm, and one had a puzzle of a skeleton to put together. Games are great fun—the atmosphere is all play, learning outside the sea of right and wrong.

This led to one last full group game—the maze. We literally took the chairs in the room and created a maze. The maze had an entrance and a destination, an exit. The first round was simply to find a way through the maze, asking to *imini* at each change of direction within. Everyone had to find their own unique way through the maze. Then my assistants became "obstacles" in the maze, literally getting in the way of progress. Again the instructions were to *imini* when encountering the obstacles, and find a new way around. A lot of laughing—and learning—takes place:

During class last night, I really loved doing the games in groups and walking in the maze. It shows that we can use AT in all kinds of human movement. (Ju)

Especially in the maze and my personal experiment, the maze helped me understand that we can use AT whenever we are facing a problem. (P)

Student Responses on the Course

This echoes the theme from yesterday's reading of "Take care of yourself before helping others." It affirms something I've heard from many coaches and teachers before this class. What I realize now about AT is that it gives me the tools to use a process to actually put this into practice to be kinder to myself instead of just believing it in theory. (G)

I really appreciated this class in that I updated my information about human anatomy and our head/spine relationship. It also changed my perspectives and corrected my old beliefs. Now I just think this class should be required for all performers. I was wondering how could I relate AT to psychology? (Ju)

Last class session I finally understood the essence of AT. During class, I repeatedly changed my body from going to and from *imini*. I even practiced trivial actions such as holding a pencil, drinking a water bottle, and opening a door. I didn't realize how often I was using so many muscles unnecessarily at a time before finding out about this method. Now for every action I was doing the technique, it made me understand my own anatomy in a more focused way. Actually, when I typed that sentence just now, I fixed myself so that the way I was sitting at my computer desk was more relaxed, which is kind of funny because I'm starting to become more conscious in my actions. (Je)

I think one of the things I've really enjoyed about AT is that there is no one way to do it, so I never feel the need to be "correct." Learning about how F.M. Alexander created the technique seems so true to how the technique actually is—he had a question, had a need to answer the question and improve his head/spine relationship. Today as I went to rehearsal, as I was waiting to get into the scene work, I found time to *imini* so that my head could move so that the rest of me could follow and consider my given circumstances and jump into the scene with a level of excitement rather than "relaxing." I felt so validated when my director commented on my energy today, and I don't feel like I'm anymore energized than usual, but I suppose my expression of that energy is clearer because I'm no longer scrunching my neck/spine when I'm doing any sort of activity. (N)

Conclusion

Each time I teach an introductory series, I relearn how utterly simple and useful AT is. I have explored it for years—and people don't need to study it for years to be able to use it. They use it successfully in inspiring ways from the first day they learn it.

Throughout the description of the classes, I have noted sources for teaching ideas when I remember them, and I list some of the many resources at the end of the chapter. I have been blessed to have many models of good teaching, as well as many classes to help me refine what is most effective. My overall intent is to present the information from as many angles as possible, in a wide variety of ways, offering abundant opportunities for repetition, omniservation, reflection, and repetition.

I mentioned at the beginning of this chapter that my introductions evolve. As I revise this chapter, I am planning my next introduction—and noting that my plan is different from how I started this class.

EXHIBIT 1: DAILY PROJECT REPORTS

Active investigation is the heart of the class, and these three daily project examples illustrate how I facilitate student confidence in the process. Key to this project is their volition—they choose an investigation they care about.

Ar's Project: Sitting

After Class 1: I have always found it hard to sit comfortably, especially in school chairs, because it never feels like they support my back properly. Last night, while sitting back into my couch, I asked my head to *imini* so that my head could move so that I could rest it on the couch, and I found my head "needed" to move backwards into the couch, and then I felt so relaxed that I realized how tired I was and almost fell asleep right there!

After Class 2: In class, when you taught us that the bend at the hip when sitting down was a leg movement, it completely changed the way I thought of sitting. I have been trying to bend at the hip first while sitting down, but it's kind of hard to remember what I did. I think I'm trying to re-create the feeling. I forgot what it was that you said about why the hip needs to bend first when sitting down. Is it because that is the first point of contact and so we need to "lead" with it?

After Class 3: For my out-of-class experiment, I tried sitting on a bar stool, so a chair that does not have backing. I always feel pain in my lower back from sitting too long in a bar stool. I tried last night to sit with AT, but I was too tired so I think that's why it didn't work. When I tried it again this morning, it was better, I felt like I wasn't "squishing" everything into my lower back. The problem with bar stools is that they tend to be higher off the ground, so I have to push myself back farther with my hands after initially sitting on the edge. I think in doing this, I "let go" of AT, and then I try to do it again once I've properly sat on the bar stool. I need to work on using AT throughout the movement.

After Class 4: I tried sitting on my bed for the out-of-class experiment, and found that like the blue mat, my body swayed with every breath I took. That way, I had an internal rhythm that I was subconsciously rocking to while sitting down. I used

AT to cooperate with this internal rocking of my body so that I could curve my spine in a way that was more comfortable to sitting on a bed.

After Class 5: While I was sitting on the bar stool last night, I tried using AT throughout the whole process, and I think I managed to do it :) I'm working on not obsessing if I'm doing it throughout the whole process. I'm learning to start with AT, and then just trust myself that I will continue to use it throughout the process.

T's Project: Drumming

After Class 1: I used AT today in playing a drumming exercise called 8/25. I played it three times, once without thinking of my head/spine/body, once scrunched, and once with AT. The first rep felt a little tense, the second rep felt especially tense in my shoulders, and I believe I lost concentration on the third rep, because it felt wonderful for the first half and then switched to restrictions halfway through. In any case, I did experience some sort of connection between my head/spine relationship and how my hands/wrists moved throughout the exercise.

After Class 2: How do you differentiate between necessary and unnecessary tension when you're executing something physically (what's necessary and what's hindering)? My attempts at 8/25 today helped to originate that question. I did the same process as yesterday (no concentration, reverse Alexander, Alexander). In the reverse Alexander, I overexaggerated the head/spine scrunch and slouch, whereupon I noticed that not only were my upper arms unbearably tense, but I actually was physically unable to play as high/loud as I normally could. With the application of AT, I still feel stuck, and I can't continually apply it throughout the exercise.

After Class 3: In my reps of 8/25 today, I again have a problem of mental cognizance, and I don't really think too much about a mental approach to playing the exercise, instead asking myself a myriad of physical corrections when I attempt to use AT (are my arms in the right place, is my head over my hips, am I leaning forward far enough, etc.).

After Class 4: Going back to what I said about not thinking about something as impossible, I applied a better mental approach to my 8/25 exercise, because despite my physical adjustments, I was still having trouble playing it cleanly. After reading the aforementioned "detective work" at the end of Chapter 9, I said to myself several things before starting the exercise today. "You're really only playing double strokes, which even at this tempo is not entirely impossible, and you want to play this because it'll make you a better player and it's fun to play this fast! You can do this, and it'll feel great." And just with that mental preparation, I played arguably the best rep of that exercise I've ever played in my life. I'm completely speechless!

After Class 5: My final reps of 8/25 today sounded "free." That is, I felt like I was playing it for me, and not for CLASS, and that improved the sound quality.

Ad's Project: Suzuki Training

After Class 1: This connection is something I am exploring with my out-of-class experiment (basic 2 w/text). In class I got the opportunity to do basic 1 and focus on the connection between my head and my spine, which allowed me to "stomp harder" with clarity. This is something I want to explore further while also keeping in mind to think without the use of the "pink elephant" as described in Chapter 1. "The most effective way to create change is to replace the old idea with a new one," which is something that I'll have to work on to get the vocabulary right in my head as the week progresses. After working my experiment, I realized that I was tightening my neck and chest as I spoke while doing the basic, probably as a call to my inherent potential energy equals tightness tendency. I recorded myself doing it before, and then while I asked myself to *imini* so that my head can move so that the rest of me could follow I recorded again and saw a slight change in my vocal quality. The resonance changed and I looked longer (which I know I'm not actually, but to where my body is likely designed to be at).

After Class 2: I also worked with my experiment further implementing the voice aspect. After yesterday's lesson and with Crispin helping me really visualize and inviting the audience who is with you to be with you, I feel myself going deeper in the text even while concentrating on the Suzuki movement. As I train, I get into the trap of going into a loud chant of the text with a very small focus rather than taking in the whole room as well, so it was a welcome adjustment.

After Class 3: I applied this same practice when I did my Suzuki experiment again and mostly work on the moment leading up to actually doing the exercise. There's this moment where I'm getting ready to go in and do it and in my mind I'm focusing in on the activity and ready to receive information around me, and I think the intellectualizing and the "relaxing" taking place is actually doing the opposite of what I want to do.

After Class 4: In Chapter 9, I was inspired to really think about this when I did my task today. So I asked to *imini* so my head can move so the rest of me could follow so I could do my task after acknowledging my want (to stomp harder), my recognition that I wanted to improve the skill, and my goal to connect my foot to the ground. I gathered the information about the activity I needed to complete and how my body was fitting in the design that best suits itself, and created the plan keeping in mind my body and the task at hand. And then I did the task using AT. Usually the first time I do it during the day, it really doesn't do much, which I think is because I'm remembering the feeling not the technique, and without the feedback from the class it's a little bit harder for me to intellectualize in the moment. Then I gathered information by comparing my result with my goal, which was to stomp harder, which it was unclear if I did. So I created a new plan by filming my process with my computer to see if there was any change in case I didn't feel it in the moment or had difficulties reflecting afterward. So I experimented again and again, continually gathering information and creating a plan. And in this moment, I figured out how I can work with it on my own, internalizing this structure and just keeping experimenting and assessing and recalibrating. I suppose it was my "a-ha" moment this week where I really felt like I "figured it out."

After Class 5: Today as I went to rehearsal, as I was waiting to get into the scene work, I found time to *imini* so that my head could move so that the rest of me could follow and consider my given circumstances and jump into the scene with a level of excitement rather than "relaxing." I felt so validated when my director commented on my energy today, and I don't feel like I'm anymore energized than usual, but I suppose my expression of that energy is clearer because I'm no longer scrunching my neck/spine when I'm doing any sort of activity.

EXHIBIT 2: SKELETON DRAWING

Draw a picture of your skeleton. Your drawing will be perfect. (Instructor can put "stars" at the top of the page, or invite students to put "stars" on themselves.)

EXHIBIT 3: AT PROCESS WORKSHEET

Steps	Frequency	Description
Wanting		
Recognizing		
Deciding		
Gathering information		
Creating a new plan		
Asking/thinking/ wishing		
Deciding again (if applicable)		
Experimenting		

Note

1   By plan, I mean using the wish to cooperate with my design to do what I am doing. One of the ways that I could phrase this wish:

> I ask to coordinate
>
> So that my head can move
>
> So that all of me can follow
>
> So that I can do what I am doing.
>
> (F.M. wording: *"directions, means whereby"*)

References and Further Reading

Ackerman, D. (1999) *Deep Play*. New York: Random House.

Alexander, F.M. (1984) *The Use of the Self*. Downey, CA: Centerline Press. (Original work published 1932.)

Alexander, F.M. (1995) *The Alexander Technique: The Essential Writings of F.M. Alexander* (3rd edition). New York: Carol Publishing Group.

Alexander, F.M. and Fischer, J.M.O. (eds) (1995) *Articles and Lectures: Articles, Published Letters and Lectures on the F.M. Alexander Technique*. London: Mouritz.

Boal, A. (2002) *Games for Actors and Non-Actors*. New York: Routledge.

Conable, B. and Conable, W. (1992) *How to Learn the Alexander Technique*. Columbus, OH: Andover Press.

Fluegelman, A. (1981) *More New Games*. New York: The Headlands Press.

Hagen, U. with Frankel, H. (1973) *Respect for Acting*. New York: Macmillan.

Illsley, C.J. (1998) *Who, Me Lead a Group?* Seattle, WA: Parenting Press.

Kapit, W. and Elson, L. (1993) *The Anatomy Coloring Book*. New York: Addison-Wesley.

Madden, C. (2012) "Deep Play Variations." In S. Jones (ed.) *The Congress Papers: Learning from Each Other*. London: STAT Books.

Madden, C. (2014) *Integrative Alexander Technique Practice for Performing Artists: Onstage Synergy*. Chicago, IL: Intellect, University of Chicago Press.

Glimpsing the Collaboratives

Alexander Technique Teachers Working with Teachers of Other Disciplines

Cathy Madden

When Jack Clay, then head of the University of Washington Professional Actor Training Program (hereafter UW), realized there wasn't enough time in the schedule to have both singing and Alexander Technique classes, he asked the singing teacher and me to combine them. Connie Koschman Haas and I approached that first class with curiosity. Unlike with the case histories offered in this chapter, Haas and I met as we arrived in the room to teach together for the first time. After a quick few minutes of orienting ourselves, I suggested that I give AT lessons to the students while she led them through their vocal warm-ups. Haas told the students that she could hear them improve as I taught each person during the warm-up. When the students sang individually, we taught simultaneously. AT was an immediate catalyst for singing improvements. I realized as we taught together throughout the term that the students were learning a great deal about how to integrate AT into all their acting work.

Professor Clay's scheduling needs led to many co-teaching partnerships at UW, including voice, movement, Suzuki training, acting studios, camera acting, dance, and stage combat. My role has been as a "mostly" quiet partner in the class. In a recent alumni survey, one of the actors said, "Cathy was very good at being a silent supporter of the work being done, adding a helpful hint when it was needed, or magically appearing beside you during your work to offer a suggestion on your alignment/coordination" (Mullen; see full response later in this chapter). The mutual goals of the UW faculty—to give each actor the tools to be their most creative and powerful self—guide all the interactions.

In this style of collaboration, I teach students as they are doing what they are doing without interrupting their process. They sing their song or play their scene with me as a vocally silent partner, moving with them as they ask themselves for optimal coordination. Before I double in a class, I explain the process to the actors. They understand that their conscious participation is a prerequisite for success. From their AT classes, they have the ability to ask themselves "to coordinate to do what they are doing."

My presence reminds the students that integrating AT with acting is the point of learning AT. Both the students and I benefit from having a common point of reference for the skills they are learning. What I indirectly receive is a broader view of each student's patterns by observing them in many different classes. The article "Integrated actor training" (Madden 2003) gives more information about my work at UW, including quotes from my colleagues and the students.

While the teaching partnerships at UW are set up fairly simply, open communication and shared goals fuel the collaboration. I would say that these partnerships galvanize the teaching process. What my collaborating teacher sees and needs enhances my observation skills as I analyze what is happening through the prism of another expert and discipline. It makes me a better teacher.

Collaboration and Galvanizing Performance

This chapter acknowledges that teaching collaboratively is a potent way to use AT to galvanize performance. As with many of the teaching approaches described in this book, there is little documentation available, even though many people do it. Earlier, I summarized my experience of teaching collaboratively at UW; I have also co-taught outside the academy: horseback riding and AT, singing and AT, life questions and AT, Meisner and AT, for example. Unlike the classes at UW, where teaching relationships are already in place, these workshops generally require more preparation—refining goals and methods of collaboration. Each is uniquely designed.

Following are three case studies from others who collaborate in teaching. I have invited teachers to tell the story of their partnership in their own way (guided by a set of questions), asking them to have their collaborators contribute as well. These stories offer a glimpse of what is possible, offering means and inspiration for others to explore.

Teaching Collaboration Case History 1: Jennifer Schulz and Richard Gilbert Hill

JENNIFER SCHULZ, AT TEACHER

The collaboration began when voice teacher Richard Gilbert Hill took an eight-week introductory AT for performers course that I co-teach (with fellow AT teacher Nick George in Los Angeles). Richard is interested in many different modalities and curious about their conjunction with the voice work he teaches. A few months after taking the course, he invited me to join him in an experimental collaboration for an advanced voice class he was creating called "Muscularity." He wanted to offer his students the opportunity to explore how the sounds of words could inform their meaning. The class was four weeks, and I designed the curriculum for the third week. In the final week we teamed up to help the students apply the methods to monologue work.

It was a great success, and the class has evolved into a six-month vocal survey course, in which one month Richard focuses on the work of Cicely Berry, for example; in subsequent months, Fitzmaurice, Alba Emoting, and so forth. The underlying link is allowing the sounds and physicality of language to inform the text rather than focusing on the literal meaning of the words. A core group of students signed up for an additional six months and have expressed interest in a third cycle.

In the week dedicated to AT, I worked on dovetailing the theme of my class into the overall theme of the month. What especially excited me came in the fourth week of every month, where it all came together with text. We found that the AT principles ran seamlessly under every vocal philosophy. Within every exercise, when a student was able to allow for freedom and coordination, they found more resonance, were more connected to the text, became more present, and stopped trying to get it all "right."

I'm fortunate to have taken several voice and speech courses in my undergrad and graduate work, so I wasn't completely unfamiliar with Richard's work. My training, however, was grounded in Linklater and Lessac, two traditions that aren't really included in our shared curriculum. Consequently, it's been a joy to learn more about these new philosophies and observe Richard take the class through exercises I've never experienced myself.

Collaborating on this class has encouraged me to investigate the work of embodied cognition (a curiosity that began during my studies with AT teacher Sarah Barker and deepened when I read Madden's book *Integrative Alexander Technique Practice for Performing Artists*). We've been exploring how the body takes language literally, often considering where the words the author has given us live. Is it the belly or heart or hands of the actor? Within expansion and contraction of the spine? In the three-dimensional space around the actor?

I also shift the AT language I use in my teaching to connect on a more intimate level to the student. The best example of this comes from a student who worked with me privately. We were having some trouble communicating, and I realized after a lesson or two that every time I asked her to release her neck, she would tighten. After I tentatively brought this to her attention, she admitted that she had recently left Scientology and that the word *release* is a Scientology term. So we had to find a new languaging. One of the phrases that was really successful with her was "allow your neck to be *silly.*" As soon as we introduced this word into the work, her face lit up and her neck released. And it gave her the added benefit of not having to get anything right.

Richard and I have developed a "dance" of communication in our teaching. For the first part of class, he takes the students through a 15-minute vocal/physical warm-up, while I walk around using touch to communicate to students. I may also give them a tiny bit of whispered vocal guidance when I believe it won't interfere with the focus and flow of the warm-up for the student.

During exercises and monologue work, I find I have to rely on instinct to know when and how to communicate. There are times when I find I'm interjecting a lot, verbally and nonverbally, and there are whole classes where I feel that any interjections would hinder the progress being made. I ask myself: Is the student already getting a lot of information from the other teacher? Do they seem to be coordinating well within the exercise without direct guidance? Are they really pulling down on themselves, but an interruption from me at this point would not be fruitful?

After working with many of these actors for a full year, I've realized that certain students welcome the use of touch no matter where they are in the process; other students feel jolted, as if I've caused a disruption. Some find touch without verbal guidance confusing, and others would rather I communicate solely through touch. Each actor and I develop an idiosyncratic teaching/learning language.

Richard and I make ample time for discussion and feedback. If I was quiet during an exercise that Richard took the class through, I have the opportunity to ask questions of the students or give feedback after.

Cultivating easy communication with Richard has been important. We talk about moments in class afterward and I may ask, "Was that okay when I jumped in there?" If Richard is teaching and I want to interject, I'll make eye contact with him before jumping in when possible. I don't think he's ever said no or given me a look indicating my interruption was unwelcome. For us, the teaching has to be generous and egoless. If I am beginning from a place of trust and joy, if my ideas about AT are not above or more important than his ideas about language and breath support, then there is room for an immense amount of success in our collaboration.

Teaching Collaboration Case History 2:
Belinda Mello and Julia Lenardon

BELINDA MELLO, AT TEACHER

Julia and I met as faculty members at the newly formed Tom Todoroff Conservatory. The system there was to alternate two groups of acting students between voice and AT, sharing a three-hour block. One group would start with me for AT, then go to voice class, while the other group started their morning with Julia and then came to AT. We essentially warmed up a group for each other. We later discovered that the students had given the whole morning one name: the "Julinda" class. They experienced that there was continuity between the lessons, even though Julia and I had not discussed our class plans. So I guess we started building our collaboration before we knew we were a team. It was collaboration *through* the studio walls.

It seemed like a logical step to meet and plan co-teaching in the same room. For a while we met for coffee before class to socialize, also discussing the students and ideas for our classes. One of our first collaborations was sharing the same end-of-year evaluation tool. We modified a video assessment I was using for AT, integrating it with more vocal assessment. The students recorded themselves performing simple activities. In addition to moving through space and working with objects, they were asked to sing a short song, recite some text, and speak about themselves.

Our discussions and evaluations revealed our shared values. I learned how much Julia understood about the principles that underlie AT by listening to her description of what she observed in the students. She recognized learning habits and prioritized a process-oriented approach. Julia inspires students to embrace consistent practice, taking the long view rather than the quick fix. But most importantly, her voice work is based in authenticity of intention. She understands that the mind, body, and voice are intertwined. She teaches that actors can be best heard when they are understood. Rather than having actors work toward being louder, she teaches them to communicate, to express specific meaning.

When I first considered collaborating with Julia, I was a little nervous that I would be exposed for what I didn't know about voice. But this was not from Julia—this was an old self-critical pattern of my own. I believe that facing my discomfort was an important part of building the collaborative relationship. Acknowledging my tension opened a window onto how invested I was in serving my own growth by co-teaching with another specialist.

I realized that I had to let myself embrace what I knew about breathing coordination, vocal coordination, and the psychophysical nature of vocal expression. Then I could enter the shared teaching space with open-hearted confidence, with the hope and expectation that I would learn more.

Julia and I took private sessions with each other. I brought my voice questions to her, and she brought her movement questions to me. This not only built more trust, but also deepened our collaboration. I have a better understanding of the experience of breath and voice exercises. This allows me to see where AT can fit into the practice of voice and speech work for actors.

Julia and I co-teach workshops as part of my summer studio class series. We have chosen topics that we can illuminate together. "Resonance" was the subject of our first workshop. In the summer of 2016 we taught a series of weekly classes, "Speak/Move/Breathe," and an intensive workshop, "Emotions Embodied and Expressed."

We meet and create a class plan in which we alternate leadership of the group. We lay out a series of complementary exercises with a progressive sequence in mind, and we set a timetable. We look at how we can build the class progression and move the student experience forward. Discussing the plan ahead of time keeps us on the same page and helps us share the time equitably.

In the actual class teaching, we improvise. We spontaneously offer supportive ideas, help silently with touch, invite each other to step in, and at times choose *not* to step in. We ask first. From the beginning we have treated each other as respected experts. Watching the students respond to Julia's teaching has often inspired me. I might shift my next exercise to better follow up on what is happening in the room.

As an AT teacher, I've explored different ways to use hands-on teaching while my collaborator is leading the group. When I assist students to follow the exercise more fully, they are not distracted by me—they become better able to follow instruction. For example, I might gently cue a student who is holding unintended tension or an awkward pose—but I wouldn't pull that student's attention into a mini-lesson. Because we have an ongoing relationship with many of our students, I might give a nonverbal reminder when I know someone is working on changing a specific pattern. My intention is to aid the actor in what they are already trying to do, rather than interrupting their process. When I observe some consistency of confusion or struggle, it's been more effective for me to ask for a brief pause, then to offer an idea to help the whole group. And Julia does this for me as well. It's like having an extra set of eyes in the room.

I'm really impressed by the quality of learning I see in our students because our work is so deeply integrated. Students in our collaborative classes learn how to psychophysically carry out the vocal exercises they already know, as well as gaining new approaches. We provide vocal, breathing, and movement solutions, while trusting in the ease of coordination that is a natural aspect of authentic expression. The attention on resonance opens up the actors' perception of themselves and their honest sound. With application to text, the actors have a platform to integrate AT, voice, and acting.

Last week we co-led a monologue workshop, and I noticed another way in which our collaboration has grown: We were able to effectively address acting issues of timing and rhetoric from a psychophysical perspective.

JULIA LENARDON, VOICE TEACHER

What started my interest in collaborating with Belinda was that the students would consistently and spontaneously share that the principles in my voice class matched and deepened what they had just done in AT class. They thought that Belinda and I had planned out classes together ahead of time to achieve this cohesiveness. Obviously, my colleague, quite literally on the other side of the wall, shared similar perspectives in voice/body training. Collaboration is rare in the teaching world, as many instructors hold close their teaching, fearful of criticism and destructive "competition." In my opinion, true professional collaboration is sharing, exploring, and mutually venturing into the unknown with no net; hence, it is the only effective way to promote true integration of skills into creative work.

My knowledge of AT comes from active work in workshops during my professional actor and voice training. Therefore, I have always seen the value of the practice, particularly in my world of the arts. Belinda and I continue to take our personal time to give each other coaching sessions in our disciplines. Her direct work with me in AT has been beneficial in addressing my own physical challenges in life. Our teaching together, directly integrating both the voice and AT work, enables me to consistently discover more embodied routes toward a whole voice and vocal communication.

Teaching Collaboration Case History 3: Kate Conklin and Benedikt Negro

KATE CONKLIN, AT TEACHER

My collaboration with Benedikt Negro started with our being friends and colleagues in *O*, the Cirque du Soleil show where I was the vocalist, and he is a lead character and pantomime. As I began to teach, we experimented with applying AT to Benedikt's work in the show as well as other acts he was developing. We had a humorous and constructive collaborative way of working that was joyful and productive. We both have a deep commitment to doing detailed work, and while we are both goofballs, we take our performance work seriously. It was a good match.

A few years after I left *O* and was living and teaching in Los Angeles, Benedikt started producing *1230 Show*, an after-hours clown show featuring the best performers from the Vegas strip doing clown acts after their nightly shows were over (at 12:30 a.m.). He brought me in to the Onyx Theater to work with his performers on movement and stage presence. Soon after, I asked Benedikt to guest teach in a few programs where I was teaching: an intensive opera program, a summer theatre conservatory, and at CalArts as a guest artist. He worked with students on ways to develop stylized movement for particular characters and talked about being a professional performer.

We then put together our first collaboration, a workshop for performers called Mime and Alexander Technique. For this, Benedikt led a warm-up for about 20 minutes, then I did 20 minutes; we switched off leading a couple times each, then did coachings for each performer or group of performers. We took turns there too, and often Benedikt would give specific ideas for movement, ways to explore the physicality of a character, or ways to create story arc through an act. For my part, I would respond to the performers' expressed desires, which may have been vocal or overall coordination needs, or help the performer to better coordinate so as to integrate Benedikt's suggestions. We have an organic back-and-forth that works really well. We both respond to questions and ask each other for feedback and comments. (I have had other collaborations that are decidedly not this way, and therefore require much more structure.)

In a few other workshops in Las Vegas, we focused mainly on mime technique, working with performers who wished to move from being mostly an athlete in a Cirque show to being a character. There, Benedikt led a lot of movement exercises and games that integrated what they had learned in the exercises. Most of those were interactions that had some sort of story arc and physical transformation, even in a simple exchange. My role in these was often to help the participants better appreciate and replicate what Benedikt was doing. Having analyzed Benedikt's movement (in general and in the workshop itself), I could observe subtle (or obvious) differences in the particular movements, as well as in the overall movement quality. I could intervene and help the participants achieve more flowing and precise movement. In this exploration we would interface with their ideas about executing sharp, fast, slow, etc. movements generally. We did more workshops in Los Angeles for performers of all kinds to help develop and hone performance and storytelling skills through both simple and stylized movement.

Before every workshop we talked together about what we wanted to cover and what the participants were interested in—why they were taking the class. I asked a lot about the history of mime and how Benedikt had trained and taught. We had a good foundational appreciation of each other's work and ability to communicate and teach. In the workshop itself, we would introduce our work and what we would be doing—I spoke about using AT as a framework to support performance goals: using overall coordination to perform more effectively and sustainably, as well as to do more detailed and extraordinary work. Benedikt spoke about Étienne Decroux and corporeal mime, as well as the difference between pantomime and mime (mimicry). In all our teaching collaborations, we got people moving first, then used that as a way to enter into exploration and coordination.

Benedikt reports that from this collaboration his teaching became more structured, and he developed new themes and preferences. Previously the class was more of an improv, and working with me gave it a different flow. The work gained more specificity and depth; it became less immediate and more of a journey where, instead of instantly learning something superficial to take away that's somewhat limited, participants were on a journey of experimentation and deeper training. He adds that you can really see in a performer the difference between someone who is "gigging" or "self-taught" and someone who has deeply trained and developed their craft.

For my part, I use more games and warm-ups—specifically ones I learned in these workshops—in all of my classes. I always did the exercises along with everyone else in the workshops, and this deepened my sense that you can learn more dimensionally by having a go at something, while better understanding the predicament of those who are learning it as well. It made me aware of how limited many people are in allowing themselves to move. This has an overall effect on their coordination, and actually moving in lots of ways can help them discover what is possible. I have a much more profound sense of the need to help people develop their imagination and curiosity—and to play.

Hearing from the Students

In the aforementioned article "Integrated actor training" (Madden 2003), UW students describe how dual-expert classrooms have worked for them. As an update for this chapter, I used Facebook to ask UW alums to answer questions about their experience in receiving collaborative teaching. Here are some of their responses.

Thea Mercouffer

(Thea had experience with AT and voice, singing, and scene study.)

Did having an AT teacher in class help your learning? If so, how?

Definitely. Paying attention to my use helped me listen better, both to my class teacher and to my scene partner, and even to the text/song at hand. I also felt it was easier to make choices that sometimes might have seemed outrageous or out of my comfort zone. Having Cathy assist my body during class gave me clarity and ease.

Did having an AT teacher in class get in the way? If so, how?

Not at all. In fact there might have been a danger of becoming dependent on Cathy's presence. Even just her presence was a reminder of the AT principles and it helped everyone in class, whether she was working with them directly or not.

Meg McQuillan

(Meg had AT and singing, Suzuki, and voice.)

Did having an AT teacher in class help your learning? If so, how?

It made a world of difference. At the time it was instrumental in establishing good use while learning these other practices. For me to learn to sing with ease in my body from the beginning, rather than have to come back years later after developing use problems, was a huge advantage. I experienced the same benefit in all the skills I was developing when AT was part of the learning process.

Years later, when singing, or acting on stage and needing my voice to reach the back row, AT is intrinsically a part of my process, my tool box, to synthesize these skills.

Did having an AT teacher in class get in the way? If so, how?

I remember feeling that it "got in the way" during scene work requiring deep emotional access. But that was only at the beginning. Later, I came to deeply appreciate the attention and reminders. It was also a very good skill to develop for acting on film or television—to be able to have emotional access and ease with another person working in tandem right next to you. There is often a sound person, rigger, or camera person virtually touching you while you work—so in a strange way, being able to maintain my focus and integrate all the emotional and physical requirements while someone is millimeters from my body began with my work with Cathy in scene study classes.

Chance Mullen

(Chance had AT and Suzuki, voice, and various acting classes.)

Did having an AT teacher in class help your learning? If so, how?

Yes, it helped tremendously. I (and many of my fellow students) felt that Cathy's input as an AT professional was the "glue" that made the other pieces of our curriculum make sense. For instance, in voice class, there were a number of great techniques for awakening the vocal cords, stretching out the body, "warming up," and so forth. Unfortunately, much of the language used was not anatomically correct. Cathy often said that when we give our bodies a command, our bodies usually try to do the thing we're asking, even if it's physically impossible. Cathy was able to "translate" the language from the voice world in anatomically correct ways, which allowed us to perform the exercises with more ease and "true" relaxation—which, in turn, allowed us to enjoy the benefits of the voice work in the first place. [Author note: This translation service is one that my colleagues value. There is a value to a language of images, but also a way to cooperate with the actual anatomy and benefit from an image.]

In Suzuki training, her input was enormous. There are many different versions of Suzuki training out there, and the version I received from Robyn Hunt and Steve Pearson was undoubtedly influenced by Cathy—who was often present in our classes. I've met others who have trained in different venues, with different teachers, and I'm always amazed that their interpretation of Suzuki is that it is "fierce" and "aggressive"—the exact opposite of how I see the training I received, which was centered around ease of movement (even if it was sometimes sharp and sudden). For us, the "ferocity" was really just an illusion (an intentional and welcome one) created by an actor's efficiency of movement and mental awareness, rather than the product of tension and passion. It's no wonder that so many others who've learned Suzuki have ended up with injuries, trying to project emotions and qualities in an uncoordinated and physically destructive way.

In acting classes, Cathy was very good at finding a way to translate "actions" into psychophysical suggestions. Including a person's whole self in the imaginative work was incredibly helpful throughout my experience as a performer at UW.

Did having an AT teacher in class get in the way? If so, how?

Generally, no. I remember one instance when it might have upset a teacher, but I think that was mostly a professional/territorial thing, since many of us were expressing our amazement at how so many things were suddenly making so much sense.

Amanda Zarr

(Amanda had AT and Suzuki, and Anton Chekhov scene study.)

Did having an AT teacher in class help your learning? If so, how?

Having an AT teacher helped me immensely because the knowledge of the efficient use of my body and the adjustments given by the instructor deepened my understanding of how movement adds to storytelling and characterization in acting. Cathy's valuable lesson of giving myself permission to semantically change what the director says has helped me to better understand what is being asked of me and therefore forge a stronger working partnership with others in the process. As an acting instructor, I am more confident in how I present materials. I am aware of how compression can have a negative effect at all levels of the process from table reads to performance, so I'm attentive to my students' physical form at all stages of learning.

Did having an AT teacher in class get in the way? If so, how?

Due to Cathy's belief in integration of AT, I did not feel that having the extra instructor in the room was a hindrance. It made learning easier for me as I was able to have a psychophysical relationship to every step of learning.

Concluding Words

When these alumni were asked if they would have wanted more of these collaborations, the answer was uniformly "yes." "I can't imagine a class/field of study that wouldn't have benefitted from collaboration with an AT teacher. If you are using your body, even just to sit at a table, you would benefit from the work" (AZ).

Reference

Madden, C. (2003) "Integrated actor training." *Direction* 3, 2, 7–10.

Metaphorically Speaking
The Singer and the Alexander Technique

Patricia O'Neill

AT Perspective

To my students who are also my teachers!

The Alexander Technique facilitates a return to an ordered use of the self as a whole. It encourages balance and cooperation between the various aspects of the self through the idea of *primary coordination* and the indirect process that facilitates its emergence.

This indirect process includes:

- understanding the dynamic relationship that exists between the head and neck at the head/neck joint, as well as between the head/neck joint and the entire spine—ultimately, the entire self

- being increasingly and vibrantly aware and appreciative of the self in the present moment

- finding a climate of stillness within the self from which all movement emerges

- dissuading the mind from an inordinate need to control, which invariably causes muscles to overwork

- clarifying intent, which is best born out of inspiration rather than willpower.

Through this process, balance among the various aspects of the self is restored, and a more expansive, vibrant, poised, fully present, and spontaneous self emerges—one that moves with ease and is fascinated by process rather than results.

For the singer, AT is a remarkable vehicle for self-exploration. It insists without demanding; it gives permission by saying "no"; it empowers by disarming; it inspires artists to embrace their role in the fabric of life, celebrating their oneness with all.

The Wild Bird

There are so many aspects of the classical singer's art to be mastered. There is vocal technique in all its various methodologies, along with centuries of musical and vocal styles, at least four languages, and knowledge of world history, poetry, and visual arts. A singer must hone his acting chops as well. He must be able to be expressive, using only two tiny and delicate vocal folds where the margin for error is similar to that facing an Olympic skater. This is only the preparation: for real artistry to emerge, the singer must learn to talk herself out of her reluctance and embrace, even celebrate, her vulnerability. She must be willing to plumb the depths of herself, exploring what she finds there as boldly and fearlessly as Evel Knievel motorcycling over Snake River Canyon. And ultimately, she must be as ready to sing each phrase of a song as is the wild bird utterly and irrevocably primed to wail its mating call.

Why Metaphors?

Most of my voice teachers taught through metaphor and imagery, and these tools remain a vital part of my teaching regimen. They speak to the whole person and therefore facilitate the organization of the whole being in singing. I find that metaphor transcends my students' beliefs and preconceived ideas, inserting itself with a purity and simplicity that disarms, enlightens, transforms, and sparks the imagination.

As a fairly new teacher of the Alexander Technique, I was thrilled to understand how its principles further clarified the images and metaphors I had been using for years to describe the experience of singing. When assimilating a metaphor fully, a singer might find herself easing into a state of being AT proponents know as *inhibition* or *non-doing*, gathering herself around an idea, or focusing on a resulting intent or *direction*. Throughout this chapter I examine the nature of singing and the principles of inhibition and direction using metaphors and imagery I invoke in my teaching. First off, here are three that capture the essence of my teaching philosophy.

The Elusive "It"

Like so many aspiring classical singers, I always knew I had a gift, yet struggled to unleash it. In voice lessons, I would often ask, "Is that *it*?" and my teacher would reply rhapsodically, "Yes! That's *it*! Do *it* again!" What was this *it*? This elusive *it*? This will o' the wisp? Was it a seemingly magical coming together of many aspects of the self, like the moment when the struggling beginning cyclist suddenly finds himself riding his bicycle? In retrospect, I believe that through embodying the *it*, I had stumbled onto my *primary coordination* but without a clear idea of what it was or how I had achieved it. Voice teachers often encourage their students to "let go" with little more clarification than that. AT offered me specific strategies for how to facilitate that process of "letting go." And in so doing I learned that there is no one perfect *it*—only my readiness for constant change presenting me with my next moment of life in all of its freshness, newness, and potential.

"Letting Go"

We have all delighted to the melodic gurgling of babies at play. Could it be that these coos are the essence of superb vocal technique? I believe that singers must find their way back to a state of innocence and vulnerability in order to uncover their true personal artistry.

They must relearn how to sing *with* themselves instead of *in spite of* themselves. I have listened to singers who sang with technical vocal prowess but whose performances did not move me. In my estimation, these singers were singing in spite of themselves, micromanaging their voices with an intent toward vocal perfection. They had not yet traveled the true artist's long journey of self-discovery that leads to authentic self-expression.

Finding my authentic voice was like peeling away accessories. I had various inorganic materials impeding my free sound that I needed to release during my AT study. It took trust and courage not only to let go of my inhibitions but to sing freely without their familiar security. (Former student Elizabeth Perryman)

I continually marvel at the elegantly playful way the principles of AT prime the nervous system so it can render the self vulnerable, rich of heart, creative, and carefree. These principles, or *means-whereby*, were developed by F.M. Alexander and include awareness, inhibition, and direction. The application of these principles results in a kind of second innocence that changes lives and manifests careers. This is what "letting go" means to me now!

"Being Sung"

The great voice teacher Giovanni Battista Lamperti said, "Don't sing until you'd die if you didn't!" (Brown 1931, p.141). A vocal artist who does not understand this statement has yet to begin the journey of "being sung." Perhaps she is caught up in producing a gorgeous tone, or on moving or thrilling the audience. Whatever her distraction, her artistic and interpretive decisions are merely pasted on, and her muscular effort deceives her into believing that she is being expressive. Put simply, she equates effort with success. In AT parlance, she is *end-gaining*. I define this AT principle as "misusing oneself to achieve a goal." Early in my singing life, I was a conscientiously ardent end-gainer. Even though I had always found it an unsatisfying approach to singing, I had not yet found a better way. Sadly, this approach to singing only alienated me from the present moment and my true artistic resources, those that lay within me. When I find something humorous, I do not pause to consider how to laugh. The laugh simply emerges out of my state of being and my intent at that moment. In essence, I am "being laughed." Ultimately, I would have to remember how to be sung in the same way!

Inhibition and Direction

Margarete von Winterfeldt,[1] an important and beloved voice teacher of mine, often described me metaphorically as someone chasing a butterfly in a beautiful garden. No matter how hard I tried to catch it, the butterfly eluded me. Finally, exhausted from the effort, I just sat down in my garden, only to have the butterfly flit toward me and alight on my shoulder. Self-discovery is not the result of a search. It is the result of ceasing to "try." It is born out of a sublime stillness that Alexander called *inhibition*. The singer who suspends the familiar patterns of doing, ceases to strive, and relinquishes the need to know and control is inhibiting. He just *is*. Inhibition is a state of being that reveals all his potential. It is there that all his answers lie, even if they are seldom the answers he wants or expects.

One metaphor for AT inhibition is one of nature's most powerful forces: the hurricane. A clearly defined eye indicates how well the hurricane is organized. A stable eye allows the hurricane to unleash its power. Utter stillness resides within it. So it is with inhibition. Profound in its stillness, it contains all possibilities and therefore facilitates the emergence of a direction while remaining open to all other directions. It is this state I encourage my students to cultivate in order to open pathways to their own personal artistry.

The "eye of the hurricane" truly saved my singing when I wanted desperately to make something happen. It helped me stay calm and realize the benefits of that ease. I use it with my students. (Former student Kori Jennings)

Direction is clarity of thought, not forced but insistent, like Elizabeth Walker's[2] *fairy wish*. A fairy knows that whatever she wishes will be so. She need not struggle or exert her willpower to accomplish this. She simply has a clear, precise idea of what she wants, then launches her intention, trusting that it will be accomplished. Direction is thought shepherding that encourages physical, mental, or emotional reeducation, such as "I wish my neck to be free" or "Now I get to experience singing this high C" or "How I sound is none of my business!"

Quite simply, *direction* is the quiet knowing that it is so.

In the beginning, I thought of the fairy wish as the unattainable Prince Charming. The more we spoke of the fairy wish, I began to realize that it is the ability to believe in yourself. You don't need a Prince Charming! It is the ability to "let go" while gently practicing intent, or mindfulness. It can be applied to all aspects of life, but as a performer, it means it is okay to be affected by the music. I am a vessel, and it is okay to be vulnerable and confident at the same time. The possibilities are endless with the fairy wish. (Former student Megan Barrera)

Inhibition and direction together induce a state of non-doing, from which emerges a new thought, fresh perspective, surprising turn of a phrase, startling outburst, serendipitous nuance, more extended silence—all of which are invited, received, accepted, savored, and embraced as each moment of a performance presents itself. These are some of the fruits of inhibition and direction.

Imagination

> I am certain of nothing but the holiness of the Heart's
> affections and the truth of the Imagination.
>
> John Keats[3]

To awaken her students' imagination, Margarete von Winterfeldt often used metaphors that I would ultimately understand as embodying AT inhibition and direction. Here is one of my favorites: "We do not pull the rosebud's petals apart to make it blossom, but instead, we give the bud the nutrients it needs and the blossoming occurs, often in ways we do not expect" (personal communication). This elegantly simple metaphor offers a soulful pathway toward the practice of inhibition and direction, through which a singer can become comfortably in touch with himself and his emotions. In this place of stillness and non-doing, there is no judgment. As the singer disarms, his essence simply unveils itself. One could say imagination is the love child of inhibition and direction and metaphor, whereby awareness of the self is embraced and intention is effortlessly revealed. There is no need to force it. As with the mating call in nature, singing born out of that process is spontaneous, vibrant, soulful. It is an authentic expression of the singer's entire being at that moment.

Space and Energy

Another of my voice teachers, Norman Gulbrandsen,[4] insisted, "The singer's language is space and energy!" (personal communication). For years I have pondered this profound and daring statement, considering the implications of its meaning. I have chosen it as the grand metaphor for this chapter.

For the singer, *space* and *energy* represent two basic aspects of vocal technique. *Space* refers to a singer's resonances, and *energy* represents the vitality in the moving breath that reflects the singer's state of being. Space and energy are also compelling metaphors for the AT principles of inhibition and direction. The result of inhibition is space. Space to be, space to think and reason, space to consider one's options, space to move, space to know and appreciate oneself, and space to experience life and singing. Inhibition or space gives one full access to one's energy, and direction is simply energy that is focused with clear and pure yet unforced intention.

The concept of space and energy directly focuses the singer to mentally engage the intrinsic muscles required for singing. Space and energy begin with a thought and the body responds. It's hard to say which comes first, the space or the energy. I think it depends on the phrase being expressed. Nonetheless, neither can exist without the other. (Former student Jane Redding)

Space

A benefit of attaining *primary control* is a sense of spaciousness throughout one's being. To foster this experience of a continuous ever-expanding space, two ideas I find particularly helpful are *unified field of attention* and the concept of *kinesphere*.[5] I use both of them liberally with my singers.

Understanding *unified field of attention* is particularly helpful to a singer who is narrowing himself because he is overthinking or overdoing. I encourage students who do this to become aware of their surroundings. When my students learn that it is possible to accomplish a difficult task while also aware of the space around them, they expand their sense of the spaciousness of the present moment where life may be more fully experienced and appreciated. This shift in perception can transform the present moment into an eternity.

The brainchild of Rudolf Laban, the term *kinesphere* is often used by AT teachers to encourage students to experience fully all the space and energy existing within their being. A singer simply imagines himself as an expanding sphere of energy that extends further than his physical body. The center of gravity is the center of the sphere. Its balance constantly adjusts to accommodate the slightest shifts of the body. Movement is never strained, and expansion within the sphere is never forced, but rather coordinated with ease.

It still amazes me how these ideas of unified field of attention and kinesphere can instantaneously alter a student's entire state of being, awakening her to new and enticing possibilities.

THE SINGER'S RESONANCE

The singer's resonance is the space throughout the vocal tract that defines her vocal quality and imbues it with its unique color and vibrancy. The singer learns how to manipulate her resonating chambers not only as a means of expression and stylistic nuance but also to project the voice. Especially for the classical singer who does not use amplification, creating resonating space is a vital component of vocal technique, a vehicle by which the tone is projected. The singer's challenge is how best to find that space. If she insists on creating more space than she can comfortably accommodate, her vocal production becomes forced and unwieldy. This is where her imagination comes into play. I have found that singers are limited only by how much space they can imagine in their vocal resonances. The singer can entertain the idea of a universe of space if it is not forced but instead lightly imagined. To give my students a perspective on how much potential space dwells within them, I ask that they imagine the reality that the space between the electrons in one atom in their bodies is proportional to the amount of space between the planets of our solar system!

Teaching students about the "language of space and energy" is mostly about helping them understand *what is* rather than what *should be*. It can be a daunting exercise to convince a student that she must merely imagine the space. It certainly was for this singer. I thought I wasn't *doing* enough. To aid a singer in clearing this hurdle, it might be helpful for him to understand that many common human responses cause the resonances to expand in an organic way. F.M. suggested thinking of something pleasant before and during inhaling and exhaling. In doing this, the resonating chambers are supple as they expand. In life, the same is true when one has an idea dawn upon them or when one is delightfully surprised. The passages of the vocal tract instinctively and organically expand in response to these experiences.

For singing, this is the quality we want when manipulating the resonances because it encourages the resonating passages to expand and the palate to rise naturally, without forcing either. Although sometimes suggested by voice teachers to create space, yawning probably causes a little too much muscular tension around the resonating spaces to be helpful. More useful is to remind the students that they already know instinctively how to manipulate their resonating chambers to achieve vocal colors. They have been doing it since they were little children exploring their speaking voices with curiosity, trust, playfulness, and acceptance. It is a particular joy for me to witness a student's careworn face gradually transform as he experiences the results of "being sung" as though he were being laughed, screamed, wept, or sighed.

THE SINGER'S LANGUAGE

Once the singer has learned how to find the space he needs for resonance, the next step is to understand that the manipulation of his resonating chambers is a language of the heart, a language of the soul.

Just as young singers come to realize that mere phonetic accuracy is insufficient for speaking a language like a native, so they must become aware of all the subtleties of expression available to them through manipulation of the head, chest, mouth, and nasal resonators. Singers already manipulate their resonating chambers when they speak, but making them aware of something so natural can often leave them feeling self-conscious. That awareness, however, is crucial to helping them realize that management of the resonating chambers is also a necessary part of singing and can ultimately happen with the same lack of self-consciousness as speaking. As they continue to inhibit, they are finally able to make the connection, and their singing is the irrevocable result of their experience at that moment. From there, intention emerges and often surprises them because it will only reveal itself as they inhibit or stop "trying" to be expressive. As they continue to inhibit, they are more open to dramatic shifts of intention happening within them, able to accommodate a new direction at any point.

Singers can feel quite vulnerable when letting go of a habit of control for the first time. But the nature of inhibition is to invite a step into the unknown, to permit one's entire being to cooperate organically with each musical phrase emerging from within. It is important to remind singers that the resulting feeling or sensation will most likely change subtly each time they sing a phrase. For this reason, I encourage my singers to avoid trying to re-create a feeling or sensation. Instead, I ask them simply to maintain the conditions that allow the tone to emerge.

SINGING AND SPEAKING AND BREATHING

Singing is simply speaking on pitch. Both speaking and singing begin with the same coordination of the vocal and breathing mechanisms. Singers can find it difficult to accept that they do not have to learn to breathe correctly but instead simply discover the ways they are interfering with the natural breathing process and cooperate with it. Yes, singing is more intense than speaking. Singing a phrase may mean extending an exhalation five to ten times longer than simply speaking the same phrase. And certainly, one of the greatest fears singers have is that they will run out of breath. So they believe they must inhale great draughts of air that only serve to encumber the process. Instead of learning to cooperate with the natural antagonism between the muscles of inhalation and exhalation that occurs with any vocal expression, they seek to ration their breath using only the muscles of exhalation. They believe they are gaining more control, but they are actually disrupting the natural breathing process.

The healthy attack of the tone the classical singing community calls *appoggio* results in a balanced, stable source of support and the all-important low larynx, thus a much larger resonating area—in other words, *space*. When a singer is using himself optimally, he has a sense of this space ever expanding in all directions effortlessly, and the tone appears in a delicate balance between inhaling and exhaling.

The tone emerges from there as though it were coming through a wormhole, from an alternate existence.

This sense of balance and housing of the tone is not something you find and hold on to, rather something for which the singer creates an environment, allowing the body to find its own way to balance in a way that is constantly changing. (Student Kathryn Drake Hedlund)

When they sing, the great singers of the world report that they feel no muscular effort in the laryngeal area, only spaciousness.

If a singer does not keep renewing the idea of ever-expanding space, the space inevitably begins to collapse. AT offers many strategies for maintaining this state of being. In no case do any of these involve direct muscular manipulation. Instead, they involve a subtle shift in thinking, a gentle coaxing toward the idea that space is a vital part of being and the self mostly comprises space. This approach allows for the delicate flow of air best employed in singing. I often describe the breath flow to my students as a "gossamer zephyr." An exercise that I find helpful is to have students speak a musical phrase several times in their normal speaking range until completely un-self-conscious. They then have a template for breath management when they sing. When this coordination is achieved, the muscles of support, resonating chambers, and vocal mechanism do a little dance in response to the intent of the singer.

I like to think that I am simply adding gorgeous music to a monologue. I have carried this idea over to my students as well. The idea that "singing is merely speaking on pitch" allows the students and myself to focus not so much on getting the music "right" but to allow oneself to be the character and truly tell a story. (Former student Angela Whitener Day)

TENSEGRITY

Tensegrity,[6] a word coined by architect and visionary Buckminster Fuller, describes beautifully the balance of tension that AT students cultivate. Tensegrity is the natural result of primary control. In fact, primary control is a form of tensegrity. For example, when an AT student realizes she does not have to hold herself up by stiffening muscles and joints, allowing herself to experience gravity, the righting mechanisms throughout her body engage and help her lengthen in an upward direction. Such is the function of these mechanisms that can often be reflexive and involuntary. These structures of balanced tension comprise a variety of systems designed to accomplish various functions throughout the body. For singing, it is useful to think of the breathing mechanism, resonating areas, vocal tract, vocal mechanism, even skin, and, yes, entire body as structures of tensegrity. An equal balance of muscular tension in singing resists collapse of these various mechanisms, resulting in a sensation of expanding in all directions. Singers have several common ways to describe this process: "Send the tone, but don't go with it." "Singers do not breathe to expand, they expand to breathe." "Drink in the phrase you are singing." When muscle groups function with balanced, coordinated tension, singing begins to feel quite easy, even ethereal. To experience this ease in singing can be daunting for singers who are used to armoring themselves with an illusion of muscular vocal control. When relinquishing it, they most often report, "I feel so vulnerable and exposed!" To which I reply, "Yes! Now you are on the right track!" This is the moment when the student begins to understand more fully what is meant by inhibition or space. It is a state of zero that contains all possibilities. Even when a direction is chosen, the other directions still remain, similar to the way the astrophysicist's mysterious black hole swallows, destroys, transforms, and gives birth simultaneously.

Something you said that I always loved was, "Get back to zero." You reminded me before every phrase. It said to me to let go of all of my tension, let go of control, and stop anticipating the "work" I was going to have to do because it wasn't necessary. Letting go of all that extra effort allowed the music to flow out freely. (Former student Nancy Ward Ratcliff)

THE "BUTTERPILLAR"

An elegant metaphor for holding the space is the "butterpillar." In a touching example of trust, the caterpillar submits itself to a process by ceasing to exist in its present state and being transformed anew. Like the caterpillar that dies unto itself when it enters the cocoon, my students are encouraged to relinquish any preconceived notions and be "in the moment," remaining open to fresh, new interpretations. The singer simply holds the space or inhibits and allows himself to be. For both singer and teacher, it is essential to pass through this stage in order to witness the birth of the singer's authentic voice. This caterpillar-to-butterfly process is a striking example of AT principles in action. The student's awareness is centered in the present moment and allowed to deepen. When coupled with inhibition, the student is able to let go of preconceived definitions of herself and behold her true essence emerging, free of ego and expectations. Direction (intent) flows easily from this state of being. Just as a "butterpillar" allows itself to unfold and emerge from the cocoon as a butterfly, the singer holds the space and permits the tone to be born.

Most humans probably do not realize how much space they create in their resonances when expressing themselves in speech. We singers do, and we learn to embrace that understanding by craving space, anticipating space, savoring space, evoking space, conjuring space, adoring space, and fearlessly employing space as the language of our hearts and souls.

Energy

Just what is energy? To most of us Westerners it seems a somewhat mysterious phenomenon, yet Asian cultures have known about and worked with it for millennia. Science tells us that energy can be neither created nor destroyed. It can be transformed and directed.

Refraining from mental and physical striving (encouraged by the practice of inhibition and direction) offers access to primary coordination. The resulting freedom of thought and movement allows full access to one's life force, an energy that can then be easily transformed and directed with our imaginations.

Western cultures lag far behind their Asian counterparts in understanding energy and its implications for our approach to life, health, healing, and artistic endeavor. Various Asian martial arts demonstrate that energy can indeed be focused and directed. I was fascinated watching t'ai chi ch'uan master Cheng Man-ch'ing practicing one of the forms of Pushing Hands[7] with his students. With seemingly little muscular effort as his "opponents" came toward him, he was able to throw them several yards with what appeared to be a simple gesture, and he never lost his mental or physical composure. I believe that the AT practice of inhibition and direction sets the singer up to direct energy with the same precision and intention.

In the t'ai chi ch'uan tradition, movement is initiated in the pelvic area. Many human beings tend to have a vague idea about their pelvises and the entire pelvic area that houses important chakras[8] or energy centers. Singers tend to focus solely on their heads and upper torsos because they believe these parts of their anatomy alone contain all the singing and breathing mechanisms. As they become aware of their legs and pelvises, they sense their connection to Earth and the powerful support emerging from there.

You once kind of "tapped" at my hips during a lesson and it unlocked something sooooo powerful. My body was holding onto something and it was concentrating itself there. It freed up everything, especially in the throat. I even remember that I was very much concentrating on freeing up and properly aligning the whole body, but that area must have been the key piece. (Former student Dana Head Crabtree)

Thrusting the pelvis forward is one of the most common examples of misuse I observe in voice students. Unfortunately, most of the general population seems to believe that the pelvis belongs solely with the legs rather than the torso. A brief look at a skeleton can easily disprove this notion, but for the singer who has not yet made this connection, a mismapping of the pelvis can have disastrous effects on body alignment and vocal production. First, participation of the muscles in the pelvic floor is vital for healthy breath support. If the pelvis is too far forward, the alignment between the vocal tract and pelvic floor is lost, compromising the singer's breath support. The vocal tract is an all-important vertical space, the sense of which the singer must constantly invite and cultivate to ensure a stabilized low larynx and high palate and thus the optimal vertical resonating space. In addition, a pelvis that is too far forward compromises the effectiveness of the psoas muscles that are important stabilizers of the whole pelvic region. These muscles can easily become disengaged, shortened, and weakened, interfering with the deep breath support needed for singing.

SINGERS' BREATH ENERGY

Energy is *space*'s partner as the singer's language. Energy, from a singer's point of view, is the vitality in the breath, and it is incumbent on the singer to find ways of renewing that energy in order to maintain the proper breath pressure within the vocal tract that ensures a consistent vocal line. It is interesting to note that we have a different name for air once it enters the body. Once air is inhaled, it is called breath. I like to think this is because the air we inhale is imbued with our personal energy. This energy reflects the singer's state of being at any given moment and is ultimately reflected in the tone produced. So it is that energy is the singer's language.

ALEXANDER TECHNIQUE DIRECTION

Physicists have thought for some time that matter and energy are interchangeable. Understanding this can help the singer embrace the idea that singing is indeed an ethereal and delicate process.

As an AT teacher, one of my main tasks is to help my students let go of deeply ingrained beliefs and attitudes that suggest otherwise. Invariably, young singers will "muscle up" in order to sing a note they perceive as "high," take a huge breath when approaching any phrase they see as "difficult," or "batten down the hatches" to prepare for the onslaught before a particularly complex and daunting coloratura passage. Usually, they don't realize they are doing this. They are simply reacting to their operative belief system, their default mode, if you will. Inhibiting the physical action alone may not be enough to correct the problem, because this may be a deeply ingrained mental as well as physical response. It is here that I simply ask, "What did you just tell yourself?" The response might be "Red alert! High note! I need to work hard to sing this!" This attitude probably has its roots in Western culture's principle of "No pain, no gain" or "I must suffer in order to achieve anything worthwhile." This can be the result of a deeply ingrained perfectionism, a need to do it "right," or simply a desire to please the teacher. The longer I teach AT, the more persuaded I am that our work lies primarily in our thinking. For me, the heart of the matter is exploring these deeply rooted belief systems and eventually transforming them into highly functional reasoning. AT direction embodies this process. Like Elizabeth Walker's "fairy wish," it is insistent without being demanding.

It is deeply satisfying to help singers replace their fear-based thinking with that of technical clarity, confidence, playfulness, fearlessness, imagination, and curiosity. When I work with a student who believes that he has to muscle up to sing a high note, I might explore the idea that the terms *high* and *low* are just semantics. Who decided which notes would be called high and which low? Isn't it simply because of the way music is written on the page?

I find particularly helpful the idea of approaching higher pitches in my range from above rather than reaching for them. It helps me not only to raise the palate but also keeps the core more grounded. (Student Sean Matassa)

Singers who practice AT are simply directing weightless energy, and likewise, directing the singer's tone does not require excessive effort but rather clarity of thought and the "quiet knowing" that it is so.

"SPINNING" THE TONE

The Italian singing masters spoke of a tone that is spun like a spider's silken web, yet has the power to cut through an orchestra. To achieve this spinning tone, the singer's breath energy must also be streamlined into a slim wieldable thread of concentrated energy similar to a laser beam. Because not much breath is needed to accomplish this, taking a huge breath is counterproductive. Professor von Winterfeldt encouraged me to "sniff a flower" or "take a thimbleful of air." She reminded me that when I speak I do not tank up on air, nor do I worry about running out of breath. My body perceives my intention, knows what I am about to say and how I want to say it, and inhales and rations the breath accordingly. While speaking, seldom do we find ourselves worried about running out of breath. Why should it be otherwise when we sing? Yet I remember to this day how difficult it was to make that adjustment in my thinking. Taking a tiny breath before a difficult phrase seemed risky. But in time I was able to inhibit my urge to take a huge breath, and I realized that the nature of my inhalation was primed by my imagination and intention. When my attention was focused on that priming process, I found myself "being breathed" with the amount and quality of breath energy necessary for each phrase. Fully committed to this process, I began to experience my breath energy as delicate and wieldable—yet still powerful.

I loved when you talked about "imagining and breathing for the whole phrase you are about to sing" when I was working on the Brentano Lieder. Thinking about this caused me to take a different kind of breath—a slower breath I think that opened up my resonance space for all the notes of the phrase— not just the first one. (Student Susan Ruggiero)

"THROWING MY HEART OVER"

My mother, Catherine O'Neill,[9] my first voice teacher, used to say, "You don't have to be crazy to sing, but it helps!" She meant that an exaggerated, heightened state of being sets the singer up to sing, and the singer must be able to house and sustain that higher plain of vibration comfortably. To accomplish this, I encourage singers to note and accept the energy or state of being they are experiencing at that moment. Through clean, clear direction, it is easily transformed and focused as necessary. The nature of this direction might emulate that of a famous equestrian who was asked how she inspired her horse to jump. "That's easy!" she said. "I throw my heart over first!"

MUSIC IS MOVEMENT

Music implies movement. When movement stops, music ceases. AT also implies and embraces movement. AT students come to realize that the body's natural state is that of perpetual movement and that the body juggles itself into all activity, including stillness. Great artists instinctively refine this movement to produce a wide variety of sounds and colors without reverting to a state of rigidity. Like a pendulum that perpetuates its own movement, the singer's energy is cycled and recycled, continually renewing the tone she is singing.

When the tone feels right and good to her, the student is often tempted to hold onto the sound, effectively killing its energy. AT helps singers become comfortable with and enjoy this state of perpetual movement. Even the all-important head/neck relationship is not a place but rather a climate, suspended, supported, and maintained by the balanced movement of many factors. And just as our beloved planet is suspended in the cosmic dance of the universe, so the singer's tone may be spun and juggled by all aspects of the self that respond to the climate created for them. To this end, I encourage my students to anticipate how the tone will feel and savor fully the experience—but in passing, as one might view the scenery from the window of a passing train without attachment or judgment. To help my students maintain this state of perpetual movement, I remind them, "How you sound is none of your business. Your fascination is with the process and not the result!"

And Finally...The Seedling

Throughout this chapter, I have sought to point out that metaphor and AT principles define each other, and each in its unique way offers a pathway toward self-discovery and actualization.

In my voice lessons, Professor von Winterfeldt insisted that I make friends with myself before every phrase I sang. She simply would not allow me to proceed without this benevolent attitude toward myself. She insisted I pause, be, and cherish myself and the gifts I could bring to this beautiful art that I have cherished throughout my life. This simple idea is the seedling that truly embodies all the AT strategies I have suggested in this chapter. Becoming friends with myself led me to the process of unlearning much of what I thought I had learned. This took me to the next essential step of remembering what I had briefly forgotten—that I have always known how to sing!

When I engage AT, singing really is that simple!

Notes

1   Margarete von Winterfeldt (1902–1978) was a celebrated German professor of voice at Freiberg University, and privately, in Berlin. She taught many famous singers, and perhaps most notably, she discovered and trained famous German tenor Fritz Wunderlich.

2   Elizabeth Walker (d. September 17, 2013) was the last living first-generation teacher of AT. She used the expression "fairy wish" to describe the qualities of direction.

3   John Keats, English poet (October 31, 1795–February 23, 1821). From a letter to Benjamin Bailey, November 22, 1817: www.john-keats.com (accessed on March 19, 2017).

4   Norman Gulbrandsen (1918–2010) was a well-known and highly successful voice teacher who was on the voice faculties at Northwestern University and De Paul University for many years.

5   A concept invented by Rudolf Laban (1879–1958), a dancer and movement specialist. For more information, see the website for the Laban/Bartenieff Institute of Movement Studies at www.limsonline.org.

6   R. Buckminster Fuller was a 20th-century inventor and visionary who did not limit himself to one field but worked as a "comprehensive anticipatory design scientist" to solve global problems: www.bfi.org/about-fuller (accessed on March 19, 2017).

7   Pushing Hands is one of the training practices of t'ai chi ch'uan. For further information, see Gilman (2015).

8   For those wishing to explore more fully the concept of energy centers called chakras, see AT teacher Glen Park's excellent book *A New Approach to the Alexander Technique* (Park 1998).

9   Catherine Rule O'Neill (January 23, 1907–July 21, 1997): voice teacher, who specialized in teaching high-school-aged singers, and was the first teacher of Metropolitan Opera singers Jeff Wells and Ruth Falcon as well as many other professional singers.

References

Brown, W.E. (1931) *Vocal Wisdom: Maxims of Giovanni Battista Lamperti* (enlarged edition). New York: Taplinger Publishing Company.

Gilman, M. (2015, February 15) Yang Tai Chi Tui Shou—Push Hands— Volume 1 [Video file]. Accessed on March 19, 2017 at www.youtube.com/watch?v=0F84zY6OiuM

Park, G. (1998) *A New Approach to the Alexander Technique: Moving Towards a More Balanced Expression of the Whole Self.* Freedom, CA: Crossing Press.

Of Testing Times and Hoped-For Miracles

The Alexander Technique and the Doubtful Musician

Robert Schubert

AT Perspective

I first came to AT through reading *The Alexander Principle*, by Wilfred Barlow (2001 [1973]), then *The Use of the Self*, by F.M. Alexander (2001). As a clarinet student in college, I experimented by myself with the concepts of inhibition and direction as I practiced my clarinet. I found that certain things I was thinking about while playing became easier or resulted in less anxiety. These effects were small but nonetheless significant to me at the time. My AT efforts at the outset were concerned with the thought process described by Alexander. I didn't experience "hands-on" work until about a year later when I traveled to Canada to study. My clarinet teacher took one look at me and sent me off for AT lessons! (A big thank you to Jim Campbell for that!)

"Less is more" and "Relax!" were instructions often given me during my college years. It wasn't till later, after discovering AT and then having lessons, that a way of realizing the real meaning of these instructions while performing finally opened up to me.

Now when I get into difficulty, I always have a tool to bring things into balance. I'm always aware of my tendency to over-try when under pressure, and the AT process helps me stay mentally and physically within myself. I've had some really wonderful experiences with hands-on lessons that granted a glimpse of my full psychophysical potential. Occasionally I manage to help a student have such a glimpse.

For me the great value of the work is in the transformational thought process. Those following the rigor of this process can maintain perspective while nurturing an exquisite sense of what's needed physically and mentally to meet the demands of any task. This is what I hope my students take away with them. A useful tool, the awareness to know when and how to use it, and an appreciation of the discipline required to develop and refine it throughout their careers.

References

Alexander, F.M. (2001) *The Use of the Self*. London: Orion Publishing Group.

Barlow, W. (2001) *The Alexander Principle*. London: Orion Publishing Group. (Original work published 1973.)

First, the bad news: Studying the Alexander Technique will not automatically make anyone a better musician. I can attest to the veracity of this from personal experience. There is a silver lining to my anti-testimonial, however, and it lies in the word "automatically."

I should explain that, earlier in my career, I was a full-time orchestral clarinet player. Since those days, I have maintained my clarinet playing at an expert level. I have recorded CDs of new clarinet music, performed clarinet concertos with semi-professional ensembles, and continue to play with various symphony orchestras in Australia. Most of my work now, however, is teaching. I teach both clarinet and AT.

Let me open by sharing a true story from my own personal treasure house of AT miracle tales. The events of this story occurred during a period in my life when I had been playing clarinet full-time in a busy professional orchestra for several years. Before this incident, I had studied AT for two years as a music student, but I had not been thinking about AT for some time.

On the day in question, our orchestra was rehearsing Beethoven's Fifth Symphony. In the second movement of this piece, there's a moment when the strings play a couple of light chords, then the clarinet comes in for a solo that moves through a weaker part of the instrument's range. I played the solo. Immediately the conductor said "Clarinet! Sound! Not very good!" as blunt as could be, just like that. (I should note that English was not his first language.) The whole orchestra gasped, not least because the quality of my sound was regarded as one of my stronger points. I was shocked. Immediately I thought to myself, "Right, next time, I'll show you." Well, we went back a few bars and ran my solo over again. This time, I tried really hard to play with a beautiful sound. Surprise, surprise! This time I sounded worse. I could hear it. The whole orchestra could hear it. Our conductor's contribution was to growl, "Breathing! Not good!" At this point, he called a rehearsal break.

One of the central concepts in AT is called *end-gaining*. This is the tendency we have to focus on an end result while losing sight of the process, or means-whereby in F.M. Alexander's terminology, employed to achieve the result: "End gaining is a universal habit" (Alexander 2001 [1932]). My reaction to the criticism was classic end-gaining! I'd totally lost my connection to the means-whereby involved in playing the solo, and my performance had deteriorated accordingly.

During the break, our concertmaster came over and said, "Robert, you sounded fine the first time. Don't worry about it." We knew this particular conductor had a record of needling players. I suspected this might have been his way of exercising dominance over us. As break continued, I recalled my training in AT. I began to work on myself as I had learned to do during my lessons. I practiced stopping for a moment before playing to allow mental space to give myself some reminders, known as *directions*, to allow freedom in the head, neck, and torso. In this way, I lifted myself out of my end-gaining mentality.

When we resumed, we started again at the point of my great discomfiture. Rightly or wrongly, I imagined that our conductor was waiting to pounce. No one in the orchestra dared glance at me. After a scowl from the conductor, the violins played their introductory chords. I sat in my chair thinking as "loudly" as I could, "It doesn't matter what this sounds like. I'm just going to direct myself while I play." The result of Alexander directions is expansion and freedom, both physically and psychologically. Without realizing it, my earlier shock at the unexpected criticism had literally "shrunk" me in both respects. My reaction was to forget myself, to contract into over-trying and "showing him a thing or two," which is hardly a noble musical goal. As I experienced the freeing and expansion, my perspective was restored along with my familiar relationship to the process of tone production and the musical values inherent in the solo. This time, the conductor said nothing at all! We just kept playing through the movement. The concertmaster glanced over at me and gave me a great big wink.

The moral of my story is of course that merely studying AT does not prevent a musician from experiencing any of a multitude of stimuli that can trigger a stress response leading to a sub-par performance. However, if one applies the technique when potentially stressful situations arise, the outcome may be surprising and delightful.

To someone new to AT, I suspect the most intriguing aspect of my story might be my descriptions of what I "did" once I remembered my Alexander training. Such a reader, I imagine, would be keen to know more about the processes of "release" I described as part of my preparation for performing. All these steps sound like doing something, and oh, how we are drawn, like moths to a flame, to any solution that involves doing something. Rather than offering a formula of things to do, Alexander training provided first the awareness to identify what was happening and how my attention had shifted. Moreover, AT practice gave me the strength to *not* do the things that were unhelpful. While it is true that the steps of "release" played a part in helping me perform better, I believe that the effect of these steps alone would have been far less had I not first consciously set aside all thoughts and worries about the end result of my music making.

When one is filled with doubts about whether one can achieve a particular musical outcome, preventing oneself from thinking about that outcome can be quite a challenge. What I stopped thinking about and doing on the stage of Hamer Hall was just as significant as what I started thinking about and doing after that. The quality of *inhibition* strongly influences the utility of the AT directions. Inhibition? This is the term Alexander used to denote the act of stopping one's initial, habitual reaction to a stimulus. This is usually a good idea, as that unconsciously developed habit often has many harmful aspects to it. All aspects of our reaction to the stimuli of life are collected in Alexander's concept of *use*. "When I employ the word 'use' it is not in that limited sense of the use of any specific part [of the body]... but in a...more comprehensive sense applying to the working of the organism in general" (Alexander 2001 [1932], p.22).

When he refers to the organism in general, he really means it. AT involves the psychological and the physical; it is all encompassing. Hence, he referred to his technique as being psychophysical in nature. So, in all situations we can be said to be using ourselves, and Alexander identified any harmful or irrational aspects of this use as *misuse*. My misuse at that time involved my old habits induced whenever I "tried hard" to achieve. Motivated by self-doubt and fear of failure, I expressed this increased effort through tightening the neck, jaw, shoulders, and arms along with compression through the torso and my peculiar tendency to strongly contract my calves. All of this was instinctive and unconscious—and highly counterproductive. Alexander said:

> All those who wish to change something in themselves must learn... to inhibit their immediate reaction to any stimulus to gain a desired end [and in order to stop falling back] upon the familiar sensory experiences of their old habitual use in order to gain it, they must continue this inhibition whilst they employ the new direction of their use. (Alexander 2001 [1932], p.105)

Once a musician has managed to inhibit their immediate reaction, they have an opportunity to change the nature of their reaction. Alexander provided guidelines for promoting healthier, more rational reactions in the form of a series of self-instructions he called directions.

> Once this misdirection was inhibited, my next step would be to discover what direction would be necessary to ensure a new and improved use of the head and neck, and, indirectly, of the larynx and breathing and other mechanisms...and in its place employ my reasoning processes...to select...the means-whereby a more satisfactory use could be brought about...[and then]...to project consciously the directions required for putting these means into effect. (Alexander 2001 [1932], pp.38–39)

During this experience, I ended up misusing myself, and only by becoming aware of and then stopping this could I rediscover good use through conscious direction. This experience truly changed my life and approach to my job. From then on, AT was always with me in the orchestra. It became my "secret weapon" that was available whenever any doubt or fear arose. None of my concerts or rehearsals from that point on lacked an Alexander influence. The confidence and ease in performance amazed me. Playing became easier and more artistically exploratory, and just sounded better—and I was enjoying myself! These experiences also crystallized in me the desire to train as an AT teacher.

* * *

One of the most difficult situations musicians face is being asked to perform a piece they feel is beyond their capabilities. If someone asks me to play a piece that is clearly beyond me, I may face some momentary embarrassment as I concede that I lack the necessary skills, but the matter is at least resolved quickly. Once I have uttered my painful confession, I don't have to worry about the matter anymore.

Faced with a passage we regard as almost impossible, however, we quickly begin tying ourselves in knots, both mentally and physically. If only we try hard and really work at it, we tell ourselves, we will eventually be able to play this passage. After all, isn't this how everyone does it? Almost before we know it, we are emotionally entangled with the outcome, doubtful we will reach our goal, but nonetheless determined to do whatever it takes.

Once we set off down this path, we immediately find ourselves falling back on our most deeply ingrained habits, at least some of which are likely to involve using ourselves poorly just at the time when it would be most beneficial to use ourselves well. It is our poor use of ourselves that ultimately leads to the end-gaining approach, for all the benefits this may appear to generate in the short term.

In Australia, alas, much of our system of musical education seems to have evolved to promote end-gaining. I believe this can be explained partly by the nature of the curriculum predominant in Australian music education. A privately funded corporation known as the Australian Music Examinations Board, or AMEB, publishes syllabi for a wide range of instruments, and conducts graded musical examinations covering these syllabi. These exams are known colloquially as Grade 1 AMEB, Grade 2 AMEB, and so on.

The Australian music teachers often feel pressure to organize their pupils' musical education around AMEB requirements. Fee-paying schools may look at AMEB results before offering scholarship exams to prospective students. Parents, teachers, and students alike appear to accept the notion that the development of musical skills is somehow akin to pursuing a black belt in the martial arts. True musical values can become obscured, and students risk being robbed of much of the pleasure they could have had from learning to play an instrument. This mindset has inflicted needless levels of performance anxiety on generations of children.

Of course the AMEB system can be a useful process in the student's development, when used as a good motivational tool and valuable performance experience. The problem is not with the AMEB system itself but in the way it's used. All too often, the student (and parents and teacher) become subsumed by the grading system. The end to be gained—the next grade on the list—is often achieved at the price of a more patient approach to the instrument and a clear and accurate musical and kinesthetic awareness.

The AMEB's influence permeates every aspect of musical education in Australia. It has been remarked that to a man with a hammer in his hand, all the world looks like a nail. Alas, to a student with an AMEB syllabus in her hand, our whole rich musical repertoire risks appearing to be itself "graded" and/or becoming merely a sequence of AMEB exam requirements. When musical progress is viewed as an ascending ladder with steps labeled Grade 1, Grade 2, and so on, effort and trying hard to jump the hurdles can replace true musical values.

This can be seen, for instance, in the way the AMEB syllabus requires clarinet students to explore the high register of the instrument quite early and in a way that too easily promotes an end-gaining approach inasmuch as how high the student can play can be viewed as an indicator of their level. If a student is not paying good attention to his use, he is almost certainly going to try forcing. The sight of a student going up on tiptoe (without realizing it) in the act of playing an ascending wide interval, along with all the neck and back tightness he employs to get there, is all too common. If he's unlucky, he manages to produce high notes this way, and the association is quickly established. If he's *really* unlucky, someone will praise this kind of choreography as evidence of his musical "expressiveness." "Success!" he thinks—and force becomes the default strategy.

When I teach clarinet students without any reference to the AMEB, I have them stay in the low part of the instrument for a long time. The high register then comes quite easily in due course, without gaining associations of extra effort or self-evaluation.

Students can easily fall into the misconception that they should be able to do their exams at regular intervals and feel they are somehow falling behind if the next exam grade's material is still too difficult when the regular exam time comes around. Clarinet students going up the AMEB ladder can go along quietly for a couple of grades, then suddenly find they're dealing with quite a large jump in technical difficulty. This abrupt change in expectation can become a stimulus for end-gaining and misuse. Suddenly the next AMEB exam is all about trying to get those top notes out and all those scales played fast enough. At some point, nearly every student is going to think, "This has suddenly become way too hard for me." At this point, the student is likely either to drop out of music altogether or fall into end-gaining.

These are some of the cultural "conditions present" that a teacher of AT will almost certainly have to take into account when introducing the technique to an Australian student exposed to the AMEB culture.

Here are some approaches I use, as a teacher of AT, when working with musicians who have come to me primarily because they have heard the technique may help them with their playing. Sometimes these are clarinet students who come to me for lessons in AT rather than clarinet. Sometimes they are musicians who play instruments in which I have no expertise at all. Quite often, a musician approaches me at a time when some crisis is looming; the trigger is typically an upcoming exam. This exam may be months away, or it may be only a week off. Some of these students are clearly hoping for a miracle!

It is possible that I may unwittingly have contributed to the expectation of miracles by relating stories of my own experience like the one that began this chapter. My story is true of course, but it is pertinent—and worth emphasizing—that I had a lot of experience in AT at the point when I got myself into such an anxious state. I was able to draw on this experience when I finally came to my senses. A student coming to me for help one week before a music exam has no such experience to fall back on.

If the student's exam is quite close, I won't hear her play in any extended way, because at this point it's too late to be going into musical content. Anxiety is usually high, preventing the student from performing as she knows she can. AT addresses both the mental and physical dimensions of the performing experience, and if the student can become aware of the nature of end-gaining and its relationship to performance anxiety, a great deal can be accomplished in a short time. It is often a source of great comfort for the student to be told that it's okay to work with "the conditions present." In other words, to inhibit the striving to attain the next perceived level and work with herself as she is today. This change in mental attitude alone tends to produce a release of physical tension, and then the student learns to give herself the self-instructions (Alexander directions) to promote release of the neck, head, and back, which further aids in obtaining freedom. These conditions often produce exciting results. Beyond the improved quality of sound and finger smoothness, the musician perceives that they have been given a key to their own performance improvement as an alternative to their old reliance on striving.

If the exam is further away, I ask the student to play one of the pieces she is preparing. Nine times out of ten, it becomes clear that the repertoire she is playing is too difficult for her. At this point, I explain the concept of end-gaining to the student, pointing out the risk she faces of developing bad playing habits if she tackles an over-difficult exam without paying close attention to her use of herself. At this early stage, of course, the student is still very much outcome-focused, despite any fine words I can muster pointing to the dangers of this approach. Nevertheless, it's important to begin helping the student gain some degree of detachment from the (probably unrealistic) musical outcome she is hoping to attain in a relatively short period of time.

By now, the student starts to grasp that whatever this AT is about, it doesn't seem to be about concentrating more or trying harder. The student may not say so aloud, but she is almost certainly wondering by this point how AT can possibly result in her performing any better if such an obvious prerequisite to success as "trying harder" is not engaged. This is implicitly the point I address next as I ask the student to play an excerpt from one of her exam pieces again. At some point, the music becomes more difficult, and when this happens, I have the student make some changes that will make it easier. If the student is playing a wind instrument, for example, and the pitch begins to rise uncomfortably, I ask her to play that section an octave lower. Or I might ask the student to slow down at the point where the going becomes difficult. In doing this, we are in effect short-circuiting the anxiety response that typically gets in the way of the student's instrumental technique, allowing the student to play without any doubt whatsoever, which is the approach I want to encourage. Once she has done that, I get her to notice the difference in herself and in the quality of the musical result, particularly in the quality of sound.

So far, I have done nothing with the student that resembles a conventional AT lesson. I can now add some primary Alexander directions, both verbally and with my hands, while the student continues to play the easier version of the piece. After a little of this, I may ask the student what she has noticed while playing using these directions. Sometimes she comments on how strange the experience has been, or she may report that certain parts of her body that are normally tensed when she plays were not so tight on this occasion, and yet she was able to play regardless.

I have noticed that musicians who play wind instruments often report dissatisfaction with the sound they hear themselves making as they play while I am giving them directions. To my ears, the student's sound is typically more vibrant and alive under these conditions, with a richer set of overtones present. But the student herself often experiences this same sound as harsh or unpleasant. When this happens, I reassure the student that this is quite a common experience and tell a story of sitting in a chamber music ensemble playing with a world-renowned clarinetist. I thought that his sound close up was very intense, realizing later that it was precisely this vibrant quality that sounded so wonderful from the vantage point of an audience member in a large auditorium. I encourage my student to consider the possibility that the unfamiliar, overtone-rich sound she is now producing may in fact be superior to the one she is accustomed to hearing from her own vantage point.

Alexander noted this phenomenon of "faulty sensory perception" during the process of learning a new use of oneself, referring to the perception of one's own physicality that a new process may "feel wrong." It is just as alive in the musician's perception of her own tonal quality; the new quality of sound "sounds wrong." Many are the performers who desire improvement but resist change because it feels or sounds unfamiliar.

As the student continues to play, I ask her to increase the level of difficulty slightly (for example, by raising the overall pitch a step or increasing the tempo by a small degree) while I continue to give the student directions, both verbally and with my hands. Before and during each repetition of the passage, I remind the student to allow the neck to free, head to go forward and up, and back to lengthen and widen.

With my hands I hint at these directions, particularly the release of the head forward and up. If there is even a small reappearance of the poor habitual use, usually in the form of tightening in the neck, I point it out to the student. This often needs to be done a few times until the student can identify the misuse and which particular aspect of the activity tends to produce it.

We continue to increase the level of difficulty progressively until we reach the point where the student's doubts begin to creep back, and then we immediately drop back to an easier level. Usually the student begins to notice the subtle misuses that accompany the doubts caused by the perceived difficulty of the material and corresponding fear of failure. An appeal to extra muscular strength and tension in the face of this doubt is the norm, as is the musician's lack of awareness of this response. However, once the student is aware of her reaction to the difficulty, she is now in a position to work on preventing it (*inhibiting*, in AT parlance). Then the student may well appeal to extra muscular strength and tension again in her desire to prevent the original misuse! All this in the service of protecting the result, of "gaining her end." "Allowing" as opposed to habitual "doing" gives rise to a real fear of failure. This fear is actually the root cause of the misuse. Many students go to great lengths to avoid acknowledging this, hurling themselves into their practice in order to feel themselves working hard. This feeling of strenuous work can provide its own satisfaction and musical results, with any subtle failures along the way remaining masked. I'm often reminded of people in the gym, sacrificing form and technique, using speed and momentum to lift too-heavy weights and measuring success in kilograms and sweat. In this scenario, they can even view injury as a badge of honor. Musicians are not immune to this, particularly the young and ambitious.

Once the student has had this experience, I explain that what we have just done together is an excellent model for how she should approach her own musical practice from then on. Rather than spend her practice time worrying constantly about results ("Can I play that high note, can I finger that fast tricky passage, can I play fast enough, soft enough, loud enough? Will I obtain an A grade in my exam?")

and trying constantly to force the issue, I want her to practice with much less stress and tightness, focusing instead on the quality of her use of herself via the AT self-instructions to release tension in the head, neck, and back, as well as any changes in her sound. There should be no sense of rushing on to meet a demanding goal.

Gradually we increase the level of difficulty of the passage, all the while keeping an eye out for doubt and fear and inhibiting the accompanying misuse that she can now recognize. In this new way of practicing, the student should not constantly be asking herself "Can I achieve my musical goal?" but rather "Can I remember to think about my use of myself and let the 'ends' take care of themselves?"

In practice, I tend to intermingle many of these conversations and activities with AT work away from the instrument, teaching the student over multiple lessons how to apply its principles in activities less emotionally charged than playing their instrument. In many lessons, there may be no actual music playing at all, though I do typically ask my student how they are progressing musically, and we often talk over some of the matters previously described while sitting, standing, or walking, always reminding them to attend to their use during movement and conversation. I think the ability to consider one's use and direct oneself during any activity, including conversation, is an excellent method for the musician to practice practicing and performing. Musical performance is always a dialogue of some sort, with yourself and the listener, your ensemble partner(s), and within the musical argument itself. What do we do to ourselves in order to make convincing musical statements? At what cost do we win the argument?

As I get to know a student better, I come to recognize areas in which he tends to try too hard, and when it seems appropriate, I may challenge him to develop his inhibition in a specific area. For example, often a wind player exerts too much effort in taking a breath, losing his good use of himself in the process. This is usually a symptom of fear of running out of breath, similar to the misuses in string players who often have a deep-seated fear of dropping the bow or the violin. I may challenge him to do all his music practice for the following week using only a minimal intake of breath, again keeping an eye on the misuse and inhibiting it. If I see a student is getting so anxious about memorizing a piece that she is forgetting it as quickly as she learns it, I may challenge her to start again at the beginning and to memorize only a single phrase on her first day, a single additional phrase on her second day, and so on. If a student is attempting to practice every note for an upcoming exam at least twice a day, I challenge him to focus most of his practice on just a few selected passages, giving relatively scant attention to the remainder of his exam repertoire. Students may find challenges such as these difficult to take up—but they are likely to report a surprising degree of success after working this way.

Occasionally a student asks me what sitting, standing, and walking have to do with playing music. The connection between music making and other activities can be explained quite simply: they help a student understand end-gaining, inhibition, and direction in a simplified (non-musically triggered) environment. You're going to sit down. What is your habitual way of sitting down? Once you have noticed any unnecessary tension in the movement, can we experiment with moving and choosing not to enlist that tension, introducing directions instead to encourage more ease and simplicity in the movement? Now you can move in a different way while still maintaining your directions; "thinking in activity," being mindful.

A student who practices all this in the chair is basically practicing the same techniques he will apply when he takes up his instrument but in a less fraught context. The instrument is such a strong stimulus for a musician that it's difficult for the player to keep the directions uppermost in his mind unless he has first had some considerable practice giving himself directions in an easier context. Once he has a musical instrument at his fingertips, he always risks slipping back into asking himself "How was that? Did I get what I wanted to get? Did I sound any good? Did I play well?" We so easily get sucked into thinking about end results. However, if we can remove that powerful stimulus and work instead with simple activities like standing and sitting and walking, we can help the student experience successful inhibition and direction giving, improving the student's chance of success in using himself well while playing his instrument.

So, how well does the approach I have described work in practice? Overall, I would say that most of my students have been happy with the improvements they notice in their music making once they have begun to lower their stress levels.

I have seen big age-related variations in how quickly students understand. Students of primary-school age tend to grasp the key concepts almost immediately, with little fuss, and they retain what they have learned of the technique very well. Older students typically persist in trying to do the AT directions for quite some time, and this is never helpful. They tend to over-try by enlisting muscular force and stiffen when thinking of the directions. Young children also try to "do" the directions initially, but they're much quicker to let that go when I say, "It's just a thought. Just have the thought that your neck can be nice and free. You don't have to move anything." Older students tend to want kinesthetic feedback, so they persist for longer in performing actions physically with their necks to reassure themselves that something is happening or that they are "doing the right thing."

I have certainly had some students who were simply not prepared to follow this path, or to follow it very far. Even for students who are highly persistent and motivated, progress can be a case of "two steps forward, one step back." Some degree of recidivism is normal: Our habits tend to reassert themselves when we are under pressure in a performance situation. The AT work enables us to build a more solid psychophysical base, and the more we practice, the more stable our "default" state of overall coordination becomes. Over time, we become more sensitive to the effects of misuse and can rebalance ourselves sooner.

I have often been genuinely astonished at how well a student who has come to me in a great state of crisis has performed in an exam that both of us may have thought was beyond her. "Miracles" of this kind do occasionally occur. When a student faces an imminent exam that is really too difficult for him, there can be considerable fear about the result. We work to shift his focus and temper his attachment to short-term musical goals, refusing to end-gain, focusing instead on his use of himself. To be able to play through an over-challenging exam while retaining this kind of mindset may not be the miracle a student was hoping for, but anyone who has experienced this kind of change can attest that it is a wonderful and liberating transformation. The student is usually pleasantly surprised at how well they actually performed in the end.

I was reminded of another way that I believe AT helps performers when a college music student who had just had four or five lessons with me remarked with a quizzical look, "I've noticed I'm feeling happier. It's weird, my mood is a lot better since I've been having AT lessons. Is that normal?" This reaction is not uncommon. I have always attributed this to the fact that in mindfully developing a freer relationship in the head, neck, and back, AT continually reduces the ill effects of any anxiety by preventing or at least not allowing a full expression of the physiological "startle response." Also, in attention to ease and freedom in breathing, AT tends to foster the parasympathetic nervous system, switching off the typical "fight or flight" response that performers know as stage fright or performance anxiety.

Recent research by Amy Cuddy and others has shown the remarkably positive psychological changes that posture and "power posing" can have. A clear relationship has been shown between increasing or reducing one's stature and perception of personal power and self-esteem. Postures were summarized as either "expansive" or "contractive." The research shows that "taking up more space" (expansive posture) feeds our feelings of personal power and well-being, and the opposite is also true. Contracting, slumping, and collapsing, thus taking up less space ("contractive posture"), can cause us to feel powerless and give up on challenges more easily. These changes have even now been measured at the hormonal level: "These intriguing findings showed that holding a single expansive pose can make significant, measurable differences in the hormones related to confidence and anxiety" (Cuddy 2016, p.205).

Now consider what we are doing in AT. Alexander noticed that his functioning improved with a "lengthening of the stature" (2001 [1932], pp.29–30). His technique is based on inhibiting contractive reactions to stimuli and mindfully learning self-instructions aimed at allowing psychophysical (his terminology for mind/body) freedom through expansion. AT teaches expansive posture as a way of life. In fact, rather than "posture," which implies something static, AT teaches a use of oneself that fosters expansion in every moment of every act. Imagine a series of still photographs that when combined show the complete action of standing up from a chair or playing a melody on the violin. The AT student will tend to release into unforced expansion in every photograph; each moment is an "expansive posture." With this approach, the "default" level of expansiveness rises considerably over time and, as my students have discovered, often in quite a short time, with positive results.

Were my Beethoven Fifth Symphony moment and the many wonderful experiences of my students over the years miracles? Perhaps not, by the standards of some, but they certainly felt like it at the time—because we were granted the freedom to produce our best in that moment. Does applying AT always enable a musician to pull a rabbit out of the hat? I think it would be naive to expect that. The quality of any musician's performance is always dependent on the quality of his training and preparation. Nevertheless, there are many circumstances in which even the most skilled performer can succumb to doubt and end-gaining—and when that happens, even the best musician may start to shrink and resort to contraction and force, ending up sounding (and feeling) rather ordinary.

If, in challenging circumstances, I am willing to risk surrendering my attachment to an outcome and focus instead on my use of myself, the result may be pleasantly surprising more often than not; it might even at times verge on the miraculous. To me, this sounds like a risk worth taking.

References

Alexander, F.M. (2001) *The Use of the Self.* London: Orion Publishing Group. (Original work published 1932.)

Cuddy, A. (2016) *Presence: Bringing Your Boldest Self to Your Biggest Challenges.* London: Orion Publishing Group.

Is This Dance Made of Cake?

An Exploration of Alexander Technique in Choreographic Process

Crispin Spaeth

AT Perspective

My current description of the Alexander Technique is that it is a tool for self-education that helps the user be a better vertebrate. A person using AT may enrich their thinking, moving, and communication in all the things they choose to do. In this chapter I am focusing on choreography—having ideas, expressing these ideas as intention, and working with dancers to usher the ideas into time and space.

I write this chapter from the perspective of having used AT for most of my creative career, and now, 20 years into my deep AT fandom, becoming an AT teacher. Within the wide-open plain that is a choreographic process, AT supports creativity by opening up new possibilities and helping to focus a dance into a coherent work of art. In addition to its wonder as a choreographic aid, I believe that AT would be invaluable as a fundamental component to all dance education—as I wish it had been part of mine. Dancers already talk to their whole selves, even while they are frequently distracted by the parts. How exciting it would be to work with dancers armed with AT as a tool to refresh the whole and to perform with full access to that wholeness—a heightened literacy of choice. This is what I would like to bring to all of my students, in and out of the dance world.

I am a choreographer and producer who has used the Alexander Technique in all aspects of my life and work for the last 20 years, including training with Cathy Madden to become an AT teacher. My personal definition of AT always includes some variation on the words *thinking*, *movement*, and *communication*. To me, this tidy trio represents all volitional human experience, pointing to the myriad ways a person might use AT to enrich all aspects of life. I have deeply explored how AT can help choreographers in the studio to create dances and align performers with the intentions of those dances. In this chapter I share some of these explorations in choreography—having ideas, expressing these ideas as intention, and working with dancers to usher the ideas into time and space.

When I first started learning AT, I knew that it would have profound effects on my physical abilities and self-care, but I didn't immediately recognize its potential application for creative process. I am, admittedly, a process nerd. The way people make things is often as interesting to me as the product. Happily, there is no one way to make a dance, so process can be ever-changing. Because of this, however, choreography can seem mysterious from the outside. At its core, choreography is acting with clarity on an idea through movement.

In 1995, I was working on a dance, *Hand Over Fist*, which loosely examined the transition from industrial to technological economies. Things felt really right, everything in place, all energy going the right direction, but I was in territory that I didn't quite grasp. I wasn't sure what I had made—actually a happy place of surprise—and needed to understand the character of the work better before supporting it with lights and costumes. I remember asking myself, "What is this dance made of?"

The answer was—metaphorically—cake and Styrofoam and cheap velvet. I had created a dance combining different forms and textures that together reflected the rich pleasures, decay, and artifice I wanted the dance to embody. This is the first time I remember using AT as a critical overlay to my own process. In the first chapter of *The Use of the Self*, "Evolution of a Technique," F.M. Alexander calls out "analyze conditions of use present" and "reason out means whereby" (1996 [1932], p.39) as key steps in his unfolding process of reasoning, what we now call AT. Of course every choreographer has their own way of assessing the direction of their work. In this instance, my applying the "conditions of use present" inquiry to my dance included the existence of those imaginary textures. This brought me to the realization of the broader applications of AT, including application to thinking itself. Having a tool to improve my thinking means an improved creative process. Simple as that.

An improved creative process means higher satisfaction in the dances I create. For me, each dance presents its own rules, and I have to complete a dance on its own terms rather than do what I have done before. The previous "What is this dance made of?" exemplifies this conceptual alignment, because the non-narrative thrust of the inquiry matched the dance. "What is this dance saying?" would not have made sense. "What is this dance made of?" did. F.M.'s "analyze conditions of use present" step may be reinterpreted as "What is the right question to ask at this moment?" Or modernized: "What exactly is going on here?" AT helped me acquire the perspective to see ("analyze conditions of use present") and to create a conceptual framework ("reason out means whereby") for the dance so that the ideas for the finished piece were in alignment with the ideas I used to generate it.

Let's see how this might get extended across a project. Say I want to make a dance whose inspiring idea relates to creating personas and social media and something about changing one's mind in public. I have no clear thesis, only questions. I follow the steps outlined by Cathy Madden in *Integrative Alexander Technique Practice for Performing Artists: Onstage Synergy* (2014) to show how I might use AT in this creative process:

1. Wanting: I have this collection of thoughts about society that I want to explore in a movement context.

2. Recognizing: I suspect the tension in my assemblage of thoughts relates to how hard it is to change one's mind in public. There are potentially complex ideas.

3. Deciding: Do I want to bring together a group of dancers to explore these ideas and perform the resultant piece? Yes.

4. Gathering information: What kind of research is right for this? Should I think about famous people? Do I know people who shared a change of mind with a smaller group, such as at work or with their friends on Facebook? Who are the right dancers to work with?

5. Making a plan (which starts to fork into a few plans, one of the management problems of creativity):

    • I'd like examples of people changing their mind in public, not just in the digital age, so I will research this.

    • The concept's inherent tension has something to do with a group versus a single person emerging and standing out, so I know I need a group. I will create a "public" onstage by working with a largeish group.

    • This feels like a complex set of ideas. I will develop a series of improvisational dance experiments to help me filter this idea into its core human dynamics. This dance needs an internal logic, a plan of expression. I'll select this plan first.

6. Asking: Ask to coordinate so that my head can move so that all of me can follow so that I can work on the movement-generating improvisations.

7. Experimenting: I know I want to explore changing one's mind. To put this in movement terms, I'll explore people making one decision and then the opposite. One person will dance a short, one-note movement phrase, then the next person will dance their interpretation of the opposite. We will refine this experiment as we go, prioritizing what is generative and

what shows "opposite." Likely candidates are directions—forward/back, up/down, over/under. Assessing what looks interesting will happen in a later phase.

This fictional process shows where I might start and what might happen. In the process of developing my work, I use AT to coordinate myself so that I can apply the AT sequence to my dance.

A real-life example of using this process is a piece I made in 2010, *Only You*. This series of intertwined duets dwells in the moments of a new relationship, that golden hour of focusing on a person just as they are—carnal, alive, complex, whole. I started with the idea "Don't look back," turning this into the positive activity "Look ahead." I extended this into movement ideas that always moved forward while remaining onstage, which required bending, twisting paths. The cast and I developed a series of duets and group transitions in between that did just that—always moved forward. There was no gazing back at a partner during a separation, no regretful exits, no troubled entrances. Rather, the dancers looked at the person they were going to meet, were fully with them while together, and went somewhere else when leaving them. In the creation of this piece, I used AT to help identify the core characteristics of the desired movement. I also used my AT-trained powers of observation to see small conflicts with the "look ahead" movement direction, working with the dancers to coordinate through the challenging transitions. The effect was even more ephemeral than a dance usually is, completely matching the idea I was working with—the brief mystery of new love.

* * *

I learned AT in the tradition of Marjorie Barstow, largely via group classes. Working in the Barstow tradition, *learning* AT in activity—just as you will *use* AT in activity—rather than as a siloed practice is a core tenet of teaching and learning. I really believe in this format because I know how powerful it is to see others make new choices while engaged in an activity they care about. Observing others has been a key step in learning to observe myself.

Choreographers create and communicate movement ideas, and key to this is knowing how dancers are taking direction. Because I am trained to observe, I have learned to see quickly how dancers respond to instruction, to recognize learning styles, and to sequence my communication appropriately. I see cause and effect more clearly. I see my words interpreted differently by different people. For instance, I was working with two dancers on a partnering move. They couldn't make it work. The move called for them to grasp hands across a distance, then for one to pull the other into a lifted hold, essentially flying into a big hug. The flying consistently fell short. I noticed one of the dancers, the catcher, was doing a tiny thing in preparation for the jump, a teensy-weensy handshake movement. I suspect she was assuring herself and her partner that all was well, that she was strong and they were ready. The net effect, however, was a small push away, which confused the jumper's system: "How will I be caught if my catcher is pushing me away?" (I found it all rather sweet and funny: What could be more charming than a person trying to help another and giving exactly the wrong message?) Leaving out that tiny handshake made way for flight. This event highlighted the idea that we do a lot of unnecessary preparations for all sorts of things. AT has taught me to see this level of detail, bringing great depth and pleasure to my choreographic life.

A choreographer wears many hats, and their daily life is chock full of communication needs, largely in the realm of leadership. One of the trickiest parts of leading within the intimate dancer–choreographer relationship can be wanting a democratic feel, but actually holding all the decision-making cards. In order for a dancer to perform a work with the quality of freedom and surprise I always want, I need to create an environment in which they willingly decide each step. Leadership in a creative setting is a living contract, constantly being renegotiated, agreed upon again and again.

One way to clean up communication around leadership is in role differentiation. Expectations around roles are often assumed and therefore overlooked. "Analyze conditions of use present" is once again useful—what is the role differentiation in this moment? I may then say, "My job is to make all creative decisions but I am asking you to offer ideas or an opinion, so I am sharing the job with you while we solve this dance puzzle." Clarifying role differentiation within oneself is also crucial. I performed in my own company for many years, and while communicating to my dancers what to do and why was a good start at charting the course for a dance, talking to myself both about what I was making and what I should do as a performer was tricky. Thank goodness I could use AT to parse the creative versus performative tasks at hand in any given moment.

* * *

Dancers are heroes of creation: brave, smart, devoted, willing to change. They may have trained in a variety of dance techniques, often from childhood. In a world where how well one "takes correction" is valued, a dancer's mind is nimble at receiving and interpreting information. I believe that dancers are more available to change than most people. I also believe, however, that in their eagerness to get things right, they become experts at layering new information on top of old information, making it look like a new idea is the only idea when in fact the old idea has been squirreled away just in case it's needed again someday. Not the worst plan, I guess, to keep a bag of tricks handy. But inevitably, there are conflicts among those tricks. Sorting through the mixed messages of dance training is an essential application of AT.

When I work with dancers, I have not trained them myself and am largely unconcerned with what dance forms they have studied. I am more interested in how receptive and responsive they are to ideas with their whole selves. Not uncoincidentally, this is what I enjoy seeing onstage—a whole person responding to and interpreting new ideas in the moment in a way that has the potential to surprise. As I think about my own dance training, which was lovely in so many ways, I wonder how AT might have given me more agency within what I felt was the constricting environment of dance technique class.

Using AT to refine expertise in dance has a few specific challenges, one of which is that dancers are often trained to rely on feeling to measure change. External mechanisms of feedback—a mirror, another person, or video—just can't keep up. I am of the school that sees feeling as a symptom, the net effect of change registering in the senses, not a goal. Sometimes when movement is right, it feels like nothing. And yet, you have lifted your leg or spun before moving on to the next thing. It is possible to have freedom of movement without a rush of sensory feedback. "The unwillingness to accept that what we feel is not a reliable guide to what we are actually doing is one of the biggest reasons performers get 'stuck'… [AT] provides the road map that could help the performer avoid the 'stuckness' or even prevent it in the first place" (Madden 2014, p.84).

Reliance on feeling can have a recursive aspect. A dancer strongly tempted to look to feeling as a way to gather feedback may create extra feeling in the body, to really *feel* it. This italicized and bolded ***feeling*** probably comes from extra tightening or something else unnecessary to the desired movement, simply created to provide feedback, even if such feedback is erroneous. After all this time, I still have to catch myself when starting to extend from a plié—I want to give a little extra push in my hip joint to "make sure" my "up" message is working. But many decades into this body and I have had to ratchet up the push to get this or some such feeling. And what happens when you have been subtly ratcheting up pressure every time you un-plié? Joint damage.

One of the great benefits of AT is in clearing up some of the helpful messages we may have received, or invented for ourselves, in dance training. Just as Alexander was trained to "take hold of the floor with [his] feet" (1996 [1932], p.33) in his theatre training, dancers are told all sorts of dubious things—"your head is a balloon," "grounding gives you power," "you must straighten or flatten your back"—and by gosh, they will move heaven and earth to accomplish them.

I have learned to see when a dancer strangely interprets a physical direction, making me wonder about their ideas about anatomy. Here are a few updates that I think would benefit dance training:

- *Metaphors are not anatomy.* Creative images are often used in training and directing dance, and an eager mind can misuse the information. It is important to let dancers know that while images may provide a useful metaphor for a creative idea, they often do not accurately reflect anatomy. Your head is not a balloon on a string; it does not float. You cannot breathe into your legs. Because dancers are trained at accepting ideas fully into their systems (I once gave it my all when asked to breathe energy from the floor and release it up to the sky...wait—nothing left for me! I fainted away, clonk), it is critical that they get relevant, accurate information.

- *Gravity works.* So many dance ideas use the word *grounding.* Gravity needs a lot less assistance than dancers are often taught. The floor is where it is. You cannot (usually) go through it, and you cannot actually send roots into the ground to plant yourself. The idea of grounding often results in people putting a lot of unneeded pressure into their system, locking down joints to get some internal feeling of strength or solidness, some outward impression of immovability. "I am ready to take what comes!" "I draw the energy from the earth and it makes me really magnetic!" I can see how in certain aesthetic situations this might prove useful, but as a universal choice, layering on false strength creates an immovability that seems especially undesirable for a dancer. I prefer to see and work with a dancer who can do what she needs to do when she needs to do it. The layer of false strength or readiness reduces options.

I once worked with a dancer who was walking very loudly, almost slamming his feet into the ground with every step. The effect was militaristic, not at all what the swirly, sexy dance we were working on required. He was holding an idea of walking with purpose, of really feeling the distance he was traveling with every step. The effect was the opposite: I was distracted by how little progress he was making. By pushing himself down with every step, it didn't seem like he was traveling through space at all. My note was "Don't worry about the ground—it will be there as you move forward. Your foot can respond to the shape and texture of the surface you are dancing on, and this can happen while you move. No moment of confirmation required." He blazed a trail then, creating the swirl required to draw another dancer to him. Lovely.

This is an example of trying to ground while also locomoting. How about grounding in stillness, to balance? (This is something dancers train for a lot but I have rarely used as a choreographer.) Well, we are never still. Our blood flows, our lungs expand and contract. We are in a constant concert of movement and change. You need not ground to go up. You are on the ground. Just go up.

- *You are not flat.* There are a few culprits in the conspiracy to flatten dancers. The spine has curves, and yet we are taught to "stand straight" or go into "flat back"—sometimes a useful shorthand for getting dancers to take a certain shape. But such instruction is so often given in training that it tends to communicate some kind of ideal. These are places to pass through, not places to live.

    Another is the mirror. It is natural to try to imitate what we see. Dance technique classes are taught in lines with dancers looking in the mirror, which while reflective is also a wall. Dimensionality has to be constantly refreshed. What if we didn't lose that dimensionality in the first place?

    Another player in this conspiracy is that old chestnut, body image. Flat people don't stick out in funny places or ungainly fashion. How do most people try to accomplish fashionable flatness? By overusing their external torso muscles (abs) and tucking their pelvis, which limits movement in all sorts of ways, compromising the natural functional design of a big, beautifully curved lumbar spine and the finesse of the near-spine muscles. Curves are good.

Clearly, I see great potential benefit in teaching choreographers and dancers AT to support their creative thoughts and movement. One challenge is that dancers generally like to keep moving, so stopping to look at a movement or activity can seem like a false learning situation. Why would I stop moving to learn something I use while moving?

* * *

In addition to continuing to teach the Barstow approach—again, *learning* AT in activity, just as you will *use* AT in activity—I am also exploring improvisation as a vehicle for using AT while moving. I asked dancer Kathryn Padberg (KP) to join me in the studio for some open-ended dancing experiments. My time with KP was meant to develop a practice of improvisation, without a performance or production goal. A practice so private we called it Dancing for Introverts. We started with some open improvisations, fairly quickly finding ourselves on the floor, disinclined to get up. Too open. We added some ideas, largely of the "noticing" kind. Not a good path. Self-awareness is a lovely thing, and noticing is a critical part of living ("Hey, that's a bear!") and practicing AT, but it is not a fruitful activity in and of itself. When we tried to use awareness in the studio, to make it an activity, we stopped moving.

Noticing as an activity in and of itself puts our present in the past. The pursuit of awareness requires constant diagnosing: "What am I doing?" is really "What did I just do?" We decided it would be more immediate, productive, and enjoyable to respond to, rather than wait to reflect on, something, whether internal or external.

Following is an account of three sessions during the evolution of this practice, along with specific improvisational scores. Each improvisation has the underlying question, "How can I use AT while I am dancing?"

Session 1

We kicked off this series by employing our friend, the metronome. I had started using a metronome to trick myself out of having to compose every moment, to get me out of always having to choreograph and occasionally getting to dance. When introducing it to my work with KP, I realized that when I felt "bogged down," I was trying to remember things or perfect them, both things that are *about the past*. The metronome provides freedom by reminding me that I always have the option of doing something new. This is an opportunity to practice a conscious newness: "I must replace my old instinctive (unreasoned) direction of myself by a new conscious (reasoned) direction" (Alexander 1996 [1932], p.39).

We use the metronome to delineate a period of time during which we will do one thing per beat. The pace of the metronome is significant: 96 beats per minute (BPM) is fast enough to "force you forward" in time, unable to worry too much about the choices you make. Eighty BPM is a whole different beast. Then the space between beats is long enough to do more than one thing, or (if you are being strict, or devoted) to spend some time deciding and then doing. Ninety-six is for fun. Eighty is for training the mind to be active without judgment.

> Session 1 score: #bpm:#mm (beats per minute for a number of minutes). Find a metronome or metronome app with a timer function. Try 80 BPM for three minutes, then 96 BPM for five minutes. Do a new thing for each beat. Just do a thing, then another thing.

Session 2

We introduced dancer/watcher. We took turns improvising and watching each other. The act of being watched expanded the way we were thinking while dancing. We included the whole room and were able to deal more directly with the act of being watched. Not a radical notion in performance, but remember that we had been calling our explorations Dancing for Introverts. This is the day we started Dancing Alone, Together.

> Session 2 score: Timed solo switches. Take turns dancing solo for three minutes at a time, four turns each. Use a timer. It can be helpful if watcher can change position to relocate "front." Can be layered with #bpm:#mm, but silence is also a terrific challenge.

Session 3

We came up with the idea of "verbing." Verbing is where we name what we are going to do in our minds, then do it. In Alexander-speak, this might be a micro-plan, or a small plan (move all of me on a diagonal) inside a larger plan (improvise continuously for three minutes with a witness). In an early iteration, we described what we were doing while doing it. This felt terrible, because something you describe has already happened, and we felt stuck. Verbing encourages quick decision-making and action without judgment.

> Session 3 score: Verbing. This can be done in any situation, but to develop the skill, set up a series of short improvisations with increasing durations: two minutes, then five minutes, then eight. Decide to do something specific and then do it; decide something new, then do that. As you dance, your imagination may start to warm up and you may think you have spaced out. Re-up on verbing alongside that imagination. Remember that imagining is also something we do—a verb.

* * *

At the beginning of this chapter I talked about thinking, movement, and communication as the three facets of human volition. I believe that insofar as dancers and choreographers embrace AT, their dances—fueled by choice—will become ever more meaningful, more beautiful, and more reflective of humanity. Can't wait.

References

Alexander, F.M. (1996) *The Use of the Self.* London: Gollancz. (Original work published 1932.)

Madden, C. (2014) *Integrative Alexander Technique Practice for Performing Artists: Onstage Synergy.* Chicago, IL: Intellect, University of Chicago Press.

Subject Index

Author Index

Made in the USA
Lexington, KY
21 August 2017